LEMMY

LEMMY

THE DEFINITIVE BIOGRAPHY

MICK WALL

This edition first published in Great Britain in 2016
by Orion
an imprint of the Orion Publishing Group Ltd
Carmelite House
50 Victoria Embankment
London EC4Y 0DZ
An Hachette UK Company

3 5 7 9 10 8 6 4

A CIP catalogue record for this book
is available from the British Library.

Hardback ISBN: 978 1 4091 6025 0
Trade Paperback ISBN: 978 1 4091 6026 7

Typeset by Input Data Services Ltd, Bridgwater, Somerset

Printed and bound by CPI Group (UK) Ltd, Croydon, CR0 4YY

www.orionbooks.co.uk

For Lemmy
Win or lose, it was all the same to him

CONTENTS

Acknowledgements   ix

1. Do I Look Ill To You?   1

2. The Watcher   14

3. Holy Shit   39

4. The Captains   71

5. The Three Amigos   106

6. Don't Forget the Joker   141

7. Nobody's Perfect   168

8. Killed by Death   199

9. Dead Man's Hand   234

10. I Have Never Drunk Milk   269

Notes and Sources   299

Index   301

ACKNOWLEDGEMENTS

Without the enormous help, kindness and generosity of the following people both past and present, this book would not exist. They are: Linda Wall, Anna Valentine, Robert Kirby, Malcolm Edwards, Joe Daly, Dave Everley, Joel McIver, 'Fast' Eddie Clarke, Doug and Eve Smith, Phil 'Philthy Animal' Taylor, Brian 'Robbo' Robertson, Phil Campbell, Würzel, Phil Carson, Ted Carroll, Dave Brock, Nik Turner, Stacia Blake, Chris Salewicz, Barry Miles, Allan Jones, Mick Farren, Tony Platt, Motorcycle Irene, Wayne and Dorine Bardell, Mörat, Dave Ling, Jamie Blaine, Nita Keeler, Ute Kromrey, Steve 'Krusher' Joule, Pete Makowski, Ross Halfin, Roland Hyams, Emma Smith, Jessica Purdue, Mark Handsley, Craig Fraser, Mark Thomas, Vanessa Lampert, Martin and Sarah Sando, Steve Morant, Ian Clark, Stephane Brun, Maureen Rice, Lynnette Lawrence, Harry Paterson, and road crews everywhere.

ONE

Do I Look Ill To You?

Lemmy lit a cigarette, blew smoke in my face and put it like this: 'I was born at eight o'clock in the morning – an only child. My father left when I was three months old. You can see why! He was a vicar in the Church of England, a padre in the RAF during the war.' His mum was 'a librarian for a while. She was a TB nurse for a while.' Working with pregnant women with TB who had deformed children. 'There was one born with a beak instead of a face. Fucking awful! She was so freaked out she couldn't do it no more.'

I begged him to stop. 'You're going too fast,' I complained.

'Either that or you're going too slow,' he sniffed.

It was a miserable dark afternoon in November, the rain lashing down outside, and we were sitting in his room at his London hotel. It was the late Nineties, cusp of a new century, and I'd recently stopped working as his PR and returned to music journalism. I'd been told, on the quiet, that

Lemmy was gravely ill. That he'd been in hospital and now it was only a matter of time. It was decided I should interview him over several hours, get his life story down before it was too late. I had interviewed him many times before over the years, and I would interview him many times more in the years to come. There had also been those innumerable occasions when we had simply talked, at gigs, at parties, in hotel rooms and bars around the world.

Yet never quite like this. When we finished it would be long into the evening. I would be ready to crash. Lemmy would be ready to go out. I was supposed to transcribe the hours and hours of tapes, put it all together, but I never did. Weeks went by and he didn't die and my life took other turns, and so the tapes stayed in a file in my office, following me around wherever that happened to be for the next several years. Until I finally got around to writing this book. And then he did die and it stunned me, even though everyone knew he was desperately ill. I had just finished transcribing the tapes when I got the news. We had been due to speak a few days before Christmas. But he was ill and it was his birthday and I thought it would be better to leave it until the New Year. And . . .

When I'd knocked on his door that day it had been with a serious face. He took one look at it and growled, 'Oh, fuck off! Let me guess. You've heard I'm about to kick the bucket, right? Well, it's not fucking true.'

Was it true he'd been ill, though? 'Yes, that part's true.' And in hospital? 'Briefly, yes, in Germany. But it was a scare, that's all.'

I must have looked doubtful. 'Look,' he said, gesturing to

the whiskey bottle on the table, 'fix yourself a drink and sit down. Do I look ill to you?'

Well. That was hardly a fair question. He'd looked like shit for most of the years I'd known him. Except for when he went to live in Los Angeles, in the early 1990s, when he'd suddenly acquired an unlikely suntan. And taken to wearing speedos. He'd even become clean-shaven for a (short) while, and talked only half jokingly of 'doing something about' his thinning hair. Living in LA, he said, 'means we now have the technology'.

The desultory whiskers soon returned, however, albeit dyed black, and he'd taken to wearing a hat. This was something of a relief. Lemmy was not the kind of rock star one would ever wish to see 'reimagined' by a Hollywood stylist.

As he reaffirmed for me that day, 'I'm not dressing up, no. What you see is what you get, man. I've only got one pair of pants and I've had them for twenty-five years, and nobody knows that. They think I get new pairs but I just paint the holes in my legs black.'

This last may or may not have been true. Or more likely had been true once upon a time, in the early days of Motörhead, before the money and the fame and the people in the band's office he would routinely send out to buy him his white boots, his whiskey and his cigarettes. Before he developed his tendency, in the words of his former manager Doug Smith, 'to be quite camp at times'. Doug was thinking of the time he'd turned up at Lemmy's Edgware Road apartment to find him kitted out in full American Confederate uniform.

'I said, "What the hell are you dressed up like that for?"

He just looked at me and said, "Yeah, it's great, isn't it?" And that's how he went out that night.'

But before one gets carried away with the idea of Lemmy sharing a Quentin Crisp-like theatricality, it's worth mentioning that he'd 'acquired' the uniform from an 'accidentally broken' glass display case in Texas during another typically piratical Motörhead tour. 'I thought, great, that's another gig we'll never be able to go back to,' sighed Doug.

But back to that day in London as the two of us sat there, huddled over a coffee table on which stood Lemmy's Jack Daniel's and Coke and his Marlboro Red cigarettes. I sat there looking closely for signs that it was over. That the story I'd been told was truer than he had wanted anyone to know. But while it was true he was now greyer around the muzzle, his belly beginning to ease over his ornate belt buckle, his eyes still held that twinkle, his mouth as sharp and funny as ever. His brain whirring away like a rat on a wheel.

'Do you want some of this?' he asked, unzipping one of the pockets in the arm of his black leather jacket.

'No, thank you!' I hurriedly replied. The short days and endless nights of wanting to have 'a taste' of Lemmy's industrial-strength amphetamines had long gone for me. I was in my forties and simply couldn't hack it any more. He was in his fifties and had no intention of stopping. Ever.

Didn't he ever worry what that stuff was doing to him after all this time?

'Do I look worried?' he said, using the razor edge of a switchblade to dig out enough to fill the nostrils of a baby elephant.

He sat back and lit another cigarette, had a sip of his

drink, and settled his sleepless gaze on me. 'You sure you don't want one?'

I don't remember the first time we met; he seemed simply to have always been there, buried deep in my subconscious: the bad man on the motorbike, come to steal your chick and fuck you up. The crazy bastard in the bald jeans and dirty hair and mirrored sunglasses that looked like two black eyes.

Mr Skull & Crossbones. Dr Swastika. The place at the crossroads where rock first met roll.

I first encountered him in the spring of 1972, playing with Hawkwind on the Portobello Road. Outside near the arches, on the green. Down the end there where all the Hells Angels hung out. Looning around on his bass behind the beautiful girl with the face-paint and torn mini-dress. He stuck out because he looked so much more fiendish than the carnival of freaks cavorting around him. But then you saw all kinds of strange scenes on the Portobello back then . . . Guys with guitars and feathers in their hair, some chick yodelling along begging for pennies . . . Some cat with a long beard everyone called Jesus you could get quid-deals from . . . Another guy selling bootlegs, selling chillums, selling the dream that this was somehow another planet you had landed on . . .

Then when 'Silver Machine' was a hit that summer the biker-looking guy in Hawkwind was on the cover of the *NME* and I learned his name: L-E-M-M-Y. Weird. But then so were Ziggy and Iggy and Ozzy and Alice. It was the age of far-out crazy-named glam rockers and everyone was getting ready for the day we would lift off to the moon. Then there was the girl who danced with them, with the breasts and the face and the legs: Stacia. Let all the children boogie . . .

Some years went by and the Hawkship crash-landed. Lemmy had gone. So had Stacia. So had everyone we had known and spaced out to back then it seemed. We were living suddenly in a new age of violently anti-hippy punks and while it was okay to admit you'd done acid it was definitely not okay to suggest Hawkwind might have once had something to do with it. Or that long hair used to mean something.

You would still see Lemmy, on the Portobello Road, a heavy presence pulling at the one-armed bandit in Henekey's. You saw him at Damned gigs, at Johnny Thunders shows. Pictured in the music papers hanging out with Sid and Nancy at the Speakeasy. Yet he never cut his hair. Never changed his look, his vibe, his whole don't-give-a-fuck deal.

And, of course, there was his new band, Motörhead. I'd heard them on a John Peel session sometime in 1978 doing their version of 'Louie Louie' and they sounded nothing like Hawkwind – who were positively languid by comparison – and more like Lemmy: raw, spiky, take-it-or-leave-it. 'We were more like a punk band than a heavy metal band,' he recalled. 'I always said that. We had longer hair, obviously. But if we'd had short hair we'd have fit right in as a punk band. Playing very hard, very fast, very short numbers.'

By then I was working at Step Forward Records, just off Portobello, and somehow Lemmy and I had taken to saying hello. Step was punk. New Wave. The bleeding edge. And of course run by old hippies. Lemmy was 'all right', I was told. But his new band was 'rubbish'.

The people that said that though were typical-for-the-times punk sheep. They would never have had the nerve to say it to his mottled, speed-gaunt face. Lemmy had a certain nightrider charisma that could incinerate people like that. So that while the Step Forward gang would be in the pub fussing over Mark P. or whoever, plotting their next move in the punk revolution, I would find my attention drawn to the devil in the dark, playing the fruit machine, solo, over there away from everybody else, an Iron Cross about his neck.

In the pub, he'd always let you buy him a drink. Always wonder if you had any speed. The biggest shock was seeing him queuing in the bank one afternoon, just like a normal person. These were still the days when you could write one of your own cheques to 'cash' and the bank would hand over the lolly. Assuming you had it in your account or the woman behind the counter didn't check. One look at Lemmy, though, and they always checked for everything. Not just in the bank.

'I'm sorry, Mr Kilmister, but you don't have sufficient funds in your account.' The whole bank could hear the old biddy giving it to him. His back stiffened. He grabbed his chequebook, wheeled around, angry, a bit embarrassed.

He saw me. Came straight over. 'Can you lend me a quid?' he said. 'You'll get it back, don't worry.'

I pulled out an old green note. He looked at it. 'Or two, if you've got it . . .'

I pulled out another one, handed it over.

'Thanks,' he said. 'I owe you.'

It was months before I saw him again. I'd been sacked from Step Forward and was now writing for *Sounds*. There had been a music press coach trip to see Motörhead play at Friars in Aylesbury and with nothing better to do I was on it. Oh lord. The bus had been tricked out with bloody slabs of meat hanging from cleavers, blow-up Barbie dolls in every other seat, and the hospitality run by a handful of barely clad biker chicks led by the overpoweringly sexy and scary Motorcycle Irene, who virtually pushed drinks down your neck while offering you speed, downers, dope, lit joints, whatever turned you on, fuckhead.

When we got to the gig it was so loud some of us pulled the tips off cigarettes and stuffed them in our ears. It didn't work. What worked was abandoning yourself entirely to the filthy noise. The review I wrote said something of the same. The next time Lemmy saw me he gave me my two quid back and bought me a drink. Then he flared his nostrils and suggested I follow him to the toilet. I thought, ooh, coke, cool.

Fool. It was always speed with Lemmy. Always. Up all night every night. He'd even written a Motörhead song about it, early on, just in case there was ever any doubt: 'White Line Fever'. It would not be his last.

Over the many years that followed Lemmy and I always seemed to bump into each other. For a couple of years I worked as a PR at a company called Heavy Publicity, around the corner from Motörhead's management office in the Great Western Road. Lemmy was always in there, ordering people around. 'Staying on their case', as he put it. Lest they forget for a trice that Lemmy and Motörhead were to be the very centre of their universe.

His manager, Doug Smith, hired Heavy Publicity to work for The Damned and Hawkwind, whom he also managed. It was always Motörhead I coveted though. They just seemed more fun. But by then they were reaching the peak of their fame, *Top of the Pops* regulars, music paper darlings. They didn't need help. Not that I could see.

Even after the shit came down in the mid-Eighties and the original band broke up and Lemmy found himself fronting new, more musically proficient, but infinitely less characterful or successful Motörhead line-ups, Lemmy's own personal fame continued to flourish on TV and in films. High-profile cameos that kept the image alive even as the record and ticket sales began to dry up.

I went to visit him at his place in West London, and it was filled with all the usual Lemmy detritus. Airfix models of Second World War aircraft, half-eaten cheese sandwiches, books and records and bottles and ashtrays, all strewn about the place like a crime scene – and the beginnings of a serious Nazi memorabilia collection. 'I'm just fascinated with the whole phenomenon,' he explained as I studied a very heavy, very impressive-looking dagger. 'Hitler was the first rock star.'

It was also the first time he told me the story of going to see the doctor and being told not to quit drugs. 'It was when that Keith Richards thing broke, about his blood change.' He said that Doug Smith had decided he was 'gonna clean us all up and make us solid citizens. So he took me down to Harley Street, to a private doctor, and he took a blood test. And we went back a week later for the results and he said, "Whatever you do don't give him whole blood, it will probably kill him!" My blood at the time had evolved into some sort of organic soup – all kinds of trace elements in it.'

I laughed of course as I always did at Lemmy's funny stories. He was a born storyteller. As the years went by, he told me versions of this story again. And each time I laughed, the story getting better with each telling.

And yet, when I mentioned this story, in passing, to Doug just a couple of weeks after Lemmy's death, he looked at me astonished. 'Absolute bullshit!' he chuckled. 'I told you he was a terrible liar.'

I laughed again. Who knows if it's true? Lemmy had told that story so often he probably ended up believing it himself. Lemmy was always his own best mythmaker. But he spoke the truth, too, and far more often. Certainly more than any other rock star I knew.

He was also surprisingly sensitive. When my mother died in 1986, he took me aside to offer condolences. He spoke to me quietly for several minutes, put his arm around me, and told me things I didn't yet know about life – and death. Another time, backstage at the Donington festival in 1988, he offered me counsel on how to dress when I appeared on TV. He'd been watching my Sky show, *Monsters of Rock*, he said. 'You're good, very funny. I like it. But you need to grow a bit of facial hair. Dirty yourself up a bit. It's more rock'n'roll and the birds will love it, you'll see.'

I did as I was told. Lemmy had spoken.

A few years later, when I learned he'd moved to Los Angeles, I was not surprised. LA was then the capital of the hairy-arsed rock world. 'Most bands want to go and tour America,' he had once told me. 'I'd like to go and just do a tour of LA. Just round and round for ever.'

It was the women, he said. Having lived and worked in

LA myself by then I knew what he meant. The rock'n'roll gals of West Hollywood always looked and behaved as if they had just stepped out of a Mötley Crüe video, and some of them had. There had always been women, though. 'I've just never been able to find a girl that would stop me chasing all the others.'

But there was something else. For Lemmy, sitting as the famous leader of Motörhead at one of the half-moon booths at the Rainbow – the notorious Sunset Strip club where Led Zeppelin had first fed on groupies – was infinitely preferable to standing still at the fruit machine of a pub in Ladbroke Grove, the last surviving recognisable member of a band many people in Britain now assumed had broken up years before.

'Anyway, you can't go back,' he said. 'You get trapped in a time warp. I still get kids going, 'Hey, Lemmy! "Ace Of Spades", man!' I say, "You're not old enough to fucking remember it! What are you talking about?"'

The real attraction of living in LA for Lemmy was that he would now be treated in the way he had always felt he should be, with the utmost respect. And overindulgence. Motörhead may not have sold many records in America but the reverence in which they were now held by acts that had sold millions there, not least Metallica and Guns N' Roses – most especially, the way their leader had been anointed as the biggest, baddest, mutton-chopped, mole-faced, speed-freaking daddy of them all – meant Lemmy's shadow never stood taller than it did when he was busy being who everyone else at the Rainbow thought he should be, whatever the so-called truth.

As Stacia told me tearfully just now, speaking over Skype, 'His real family was his fans. Lemmy had such a genuine connection with people. They loved him. He knew it and loved them back.'

It was a love matched only by his disdain for what he saw as the cringe-inducing fakery of the rock star life. As he put it, most rock stars, 'seem to think they've descended from the son of heaven. Fucking walking around . . .' Adopting an airy-fairy voice: '"Nobody leaves this room until we find David's glove!" It's fucking terrifying. They seem to think they have a message for "the kids". Mostly, they haven't. Cos if you think that, you obviously haven't got a message for anyone. Or the message is: beware.'

This then is a book both about the man I knew and the rock star the rest of the world thought it knew. There's some bullshit in here, as there is in any telling of a true story. And there's some tears, which there always must be wherever there is laughter. And noise. Lemmy really wasn't like the others. He wasn't 'crazy' like Ozzy. Or 'cool' like Slash. He was about the music but by the end of his career he was far beyond even that. Lemmy was a Great British eccentric. In the same way that Jeffrey Bernard or Peter Cook were, both of whom also lived dissolute, alcoholic lives, beloved of strangers and yet a stranger to many of their real friends.

As for the way he looked back on his own life: 'Well, you know, hindsight's 20-20, isn't it? And that's the trouble with it, it isn't true what you see when you look back. When you look back you only see the good bits because your brain blacks out the bad bits to give you a break. I'm sure we've all fucked up every year of our lives and had a good time every year of our lives. I'm not into looking at pinnacles. I like to look at the life as a life. And I've done pretty good, really. Nearly all of my dreams have come true, there's not many left. Most people, they never get one dream come true, so I'm pretty lucky, and I'm happy with that. Anyway, you shouldn't look for perfect. If you get "very good", you should be fucking on your knees thanking somebody.'

I am thankful to have known Lemmy. He may have sung about not wanting to live for ever. But the facts of his life will enthral for many generations to come. This book pays no favours in attempting to demonstrate just why that is. The good, the bad and the purely Lemmy – as he always wanted it to be. Begun in life, finished in death. Imbued with his bloody-minded spirit and unexpectedly gentle touch. God's speed old friend . . .

TWO

The Watcher

Born to lose. Live to win. It was Motörhead's catchphrase and, in the minds of his fans at least, Lemmy's personal credo. Yet like all such braggadocio its roots lay in far less certain emotional terrain.

A war baby, born in Burslem, Stoke-on-Trent, on Christmas Eve, 1945, Ian Fraser Kilmister came into the world with a perforated eardrum and whooping cough. So weak was he that the midwife on duty advised his parents to request an emergency christening for fear he wouldn't survive more than a few days. But survive he did, already defying the low expectations of those around him. Nevertheless, he didn't meet his real father until he was already Lemmy, a 25-year-old speed freak living in an Earl's Court squat. 'He was a horrible little fucker, bald with glasses,' he told me. 'They separated when I was three months old, then later divorced.'

The only reason Lemmy – a name he later swore was given to him at school, though he never explained why, while most of us who knew him always understood it to be an abbreviation of 'lend me a quid', which seems far more likely – agreed to the meet was because his father had 'started writing letters to my mother saying "I feel bad about the boy". He probably couldn't even remember my fucking name, "the boy".' They met at a pizza parlour around the corner from Lemmy's squat. Lemmy told him he needed money to buy a new amp for his band, even though he wasn't actually in one at the time. His father suggested paying for driving lessons instead. 'He offered to pay for a course for me to become a commercial traveller. I said, "It's a good thing the pizza hasn't arrived yet, it'd be your new fucking hat," and I walked out. I never saw him again.'

Did he ever discover why his parents had split up so soon after his birth? 'Who knows why people split up? Dirty knickers on the bathroom shower rail once too often, these things get huge, don't they?' He grinned as he said it but it's clear Lemmy's origins remained a mystery to him throughout his life. Moving with his mother to his maternal grandmother's place in Newcastle-under-Lyme and then soon after to Madeley in Staffordshire, he spent his formative years alone, the only child of a single mother in a post-war world where household goods were kept to essentials and entertainment was of the make-your-own variety.

As an only child, said Lemmy, 'You grow up learning to be alone, which a lot of kids that grow up in large families never learn. They're never alone so they never reflect much. You can't think can you if someone's trying to hit you with a cushion. There's always something going on. Whereas if you're an only child, especially with a working parent, I used to be on me own all day.' He became 'the watcher', he said, 'taking it all in'. But that was good, he said, because 'it teaches you how to be alone and not have it bother you. A lot of people can't be alone. It freaks them out. And I could be alone from now on and it won't bother me at all. Because I know who I am and I'm my own best friend. It's a great gift.'

Indeed, it was this aloneness – this ability to maintain his own time and space whatever social or professional situation he found himself in – that would come to define Lemmy for those that knew him. For someone who spent practically every night, when not touring, either out at a gig, or in a club or pub or party of some sort, for someone re-nowned for always being courteous to all-comers, no matter how obnoxious, Lemmy had a permanent aura about him of separateness, of never really being part of the crowd, of maintaining his own peculiar focus, whether on a slot machine or a book, or giving attention to whatever pretty face had just appeared on his radar.

He was a great talker who knew how to tune out of any conversation that didn't interest him. It wasn't just fools that were not to be suffered. It was anything that didn't quite work for him. And if that left him alone quite, the last man standing, that was fine by him. He preferred it that way, actually.

'He's always been very comfortable in his own skin,' says Stacia, 'because he has always known exactly who he is. Most people don't know that. But Lemmy did.'

He was ten when his mother remarried and moved the family to the tiny town of Benllech on the island of Anglesey in North Wales. George Willis had been a professional footballer before and after the war, an inside forward for Plymouth Argyle in their title-winning Third Division South team of 1952. George was a widower with two kids – a boy and a girl, both older than Lemmy – from his previous marriage. 'I suddenly became the downtrodden younger brother instead of an only child. But I was still an only child really.'

George willingly offered to become Lemmy's stepfather – turning Ian Kilmister into Ian Willis, which he remained known as for the next ten years – but there was a snag. 'My stepfather wanted to marry my mother and he was Catholic, devout, you know, really into it. So he wrote to the Vatican for dispensation. And they sent back this thing that said [he could] only marry my mother if they proved me illegitimate. That's the Church for you, to send a child through his life with a stigma. Wonderful people the Catholic Church, very big on guilt. That's how they survive.'

To his would-be stepfather's credit, though, 'he told them, "Excommunicate my ass" – and they did! He wouldn't obey them and they hate people that don't obey them. Sons of bitches. It's not religion, it's just politics and control.' It's interesting to note, though, how vengeful Lemmy felt about this incident in later life. For someone who had made his reputation as one of the most celebrated outsiders in rock, he never forgave the fact that in the eyes of the Church he grew up illegitimate, excluded from the norms of polite, God-fearing society. Interesting, too, to discover that his original name for Motörhead was Bastard – until an appalled Doug Smith talked him out of it.

That was about as exciting as life got in those days, though. According to Lemmy, Anglesey 'was pretty well wasteland, you know? Even today it's pretty fucking rural.' His idea of escape was 'being a train driver. Things kids think about. You don't know what you want to do until you start doing it. I didn't know I wanted to be a guitar player until I started doing it.' Nevertheless, he said, 'I learned about myself more between . . . well, adolescence is pretty much the most intense soul-seeking years. But I was pretty well set by the time I was eleven. But then of course women happened and it all went to hell. It teaches you other things.' He laughed that laugh, part devil-may-care, part bomb site.

Already a regular absconder from Ysgol Syr Thomas Jones secondary school in nearby Amlwch, where he was picked on for being the only non-Welsh kid, it was only through the persistence of his female English teacher that he eventually passed his matriculation level exam at 13. 'I was always good at English. And that's a great blessing, you know. Reading and writing is a great blessing.'

Reading and writing – and music. 'We didn't have much TV, only what we heard on the radio, which was the BBC. I got into buying American rock'n'roll records but I didn't know anything about them. There was Radio Luxembourg but that was it. And that was very bad reception. You couldn't really get it. I remember sitting with the radio and you'd get bits of songs but it would be another two days before you heard the beginning. Then you'd go and order it from the shop, who'd never heard of it. Three weeks later the record would turn up. This was in North Wales, which was like Alaska. There was nothing laid on, you had to order everything. You had to order the music papers too, and there wasn't many of them, just the *Melody Maker*.'

The first record he ever bought was 'Knee Deep in the Blues', on 78 rpm; a minor hit in 1957 for Tommy Steele And The Steelmen. The same year he started watching *Six-Five Special* featuring Gene Vincent, the Big Bopper, Eddie Cochran, Lonnie Donegan, Cliff Richard . . . shots of girls twirling in their dresses, showing their knickers.

'Don Lang and His Frantic Five – and there was eight of them! I remember that. The other one was *Oh Boy!*. *Six-Five Special* ceased to exist once you'd seen *Oh Boy!*. It was very atmospheric. It was all black backstage and guys in the spotlight. It was very well produced. *Six-Five Special* was like a kids' show, really. *Oh Boy!* really wasn't, cos you had chicks in hot pants and shit, you know? Dancing to the records. That's what set me up for life. Because there were all these birds screaming at these guys. I thought, well, that looks like quite a good idea. Being a wallflower and an only child. My first adventures with women were dismal, you know? Hiding in my shell. But that rock'n'roll don't half bring you out of yourself.'

One of his earliest misadventures, he later recalled, involved a late-night foray into a Girl Guides camp. 'I was thirteen and living in Benllech and I knew this guy called Tom who had a prosthetic arm. One night we sneaked into this Girl Guides camp and, you know, started getting down to business. So there I am bathing in the soft afterglow in some girl's tent when, all of a sudden, I hear "Whack! Ow! Whack! Ow!" I thought, "What the bloody hell is that?" And looked out to see Tom running naked down the road with this Guide mistress belting him over the head with his own false arm.'

A budding pubescent interest in the female form and a sudden flash of lightning called rock'n'roll happened at about the same time. A heady, inextricably bound conflation he would never allow himself to fully recover from. That and smoking followed by drinking – and then later, of course, drugs. All the things Lemmy would become assiduously tied to – famous for, in fact – for the rest of his life.

In the summer of 1957, after the exams, during what he calls 'that dead week before you break up for the holidays', one of the other boys at his school brought an acoustic guitar in. 'And he was immediately surrounded by women. I thought, hmm, that's interesting.' His uncle played banjo and as a young girl his mother had played Hawaiian guitar. 'She still had it hanging on the wall at home. So I took that to school. I couldn't play it but the same thing happened, I was immediately surrounded by women, which was excellent. I thought: it works! Then I had to learn to play, to justify my position.'

Lemmy's older stepbrother had a friend who could play guitar. 'He showed me the three chords and I was away: E, A and D. Like a lot of people my age, there was also Bert Weedon's *Learn to Play in a Day*. Load of rubbish, of course, it took longer than that. But that was the start.'

He added: 'I was lucky because I could always do the right hand, which is the rhythm. The left hand makes the shapes but if you can't do the rhythm you've had it. Like the big heavy rock boom in the Eighties, a lot of kids learned to solo but they couldn't play riffs to save their lives. Standing at the front of the stage in spandex soloing, kidding on they had songs. They didn't.'

Mainly he learned by playing along to skiffle groups. 'Lonnie Donegan and Don Lang. The Chas McDevitt Skiffle Group and Shirley Douglas . . . Playing skiffle was easier cos it was all do it yourself. Tea chest basses, washboards, it was all acoustic. My stepbrother was in a skiffle group that was truly awful. They used to play at dances in the village hall, usual stuff.'

The teenage Lemmy's other big inspiration came from The Shadows, 'because they all played shiny electric guitars. I couldn't get a Stratocaster because they didn't exist. Hank Marvin got his sent over from the States. I remember seeing a picture of Buddy Holly on his first album sleeve, *The 'Chirping' Crickets*, with a brown Stratocaster. I thought, my god, they make them in two colours! This is big! It was like being told how babies are made. Like, wow! So ostentatious! Then of course everyone wanted one of them. But you couldn't get one. I got a Hofner Club 50 [hollow-bodied electric guitar without sound-holes]. A two pickups job with a very small green amplifier.' He had 'begged' the money 'off me mum. She was always very accommodating, just to get back at my stepbrother and stepsister and stepfather. She loved all that intense sibling rivalry. The down payment was disguised as a birthday present, something like that, then the rest came

21

out of my pocket money. I got that at [an instrument shop] in Llandudno, which is dust now.' Llandudno was the 'big city. Had more than two streets.'

Another development occurred when the family moved up to the walled market town of Conwy. A burgeoning tourist destination on the Welsh north coast, it boasted Llandudno Junction, and even though most people there still spoke Welsh, Lemmy was delighted. 'It was the first chance to get in touch with the outside world. Anglesey there wasn't much chance. You could commune with the sea during a storm but that was about it.' Talk of becoming a jobbing musician, though, was laughed off. 'The consensus [was] "You can't do that, it's a mug's game."' Not that Lemmy was listening. 'Fifty years later I'm still waiting to get a real job. Which is bullshit, actually. Because this life is no bowl of cherries. This rock'n'roll thing is very hard to do and I've served my apprenticeship over the years, amid long periods of mind-battering fucking boredom, sitting on buses and shit. It's no job for the fainthearted, as we've seen from the casualties that have fallen by the wayside.'

When did he feel confident enough about his guitar playing to want to take it further and start to get into real-life groups? 'I joined a group with this guy called Malvin, who was a drummer who had this terrible Broadway kit, which was like two biscuit tins on a stand. His bass drum used to roll over all the time, which was very disconcerting. We did this one gig in a basement café place where I made my debut singing "Travelin' Man" by Ricky Nelson. That was the first song I ever sang with a band in front of people. It went down pretty well, actually. But then none of them had heard the original.'

Had he been nervous before he went on? 'Oh god, yeah! It was awful! But that's the real test, being able to stand up there and do it in front of a roomful of people. Anybody can be the best singer or guitarist in the world, on their own at home. But unless you can get it across the footlights you might as well pack up and go home. And that's what I was always good at. I was always good at selling it to people. Once I'm on the stage I can get across a certain . . . it isn't a knack. It's a gift.'

Not that he realised he might have the gift yet. 'No, no, no. I thought we were abject failures before I realised we were getting five gigs a week, you know?' This was in his next band, which was 'just me and this other guy, both playing guitars, we didn't sing, just played instrumentals. That's how I became a great rhythm guitarist, which was very good training for becoming a bass player. We used to do "(Ghost) Riders in the Sky"' – the Vaughn Monroe version – 'and all the Shadows' stuff. The Midnighters was another band.' Hard to imagine now but Lemmy doing his best Hank Ballard impression as he belted out 'Finger Poppin' Time' remained a fond memory.

It was the Shadows though that really drove home the message about having a strong image. 'Hank [Marvin] was the smart one, he could play solos. But Jet [Harris] was the cool one, because of the way he looked. The devil boy.' The Shadows' drummer, Brian Bennett, 'always looked sharp', too. 'He had that solo on "The Savage", you know? I remember hearing that for the first time and thinking, fucking hell, this is it! But Jet was the cool one with that blonde hair and Fender Precision bass. The first one I'd ever seen, I think.'

Lemmy wasn't thinking about actually playing a bass yet, though, merely aping Jet Harris's effortless cool. This was in the days before the Shadows took to wearing suits and bow ties and sashaying around the stage in synchronised dance steps. Check out the old black-and-white clips of the band performing their worldwide hit 'Apache' in 1960 and you'll see Jet in his leather jacket, blonde Elvis quiff and long, gaunt face, wreathed in thick cigarette smoke.

Elvis was also 'very big news. People thought those sideburns were the work of the devil. Also, Elvis was very big on style. And Cliff Richard of course because Cliff Richard's gimmick at one time, believe it or not, was that he never smiled. He was moody, with the sideburns and the pink jacket and the pink tie and the black shirt. And a big pompadour. He modelled himself on Elvis. A lot of that generation of guys were actors more than musicians, I think.'

Suddenly for the first time in his life, Lemmy became clothes-conscious. 'I got my first Teddy Boy jacket in Llandudno and my mother was most disappointed. It was powder blue with very thin red stripes, double-breasted one-button. Very hot, yeah. From the Elvis Presley shop that sold Negro clothes. It was that kind of store, you know, that lots of people bought flash clothes from. I had that typical conversation. "But all the kids are wearing them, Mum!" "I don't care what all the kids are wearing." All of that. Everybody who has ever been an individual has started out by getting a lot of flak from their parents. It wasn't like what they did and they hate that because it means you've left the nest, and parents don't like that. You take on a personality for the first time. You're not their child any more. You're just another kid that's out there on the street. You don't run home to your mum when someone hits you. You hit them back for the first time.'

As if to prove the point, he was expelled from school when he was 15. He showed me a scar on his finger, 'That goes right round to the nail here. I did that on a school trip to Paris.' He'd bought a flick knife at the Flea Market, and when he tried to snap the blade shut it chopped off a chunk of his finger. 'It was brand new so the spring was quite good. It really bled too, I'll tell you. Blood pumping with the heart. I didn't know you had a pulse in your fingers but you do. And we bandaged it up with this shit and it took ages to heal because it was a big cut. Though I played guitar with it that night, funnily enough. Cos I took my guitar with me.

'Anyway, we get back to school, three or four weeks later, it's just starting to heal, all scabby and fragile, when I was given two strokes [of the cane for being caught playing truant]. I put out my good hand but he wasn't having it. Made me stick out my bad hand. Whack! He split it wide open. So I thought, right, you cunt. And as he brought the cane down again I took the cane off him and whacked him round the fucking head with it. Well, I was in a lot of pain, you know? Two strokes is two strokes, it wouldn't have mattered where he hit you. But no, he had to hit my bad hand. A real bastard, he was. Mr Evans. Dead now. And I'm alive!' Big laughs.

25

'And he took that to his grave, I'll bet. That one of his kids had the nerve to whack him round the fucking head with his own cane. That must have gone very deep there. But it was just a spur of the moment thing, railing against the injustice. In fact, he probably did me a favour, because he gave me the sense of injustice I've been writing about for all these years.'

How had that gone down when he came home? 'I think they were just about ready for it,' he said, shrugging. 'It was just the next thing. The final disgrace.' His only regret was that he missed out on any hero worship from the other pupils because he was immediately expelled. 'I didn't get to be fawned over, I was gone.'

Forced to get a job, he became a stable boy. 'It was quite easy, really, because I'd been working at the local riding stables during the holidays for the past five years, doing beach rides, leading people up and down the beach on horses.' At the end of each day he would be allowed to ride one of the beach horses home at night. 'I was very big into horses.'

He had it all figured out, he told his parents. He would do the beach rides in the summer, and be a house painter in the winter. The latter something of a disaster when he quickly discovered that, 'I was no good at it. Crushing boredom, you know?' Being expected to paint 'anything higher than four feet was too much like hard work. And you're forever covered in specks of paint. There were two of us kids working for this terrible old village queer called – would you believe? – Mr Brownsword. Fucking Mr Brownsword! Luckily for me, he didn't fancy me. He fancied the other one. So he was always following him up and down the stairs, watching him paint and making sure he got it right, while I was downstairs doing fuck all. Mr Brownsword. And the kid he fancied was called Colin Purvis! I am not making this up!' Huge laughs. 'If that was my name I'd fucking change it! Wouldn't you?'

Next his stepfather wangled him a job at the Hotpoint factory in Llandudno Junction, working on the conveyor belt. 'Fucking horrible. What I did was, I had this huge machine, made a lot of noise, and out would come four brass nuts. And there's four little sticky-up things on this platform and I had to put them on there, bolt them down, press the red button, and very slowly this thing would come down and put a groove on the sides of these four nuts. Then when it was finished, I'd have to take the four nuts off, put them into a huge empty basket, and get four more. When you got a full basket, they'd take it away. The tedium! Then they'd bring you an empty basket and you'd start again.

'People that run factories don't know what they're doing to you. It kills you. The whole thing felt fucking pointless. So I grew my hair until they fired me. They said "Put your hair in a net or you're fired." I said, "I will not wear a hairnet. My granny wears hairnets. Real men like John Lennon and Kirk Douglas do not wear hairnets." So they said, "Fired." My stepfather never forgave me, because he got me the job.'

On the subject of hair, he recalled gleefully how when the Beatles came along in 1962 they had hair to just above the top of their ears. 'Outrageous! I remember thinking that. It wasn't, of course, but we were still in "war hair". The only reason very short hair came in, I found out later, was in the First World War, in the trenches, to fight the lice and fleas. Before the First World War a lot of people had long hair.'

At the time he was fired for having long hair, Lemmy's hair 'was just down to my ears. They said it could get caught in the machines. Fat chance! But people are stupid, you know? They'll tell you absolute garbage that you can see through in a second and they'll keep their face straight. That is being a grown-up.' After that, 'I swore then I'd never grow up, and I haven't, thank god. To be a grown-up is to be a plausible liar, to other plausible liars.'

After Hotpoint, he went back to working with horses. 'We got a farm up in Conway Mountain, about 800 feet above sea level. I must say my stepfather was very good like that. We bought two stallions and I was gonna start horse breeding.' He recalled with horror, though, the time he was forced to take part in the castration of one of the horses. He'd broken in both the stallions himself, he said. He was less proud, though, when expected to hold a horse's leg firm while his father went about his grizzly business. 'I saw the whole thing. They open up slits in the bag and pull them out and chop them up. I never felt right about that. Taking the balls off a male is about as bad as you can get, isn't it? If someone did that to me, I would never let them get away. I would stalk them. I don't know why he didn't kill me. I couldn't look him in the eye after.'

Horse breeding never held the same appeal after that. 'But then of course I heard Little Richard and it was all over.' Years later, he said, walking into the Hyatt House hotel on

Sunset Strip in LA, he ran into Little Richard and told him: 'No you, no me.' He went on, 'It's his fault. "Look," I told him. "Your fault." He said, "Oh, honey, don't say that!"'

Whenever he saw old footage on TV now, he said, he still marvelled at how 'he's in a suit and a shirt and tie and yet he's outrageous! Demonic, in those days . . . I was very impressed with Little Richard. He was the wildest one and he still is. Of all them people he was the only one who stayed wild.' More than The Shadows, or Elvis or skiffle, Little Richard was the turning point in terms of Lemmy deciding he definitely wanted to be a musician. 'I only heard him on the radio. I never saw him on TV. I didn't see him for years. I didn't know he was black. None of us did. How would you know? It was the same for all the major stars back then.'

Not until *The Girl Can't Help It* came out in Britain in 1957. 'Then when we saw him we didn't care what colour he was. And I think that was a great thing. It wasn't about whether the singer was black or white, it was just about rock'n'roll. Not black rock'n'roll or white rock'n'roll or Hispanic rock'n'roll. We just got rock'n'roll and we didn't care. It brought down so many barriers, rock'n'roll, it really did. Before that it was "race music". Don't listen to this jungle race music! It'll turn you girls into prostitutes. That was grown-ups talking again.'

It was one thing to dream of being the next Little Richard, quite another knowing which road to take that might actually lead there or somewhere near enough about. Eventually, you might say the road simply found Lemmy.

'I had this friend called Ming, after the Merciless Ming,

on the radio and at Saturday morning pictures. And we had both grown our hair and we decided we were gonna go to Manchester.' They had 'met these two Manchester birds on holiday, they had their own chalet. Their parents were fools! We were in there every night. I'll never forget being in the dark and Ming's voice going, "Don't stop, don't stop!" A lot of fumbling in a chalet by the sea. So we did all that then we went to Manchester, me and Ming, hitchhiking up the motorway, or eventually what became the motorway.'

He was 17. 'We were gonna stay in Manchester, that's all. We didn't know about any other place. Didn't know about London. We were two dossers in second-hand US army combat jackets, carrying bedrolls, and in my case a guitar. We were on the road.' There had already been practice runs. Short trips thumbing rides up and down England. 'We used to go all over the place. Used to hitch down to Cornwall.' There were these birds Lemmy and Ming knew down there, see. They were wandering minstrels, sleeping at roadsides and digging the scene. Ming didn't play, just Lemmy. But then he lost his guitar. 'It turned up again a long time later. But that's beside the point.' They survived with the help of 'a lot of hospitable women. We ended up with hospitable women all over the country because we were the pirates, right? And all the girls will hide a pirate on the run, won't they? Usually the best-looking ones, funny enough. Those are the ones that have been ostracised as well, through their beauty. Everything was about rebellion, at least in those days.' He recalled one road trip where they decided to visit a pal up in the wilds of Scotland. They got as far as a farm in John O'Groats. 'When we told the old farmer where we were going he said [affects a rasping Scottish accent]: "Don't go up there tonight, lads. It's the devil's country up there." So we stayed in his barn then came back.'

Back in North Wales, Lemmy now had his own hangout at the farmhouse. 'An old garage that my old man let me turn into a sort of rumpus room, filled it with a couple of old chairs and had a record player in there. I remember one time I had these four girls from Manchester round there. One of them was very pretty, she was called Judy, which was funny because Liverpool slang in those days for a girl was "Judy". My father came in and asked me what I thought I was doing lying on top of a girl. I looked at him. "Don't you know what I was doing? She knew what I was doing. I knew what I was doing . . ." Another crack round the fucking ear.'

Manchester, they decided, was where Lemmy and Ming would make their stand. It was 1962, Elvis was still on his throne, everyone was doing the twist, and by the end of the year the Beatles would be vying with Telstar as the biggest new comet in the suddenly very young and very swinging sky. As Lemmy later put it in an interview with the *Guardian*, 'Rock'n'roll sounded like music from another planet. The first time around, we had people like Elvis, Little Richard, Chuck Berry, Jerry Lee Lewis – all them people. And they were gone within two years. Chuck Berry was in jail. Jerry Lee's career had been destroyed by the British press. Elvis was in the fucking army. And then we got Bobby Rydell and all them cunts. It took us a couple of years to get rid of them. Then the Beatles showed up. That was all right.'

And for the first time there were drugs. 'We had all started smoking dope by then. You just had to be in a big city, cos there was none down in Llandudno. We used to call it shit, "Wanna buy some shit?" and sometimes it was. You'd buy it from West Indians, always, yeah. I don't know why, it just was. They were the ones who had it. I didn't see it as a drug-taking thing especially, it was just part of the scene. I mean, it was different from getting pissed but that's all it was – different. It wasn't worse or better.'

What really fired Lemmy's imagination, however, was a drug with an entirely opposite effect to the stoned immaculate fug of dope: speed. An older pal of his named Robbie Watson had given him his first taste one night at the Venezia Coffee Bar in Llandudno. Robbie was a junkie, he'd shoot anything into his arm, even water if he had to, just to get the buzz of the needle going in his vein. When he offered Lemmy a small ampoule of methyl amphetamine hydrochloride – 'the old buck-you-uppo!' as Lemmy called it – it came with a skull and crossbones stamped on it. Robbie had meant for Lemmy to inject it. But Lemmy wasn't having that. It was the one thing you drew the line at when it came to drugs. Instead he snapped it open and poured the contents into a cup of hot chocolate. He later recalled talking to the poor girl behind the counter at the Venezia 'non-stop for about four or five hours – I felt great!' The only downer was it eventually wore off. Lemmy decided he would have to do something about that. Another decision he would stick to for the rest of his life.

There was also the first real love of Lemmy's life: a 15-year-old schoolgirl from Stockport named Cathy. Lemmy had gone as far as telling Ming he was going to marry her. But then Cathy became pregnant and Lemmy got the shakes.

'Visions of prison bars!' as he later put it. But it was the early Sixties, when that would have done Cathy no good, either. Instead an 'arrangement' was reached between Cathy's father and Lemmy's stepfather, which resulted in the baby – a boy, named Sean, born in 1962 – being adopted at birth. Lemmy recalled seeing Cathy revising for her O-level exams at the maternity home. He nicknamed her 'Porky' 'and she'd crack up laughing too'. When it was all over though and Sean had left for his new home, Lemmy never saw Cathy again. Decades later, in his autobiography, Lemmy claimed he couldn't remember why he stopped seeing Cathy. But it's not hard to figure out. Indeed, it would become a pattern of behaviour he was to repeat with different women through- out his life: grand passion, followed by what he saw as the grinding tedium of a 'normal' relationship. Followed by Lemmy taking his leave. Usually without goodbyes.

Back on the scene in Manchester, sleeping in doss houses when he bothered to sleep at all, living on a diet of rice pud- ding and No. 6 tipped cigarettes, it was another girl whose name Lemmy would not remember who alerted him to a new musical phenomenon. Until then, the girls Lemmy and Ming met tended to be big Billy Fury fans. 'He was the one that they all went mad for. Then Billy Fury suddenly one year was no more. Gone. Consigned to being a has-been as this new four-piece from Liverpool came along called the Beatles. It was this chick told me about them. I'd never heard of them. She said, "There's this group in Liverpool, they're great." And they were. They changed everything. Not just rock music, but life, the universe and everything. You had to be there to truly understand what I'm on about but for anyone that was there, they know. After them no one was ever the same again, the young and the old, singers and politicians, sportsmen and actors. Everyone.'

Lemmy took the train to Liverpool to see the Beatles at The Cavern. 'This was while I was still in Wales. They were still wearing the leather jackets and trousers. They got all that stuff in Hamburg. No one else except motorcyclists wore leather trousers in Britain. But if you wore them and you didn't have a motorbike you were obviously queer. It's amazing though how history hangs on small things. If Epstein hadn't wanted to fuck John Lennon there would have been no Beatles. Or there might have been but in a different way. No clean-cut suits and ties. Epstein was striking out and not just waiting for phone calls.'

He recalled the audience at The Cavern as 'half and half' boys and girls. 'All the Liverpool bands played the same twenty songs, right? All of them. It was just one-upmanship. The first band would come on and say, "Here's a song by The Merseybeats called 'The Fortune Teller'." Then the next band would come on and say, "Here's a song by Benny Spellman called 'The Fortune Teller'." Ah . . . superior knowledge. Knowing who the original was. "Some Other Guy" by The Big Three. Or "Some Other Guy" by Richie Barrett.'

Lemmy was as baffled as anyone else over the provenance of most of these records. 'I was interested in knowing who the original was but I never heard them until much later. You couldn't get the originals. In Liverpool, there were guys who worked on the Cunard ship lines and they would go to America and bring back these records. Other than that you couldn't get them.' Seeing the Beatles, though, was another story. They were their own originals. 'Going to see the Beatles was like going to see Hendrix for the first time. You'd just never seen that before. The Beatles didn't have a singer. I'd never seen a band with four people playing but no singer out front without a guitar. It was very unusual. I didn't even know bands could do that.'

It brought him one step closer to believing he could have his own band like that. 'Yeah, it made me feel: I could do that. I never wanted to be an out-front singer. I always wanted to be a guitar player. But you couldn't play and sing out front but then after the Beatles you could. I mean, there were some other groups in Liverpool like that, Gerry and the Pacemakers, right? But that wasn't like John Lennon and the Beatles. But then a lot of kids formed bands because of the Beatles, didn't they?'

In Lemmy's case that turned into a string of no-hopers that began with The DeeJays, who kept shedding members until the line-up settled into a two-piece featuring Lemmy and another guitarist, named Dave. There were also the Sapphires, who lasted only as long as it took for Lemmy to call the other guitarist a cunt. Now playing a Gibson ES-330, which doubled as an electric or acoustic instrument, Lemmy thought he might have made it when he landed the gig in a well-known Manchester act called The Rainmakers. Big on the club and cabaret scene, they were managed by the same people as The Hollies but never got a record deal and were already on the way out when Lemmy joined.

'There were about six or seven of them but none of them got anywhere,' he told me. 'You couldn't be professional and make a living off that. You'd get paid but it would be a pittance. My first professional band, the most we ever got was £6.50 between the four of us for four forty-five-minute spots in one night. It was still better than being on the production line because we chose this production line.'

Lemmy didn't tell anyone because he didn't want them to think he was 'a mummy's boy', but when things got bad he would ask her to help out and she would 'send me a fiver quietly and stuff like that'. Looking back, he reckoned his mother was actually 'very subversive. She always wanted to sneakily do something like [be in showbiz], but she couldn't because in her time it wasn't possible. But she loved me doing it.'

Things finally began to look up when he hooked up with a guy called Stewart Steele, who was the guitarist-cum-leader of a band called The Motown Sect. Stewart needed a guy who could sing and play rhythm guitar. Lemmy disliked the idea of singing but disliked being out of work more and eagerly offered his services. Stewart, he recalled, 'was a great player', but not one blessed with enormous reserves of enthusiasm. 'He could never get out of the front room, except for the band we were in – The Motown Sect. We were called that because Motown had just happened and it was very big. We were a blues band but we couldn't get a gig as a blues band so we called ourselves The Motown Sect – a cross between Motown and The Downliners Sect – and suddenly all these gigs rolled in. They thought they were getting a Motown band then we'd turn up in striped T-shirts and start playing "Smokestack Lightning". We'd say, "Here's a song for all the Motown fans", and start playing Chuck Berry.'

Gigs became scarce though when the clubs the Sect were

used to playing started banning people with long hair, 'because they were all run by Mods'. One regular gig they could still rely on though was at a Sheffield club called The Mojo, run by future London nightclub owner Peter Stringfellow. 'So that's how long I've known him. It was the worst place too, terrible circular stairway, trying to carry the gear up and down them. It was a great club, though, three floors, all rocking out. Quality stuff.'

He paused. Filled his glass. Two-thirds Jack. One-third Coke. 'Those were better days,' he said, simply. 'You're not supposed to say that but they were better days. These days you get herded into a huge fucking arena where everybody hates you. The bouncers hate you. The staff hate you. The band probably even hates you. You get shoved in and told to stay like that. You can't leave your seat and all that shit. It's fucking awful. That's no proper place for rock'n'roll to be heard.

'Makes me appreciate the club days. But those days are gone, the clubs are gone and they're poorer for it. Christ, there was always a room where you could get nookie. There'd always be a corner without much light where you could try and make out with chicks, you know, knee trembling severely, amidst protestations of love and respect in the morning. Cos nobody had their own flat. Or you'd be under a railway archway somewhere outside. Fucking chicks in doorways in the rain. Really difficult, cos we didn't manage to turn them round in them days . . .'

Lemmy recalled there was another club in Sheffield which The Motown Sect could also still call on for work: the Two Plus Two, run by Shirley Crabtree and his brothers.

Crabtree, who later found huge fame in Britain as the wrestler Big Daddy, 'didn't need any bouncers. They'd just have two of the brothers coming around, you know? I saw a lot of people thrown out of there, rolling down the hill.'

It couldn't last and it didn't. But Lemmy's own spectacular roll had only just begun.

THREE

Holy Shit

Another time, another place, the same whiskey though and the same cigarettes and old buck-you-uppo.

'Life has a way of taking the piss, have you noticed?' Lemmy said, standing at the bar of the Embassy club in London. He was referring to the fact that the first band he found a measure of real fame with in the Sixties was called the Rockin' Vicars. 'My old man would have hated it, seeing me in a band that – shock, horror – took the piss out of being a vicar. At the same time he'd probably have loved seeing me having to wear a fucking vicar's dog collar on stage.'

Wouldn't we all? On the other hand Lemmy always did treat the stage as his pulpit, the Motörhead fans gathered there today as his flock. But his message to the faithful – be yourself, don't be afraid to think out loud, fuck those who would first fuck you – was not nearly so serious in the Rockin' Vicars. A hard-working four-piece from Burnley that had moved to Blackpool, where they first made a name for themselves playing cabaret shows along the pier, the Vicars were part rock'n'roll covers act – staples like Bill Haley's 'Rock Around the Clock' spiced up with whatever was currently popular on the radio – part knockabout comedy act, in the realm of Freddie and the Dreamers. The bass player, Stephen 'Moggsy' Morris, would drop his trousers, revealing 'big spotty underpants' and Lemmy would hit him in the face with a custard pie. 'Because people still love that now, seeing someone getting hit in the face with a custard pie.'

Sitting down later, away from the chatter of the fruit machine and the endless stream of goodwill merchants vying for his attention, Lemmy revealed just how much he'd loved his time in the Vicars. While most club promoters wanted the Vicars for their strange costumes and crowd-pleasing antics, Lemmy – or Ian Willis, as he was known in the band, again belying his later insistence that 'Lemmy' went back to schooldays and not to his hard-earned reputation as a young scrounger – preferred to think of the Vicars as more akin to Johnny Kidd & The Pirates, who also dressed up onstage, the singer, Kidd, whom Lemmy deeply admired, sporting a pirate's eye patch and striped jersey. 'They had a strobe onstage, the first I'd ever seen.'

He began by simply hanging around at their gigs, helping out humping the gear and chatting with the band. When they found themselves a man down though after the sudden departure of their guitarist, Lemmy immediately offered his services. Playing in the Rockin' Vicars meant money. Good money. 'I went from £6.50 for four forty-five-minute spots, to £1000 a gig. That's what the Rockin' Vicars were making per gig, and this was in 1965, cos we were a big pull in the North. We pulled in full houses at all the Locarnos. The Locarnos put us on, round and round. We all had Jags, except I had a Zephyr 6, which was big news in them days.'

Lemmy would drive his big American-style saloon around Manchester, pulling over and offering lifts to any pretty girls that took his fancy. With no legal limit yet imposed on how much a person could drink and drive, Lemmy would be 'speeding, drunk, awake for days' while driving. This led to more than one occasion where the car he was at the wheel of didn't return home with him.

Fortunately, no one was ever hurt. Lemmy, thankfully, would eventually decide driving wasn't for him, and would spend the rest of his life either in a tour bus or in a taxi, or over the last years of his life either in the back of a limo or cadging a ride home off anyone who happened to be offering at the end of the night. 'Mind you, I crashed two Jags so I can't really complain. The last car I ever had [with the Vicars] was a 1952 Chevy coupe. Straight 8 engine. Bought in Blackpool for £36 in 1966. The bloke just wanted to get rid of it. They weren't cool cars back then. They were just seen as old American cars. He'd welded a girder to the front of it and painted it in diagonal yellow and black stripes. It looked like a fucking bulldozer. It was a huge car, you know? When the window wound down you had a complete side to the car open. Old American radio, push-button stations, fucking amazing, power steering, power brakes, stick shift. A monster of a car.'

When he crashed that, he gave up. 'In this country at that time we weren't used to automatics. Coming off the motorway to Manchester I changed down. That was that – bang! Ka-chunka-ka-chunka-ka-chunka. There was a petrol station at the top of the slip road. I just coasted into that and left it. Gave the keys to the guy there. Trying to find parts for a 1952 Chevy in 1967, forget it. It would have cost what the car cost nineteen times over.'

The rest of the Vicars, fronted by the singer, Harry 'Reverend Black' Feeney, and led by the drummer, Cyril 'Ciggy' Shaw, were no less flash. 'We had this big house we lived in [but] Ciggy had a speedboat and this big flat in Salford.' In summer, Ciggy would take them water-skiing on Lake Windermere. It would be many years before Lemmy would reach such obvious heights of success again.

As Harry Feeney, now the respected owner of a second-hand car dealership in Blackpool, recalled, 'He had the image of a hard man but he was a gentle giant, and a very thoughtful person.' He remembers Lemmy being an instant hit after he joined the band. 'He was a fan of our band before joining forces with our two road managers and setting our gear up for us. We didn't pay him a wage, we just fed him and kept him. Then the band had a big bust-up and we were left with only three of us. Lemmy turned round and said, 'I can do this', and he got on stage and he was brilliant. The fans really loved him, I was the lead singer but they would scream for Lemmy.'

As well as touring the Locarnos, Town Halls, Imperials and Odeons, the Rockin' Vicars were the first band Lemmy was in that actually played abroad. Never having stepped foot off British soil, he did his best to disguise his excitement at finding himself suddenly in Finland, where the Vicars had astonishingly scored a No. 1 hit with a typically 'Swinging Sixties' version of a Neil Sedaka song, 'I Go Ape', recorded for Decca before Lemmy had joined. The gig was at the 10,000-capacity Olympic stadium and Lemmy could not believe his saucer eyes: thousands of blonde-haired girls all screaming for his group. This, he decided, 'was very big news'. There was a big party after the show, which went on all night, with the Finnish summer sun refusing to die. 'Girls to the left, women to the right', as he put it. What made it an even more eventful night for Lemmy, he said, was that they 'took all the money too. We got to the end and we said to the promoter, see you in the morning and we'll sort out the money, but we fucked off to the airport . . .'

They returned to England officially as Finnish pop stars. Hence the adoption of traditional Finnish dress when they returned home to England. Taken into a Blackpool studio, they agreed to dress up in 'these reindeer-skin boots, which we got in Lapland. And we got the Finnish national costume. These smock things with all the embroidery across it.' As if to add an even more surreal edge to their image, Lemmy recalled, 'We wore dog collars and the Finnish national costume. The Lapp smock, royal blue with orange and yellow felt stick-on stuff across – and skin-tight white jeans with lace-up flies, and reindeer skin boots.' The only downside: 'trying to undo that to take a piss. You should have thought of that before you came out . . .'

A second single, another typically swinging cover version,

this time of an old Judy Garland hit, 'Zing! Went the Strings of My Heart', aimed specifically at the Finnish market was released with the new Rockin' Finn pictures on it, but it tanked and the band never returned. 'We thought we'd made it,' said Lemmy. 'The Rolling Stones were on Decca. Not that it did us any good. The only time you heard [Vicars' singles] was on a jukebox in Helsinki. And in a café on the promenade on the Isle of Man.'

Instead, the Vicars found themselves in the even more bizarre position of being part of a 'cultural exchange' programme with the Red Army Orchestra, which found them in Yugoslavia performing for the massed troops of the dictator, General Tito. 'We were the first band behind the Iron Curtain. Afterwards we had dinner with Tito. Tito and the Rockin' Vicars. That is, we got shovelled into this big dining room, sat down and ate, then afterwards got shovelled out again. It was some sort of criminally insane swap policy with Britain. We got the Red Army Orchestra; they got the Rockin' Vicars. They loved us, set fire to their shirts and started rolling around on the floor. It was years before they had another rock concert, because it was so subversive. I mean, if you set fire to your shirt, what will you set fire to next? Usual state fucking crap.'

The highlight of the show, he remembered, was when he accidentally broke Moggsy's nose after the roadies had misguidedly (or possibly not) loaded the shaving foam used to furnish the 'custard' pies onto tin plates, the only kind available. 'I said to Harry, "It's a tin plate." He went, "Just hit him!" I did it – bong! He went, "Fucking hell!" collapsed, and the audience loved it, thought it was part of the act.

"Rock and roll!" Blood everywhere, broke his nose in two places . . .'

Mayhem seemed to follow them, if often self-induced. They had one roadie, David 'Nodder' Turner, a former Radio Caroline technician, who drove the van and humped the gear, and lived as a kind of faithful retainer in a spare room at Ciggy's gaff. Lemmy laughingly recalled Ciggy stopping the van one day on the way to a gig and telling the rest of the band: 'I don't think you boys know what Nodder would do for me.' Told to get out of the van, Lemmy and Moggsy and Harry stood balefully and watched as Ciggy ordered Nod to drive the van into a nearby shop window. Without hesitation, Nodder put his foot down. As the old Thames truck trundled through the window – wedding shop – dozens of dresses and showroom dummies flew through the air. Lemmy laughed as he recalled Ciggy turning to them, beaming. 'He said, "So you see, boys, Nodder, will do *anything* for me . . ."'

Looking back at his couple of years in the mid-Sixties with the Vicars, Lemmy said, he viewed it now as 'some sort of heyday, really'. It felt big time. Driving to gigs in a Thames 13-hundredweight van, with a big gold cross on the top. 'Chicks used to write their names on it and occasionally their phone numbers – occasionally their full addresses! The van was covered in lipstick. One said, 'I like the one with long hair.' That was me. They didn't know our names cos we didn't introduce ourselves on stage or nothing.'

One girl who did get his name and address was called Tracey. Years later Lemmy professed to know or recall very little about her, other than she had been the singer in a female vocal duo that had played some of the same US air force base gigs in Europe that the Vicars had. He made a point in his autobiography of saying he'd actually fancied her friend more but that Harry had got to her first. Looking on the bright side, though, he said, Tracey had 'bigger tits' and so they began an occasional relationship, staying over at the band's Manchester pad between gigs. When, however, Tracey turned up at six o'clock one morning to tell Lemmy she was pregnant, he affected disdain. Storming out, he wrote, 'She went away and had the kid, Paul, and brought him up on her own.'

He went on to claim that he didn't finally get around to meeting the child until he was six, and then only by chance, when Tracey happened to be at the same cocaine dealer's place in London. It was 1973. Lemmy was in Hawkwind then, and Tracey took to bringing Paul to see his dad play whenever she got the chance.

Eve Smith, who with her husband, Doug, co-managed the band's affairs, recalls those times with a puzzled smile. Paul, she says, 'was *obsessed* with Lemmy. Obsessed with music. He would just climb up onstage. And Lemmy would *never* acknowledge him. Paul was a couple of years older than Damian, my son. And he would just . . . you'd see him just go straight to the stage. He wasn't invited by anyone to come up and sit on the stage. But they all let him be . . . And I remember Lemmy used to sort of . . . I don't think he had anything to do with him, did he, when he was little? No, I don't think until he got much older . . .'

There was another reason why Lemmy never felt the need to get involved in Tracey's affairs (other than once buying her a fridge, he claimed). His genuine love for another girl, Susan Bennett. 'Yeah, yeah,' he told me. 'Susie. Black Susie. First black girl I ever went out with.' He later described Susie as 'the girl I was most in love with in my life'. He even dedicated his memoir, *White Line Fever*, to her, with the words: 'Susan Bennett, who might have been the one.' By his own admission, though, Lemmy's relationship with Susan never ran smooth. Or not for long. His friends, he said, disliked him 'associating with a nigger'. Her friends, he said, viewed him as 'the oppressor'. But they were in love, 'so no one else mattered'.

Well, no one except the endless groupies that Lemmy still enjoyed on the road, or the newfound 'friends' 19-year-old Susie discovered when she moved down to London and began working behind the bar at the Speakeasy, then one of London's most famous members-only rock nightclubs. When they weren't making love, they were fighting and falling out with each other. According to Lemmy, they split up four or five times. 'And then she screwed Mick Jagger.'

Lemmy, meanwhile, still fancied himself to become Mick Jagger one day. Or at the very least Keith Richards. Anyone but the bedraggled, unfulfilled figure he was slowly becoming in the Rockin' Vicars. Being famous in the Vicars, Lemmy said, 'was just a licence to fucking shit in the street . . . We used to do a great show though.' There was even a short-lived attempt to make a mark in London, home to the rapidly expanding British music business. 'Even the Beatles had to do that,' he reasoned, 'because it's where everything is. All the streets look the same when you first come down, all those rows of houses with pillars on the doors. The size was daunting, especially if you're from Colwyn Bay. But it was great, they really were the Swinging Sixties.'

They booked appointments at Vidal Sassoon's famous salon in Mayfair where they submitted to having their long unkempt hair cut into the geometrical 'bob cuts' Sassoon was growing famous for. Then they paid to have a photo session with Gered Mankowitz, whose brilliantly evocative shots of the Stones and Jimi Hendrix they hoped to emulate. Anything to get away from the dog collars and reindeer boots.

Armed with their new look they managed to get a deal with Shel Talmy Productions. Among more than a dozen hits for The Kinks and The Who, Shel had produced 'You Really Got Me' and 'My Generation'. But the American hit maker could not work his magic on the Rockin' Vicars, who simply couldn't come up with original material. Their first single under the new deal in 1966, and produced by Talmy's engineer, Glyn Johns, was 'It's All Right', which Lemmy remembered as 'a bastardisation of "The Kids are Alright" by The Who. It was written by Harry, who'd only heard the original once, so it was completely different [musically]. The problem was it was their words!'

The closest they came to a hit was their cover of 'Dandy', by Ray Davies of The Kinks, whose version had been a hit across Europe, and a major hit in the US for Herman's Hermits. Talmy produced this one himself. 'He'd come in and knock things over,' laughed Lemmy. 'Blind as a fucking badger. He'd walk in and fall straight over the drum-kit. "Hi, boys!" Crash through the cymbals! But he was a good producer.' The resulting track was catchy, upbeat, enough so that it looked like it might actually get the Vicars into the lower reaches of the charts. But they were thwarted by the unexpected release at the same time of yet another version of 'Dandy' by a former Butlin's Redcoat named Clinton Ford. This was not a hit either but Ford had a name – he'd had two minor hits in the recent past – and when *Top of the Pops*, BBC TV's hugely influential weekly chart show, chose to feature Ford, the Vicars' recording career was over. As Lemmy later put it, 'We didn't have the hit with "Dandy", everyone else did.'

There was a strange coda to the story of the Rockin' Vicars' 'Dandy', in that it later slipped into the US national pop charts at No. 98. But by then the band, with Lemmy in tow, had relocated back to an uncertain future in Blackpool. By the spring of 1967, 'Moggsy' had quit, to be replaced by their faithful roadie, Nod, and Lemmy was thinking seriously about doing the same. Going back up North to Blackpool was a backwards step, as far as the 22-year-old was concerned. It meant the dream was over and he wasn't settling for that. Not yet.

Meanwhile, the Vicars were turning into a joke. 'I remember Harry running out and as he reached the mike, these two chicks had hold of his mike lead and they pulled it and he went straight out into the audience! He thought the chicks would save him but they all jumped out of the way. He said, "I could see the floor coming up very slowly." He broke his nose in two places.'

Still, though, he hung on. The Vicars might not be going anywhere but being in them offered him the kind of access he could never achieve back out on his own. He recalled meeting Gene Vincent and being in awe. 'I used to chat with him. I didn't get to know him that well. Gene was in a lot of trouble. He was in pain all the time. His leg was fucked after that motorcycle [accident] and he was in pain all the fucking time. And that one black glove? That was elastic, it used to keep the tendons from springing out of his wrist. It wasn't an affectation. He'd fucked all himself up from that motorcycle [accident] in the navy. For ever after that he was just in pain. But he was such a good performer. He was very hard, man.'

Lemmy describes as 'one of the greatest moments of my rock'n'roll life' the time he saw Gene perform at the Prestatyn Lido. 'They used to get a lot of big acts there. He was lifted up out of the crowd. His feet were on the stage and he came up straight at the microphone, smiling at the band. Then he turned round and just started singing. It was great! He used to whip his bad leg up over the mike. I still stand like him onstage today, with one leg stuck out the back. The influence was there long before I realised it. Same with John Lennon. He used to stand like that [assumes pose]. He'd say, "I'm just doing Elvis, like."'

Another hero he met while in the Vicars was PJ Proby, the outlandish Texan singer who enjoyed a string of hits in the UK throughout 1964 and '65, but who quickly became better-known for the ribbon in which he kept his hair pony-tailed – and a penchant for ripping his skin-tight trousers at the crotch mid-performance onstage. An act that led to him being banned first from television, then later ballrooms around the country as the 'scandalised' British tabloids descended on him like vultures.

'I'll never forget a Rolls pulling up with blacked-out windows, which was massive in them days, and this mass of hair getting out, dressed in a striped pirate shirt and old cords, and saying, "Hi, I'm Jim." It was Proby. Ciggy never got over it. He saw the show that night, PJ Proby in a skin-tight red-velvet jumpsuit and the hair tied back in a bow and the buckled shoes, singing [does voice], 'There's a place for us . . .' Ciggy never got over it for years afterwards. It dwarfed him, you know? Being short in the first place . . .'

What Lemmy liked most about the singer, though, he said, was that he 'was real. The music industry killed him on purpose. Okay, he ripped his jeans onstage but they said it was obscene. So all the boring chains of record stores that were in league with those bastards banned him. It was bullshit. Because he wouldn't bend to their rules, I guess, I don't know. He was a truly outrageous character. He was pissed drunk by the time he went onstage but it was such a great performance it didn't matter! When I go onstage you'll never know [what I've drunk]. By the time you cross from the stairs to the stage you become professional, right, and that's it. And if you can't do that and it's visible, then you can't perform any more. You just fall and crash to the ground.' Like Proby, who defied the bans to keep on working, kept on doing his act to the full, Lemmy would stand tall, he decided, against all-comers.

He loved the showmen of the era. The 'fucking brilliant' Sounds Incorporated, whose sax player, he recalled, 'used to do a one-handed cartwheel while playing the saxophone, without missing a breath! And Tony Newman on drums.

51

The blonde bombshell! Ended up playing with Jeff Beck. And they backed Gene Vincent and they backed Proby . . . There were all sorts of characters then. Look at Nirvana, man, they wrote great songs, right? Before [Cobain] died. Great stage persona. But they didn't *do* anything. All they do is walk up to the mike, sing, then waltz back and do a solo. In them days, you were *competing* with a lot of bands with a showman. Like Rory Storm, who would climb up the scaffolding at the side of the stage and throw himself down – while singing! He fell off it once and broke his fucking arm! Nobody cared. He just went to the next gig with a cast.'

Then there were proto-psychedelic rockers Four Plus One, featuring Keith West later of Tomorrow. 'They were around for ages, very influential on the scene. They had a bass player called Bootsy who was always going to jail for some reason . . .' He also recalled seeing Junior Wood, bassist in Tomorrow, 'throw his bass guitar up in the air, catch it and play the right note exactly at the same time the singer began singing. That was very, very big! A Fender Precision bass? That's not a lightweight object . . . I thought, this guy is *good*. We used to go and see these bands every time they came around. The place would be jammed. And this was without a record.'

He had also become a regular face at gigs by The Birds. The Birds were The Thunderbirds, from West London, that had dropped 'thunder' from their name after Chris Farlowe and The Thunderbirds got there first. Featuring the future Faces and Rolling Stones guitarist Ronnie Wood and bassist Kim Gardner (who years later Lemmy would become friends with in Los Angeles, where Gardner had opened the Cat & Fiddle, aka the English Pub, popular with expat British musicians), they specialised in covers of American classics, Chuck Berry, Howlin' Wolf, Bo Diddley, tons of Motown. By the time they got to play as far as Manchester, The Birds were a brilliantly tight outfit. Lemmy loved the explosive mix of jittery Mod guitars and drums, and joyous Motown-style vocal harmonies that became The Birds' signature sound.

'They were a very big influence on my career,' said Lemmy. 'An *incredibly* large influence on my career, really. They had three singles and I used to play all of them,' he told me proudly. 'They used to play stuff you'd never heard before. And they used to do a lot of their own stuff. Ronnie used to write a lot of songs [including their first single, 'You're on My Mind', on Decca]. That was the last time Ronnie was a really good guitar player, because his stuff with the Stones and the Faces never approached it at all. He was powerful, and the look of them was excellent too, Ronnie in a three-piece tweed herringbone suit on stage and a white telecaster. And then very sharp moves and all that. One of the best gigs I ever saw was them and The Action. They were another great band.'

He recalled the night The Birds and The Action played at a club called the Twisted Wheel, using each other's equipment. 'That was a hell of a night. Like a battle of the bands kind of. See, to be big back then you didn't need to have hits. You could be huge on the club circuit. More even than a lot of chart bands, because you were popular with everybody that went there and knew you. Whereas if you'd just come out of nowhere with a chart record it didn't necessarily mean they were going to like you in the clubs. Fucking Crispian St Peters and all them bozos. We'd go for the real stuff. Bands that played three-hour sets and knocked your fucking head off.' He recalled with a glow hitching up to Preston to see The Birds. 'They noticed us in the crowd, we told them we had nowhere to stay so they let us sleep in the van. Can you imagine that happening now?' It was the height of luxury, as far as Lemmy was concerned, except for the fact that 'The doors would always come off the top end . . .'

Of course, it wasn't just Lemmy who was having his 'head blown off' by the rock scene in Britain in the mid-Sixties. With LP sales starting to overtake those of singles for the first time, you didn't need to take speed to feel the world was flashing by like the lights of a train. The Beatles, the Stones, LSD, Pink Floyd . . . The whole era spoke deeply to Lemmy, helped forge his own identity, musical and otherwise. He rattled off more names he'd never be able to forget. 'The Who, Hendrix, Cream . . . That first John Mayall album was a great influence on guitar players.'

He was still in the Vicars the first time he saw Jimi Hendrix play. It was the package tour. 'The oddest tour I've ever seen: The Walker Brothers, Engelbert Humperdinck, Cat Stevens, Hendrix, and some local band. The Walker Brothers were as big as the Beatles at the time, people don't realise now. Massive!'

Seeing Hendrix was the really big turning point. The moment he knew his time in the Rockin' Vicars was now over. 'I couldn't believe him, you know? Nobody could believe him. Hendrix changed the way people played guitar for ever. Nobody knew you could do that with a guitar. The big thing before that was Clapton. That was as high as you could get. But this guy was turning somersaults and playing. People have lost it now. These bands have fucking lost it. They think smashing up the equipment is a big show. Hendrix used to fucking do a double-somersault and come playing it behind his neck, fucking bite it, fucking every fucking thing! He was playing it with his teeth. I watched him many nights and he wasn't just pretending, playing it with his fingers. He was playing it with his teeth! And he used to fuck the amplifier and drag it around the floor. Rory Gallagher got his act from there, you know? Lighting it on fire . . .'

Ultimately, said Lemmy, with the benefit of decades-long hindsight, he eventually walked out on the Vicars 'because I was full of my own fucking self-importance, basically'. He was tired of being in a covers band. 'We showed no signs of progressing. And I knew we were never going to get anywhere based in Blackpool or Manchester. I realised we were never going to get any support from the record company, because in London you're around to bother them. In Blackpool you're relying on a phone call and even that depends on whether they want to take it. I knew we were fucked.

'I'd had enough of the Vicars. They were on a never-ending circuit of supper clubs in the North and they were becoming kind of a cabaret act. It was time to get out. Harry used to do that Herman's Hermits thing with his fingers, the windscreen wipers. We used to call him the Viper. The

Windscreen Viper! Behind his back. And there were always arguments over money, because Harry and Ciggy got most of it.'

He stopped. Surprised perhaps at the vehemence still there inside, even after all these years. He began to tell another story. How Cyril, years later, after Lemmy had become a star in Motörhead, came down to visit him. He was then living in Little Venice on a houseboat. The famous rock star. 'I had all the gold discs up on the wall and he went, "You've done it, boy! What I always dreamed of, you've done it . . ." It was kind of sad, you know? We took a picture of him with me and all my gold records and he took it home with him.'

Leaving the Rockin' Vicars didn't automatically leave Lemmy thumbing a lift back down to London. Outside the Rockin' Vicars, he didn't know anyone down there yet, wasn't sure how to make the first move. So, for a time, he became a DJ at a ska club in Blackpool. 'Playing "Phoenix City" by Prince Buster and all that. They couldn't see into the booth, see? If they'd seen I was white it would have been all over. I did that for about two months. I didn't speak between the records, as that would have been a dead giveaway. That said, the blacks up there all had Lancashire accents so maybe I'd have been all right. There was nothing weirder to me though than to hear a black man open his mouth and "Ay up, lad" comes out, cos that's one of the real, quintessentially, yobbo English accents, you know? But they're born there, so that's their accent. And what's English anyway? We've got all the Celts in us.'

When he got fed up with that he even went home to Wales

for a while. In the end it was a chance meeting with Deep Purple's future keyboardist Jon Lord, then of The Artwoods, that finally gave him the courage to come down to London alone. The Artwoods were a tough-playing blues rock band from London. Their leader, the singer Art Wood, was the older brother of Ronnie, whom Lemmy hadn't seen since The Birds had broken up some months before. Lemmy went to see them play in Llandudno, and introduced himself afterwards as a pal of Ronnie's. As a result, they offered him a lift home in their van, which is where he got talking to Lord, who gave him his address in West Drayton, a London suburb. Told him to come by if ever he was in the neighbourhood. A cordial, end-of-the-night general, rather than specific, invitation, but which Lemmy took literally.

'Jon Lord, it was his fault that I came to London. Like a fucking idiot he gave me his address. He was staying at Art Wood's mum and dad's house. So when I hitched to London the first place I went to was Mrs Wood's house. I turned up at three in the morning, knocked on the door, and this little old lady came to the door.

'"Yes, dear?"

'"Is Jon Lord in?"

'"No, no, no, dear. He's on tour in Denmark."

'Oh, fucked, you know? She said, "You got anywhere to stay, dear?"

'"No."

'"You better come inside then. You can sleep on the sofa."

'She was good as gold, you know? Ronnie Wood's mother was a good woman. A place in my heart for ever. She could have just shut the door. I wouldn't have blamed her. Then I woke up in the morning with all The Birds standing around me, Ronnie, Art and Ted. "Who's this chap? What you doing on my mum's sofa?" I ended up hanging out with The Birds for about four days, while they were doing shows. Then I went back up [North], cos I didn't know anybody else there. That was the first time I moved to London.'

There was also a short-lived attempt to establish his own London presence and get in a band, going over to stay for a while in a squat in Bromley with a friend, Murph. But the band he was in 'got nowhere; our drummer didn't have any drums – but he had some cushions. And he'd tuned them. They sounded better than you'd think, but I hung around waiting for him to get some proper drums like you do when you're young and stupid. So I went back home again.'

His next attempt at making a go of London life was no less haphazard but, this time at least, more successful. Having had a taste of what to expect, 'I was up for it. And the next time I went there [London] was when I drove back down with The Birds in their van, after a gig in Northwich. That time though I stayed with Neville Chesters, who had worked with The Merseybeats. I'd met him with the Vicars when he was working for The Who, trying to put guitars back together after Townshend had finished smashing them. I phoned him from a call box and asked him if I could kip on his floor for a while and he said, yes, come on over. He was working for the Jimi Hendrix Experience by then and he shared his flat with [Experience bassist] Noel Redding, in Harrington Gardens in Kensington. The flat was full of these guitars in different degrees of destruction that Neville was trying to put back together out of the bits. Cannibalising Rickenbackers.'

Lemmy was still wondering how to go about finding his own pad when, out of the blue, Neville mentioned they were looking for a second roadie to assist him on the next Hendrix tour, a 16-date trawl around Britain due to start with a show at the Royal Albert Hall on 14 November. Lemmy couldn't believe his luck. 'I hired on for £10 a week, and all your meals and whatever . . .'

The tour featured The Move and Hendrix as co-headliners, supported by The Nice and Pink Floyd with Syd Barrett, and Amen Corner. 'It was like the Rockin' Vicars to the power of twelve! It was madness. Two shows a night as well. Everybody got fifteen minutes each. Hendrix I think got twenty. There's something to be said for that, because you haven't got time to be boring. Just do your hits. Bang, bang, bang, bang, bang, all the hits and come off. Great fun.'

For Lemmy, working for Hendrix was an honour. 'He was like a prince, a really good guy. Very old-fashioned good manners. Get up when a lady enters the room. Pulling chairs out for chicks. Good manners are for free. I don't like anybody that doesn't have them. There's no reason.' His job was easy enough. 'Just general humping and carrying. Neville took care of all the electrics. I just humped all Hendrix's gear. When he was playing I'd watch him onstage from a chair in the wings; you could never tell how he did it. He loved to fuck off all the guitar players in the audience. Graham Nash [then of The Hollies, soon to join Crosby,

Stills & Nash] used to sit backstage with his ear on the stacks all night – none of this glad-handing you get backstage now with the fucking canapés. In those days people wanted to learn and improve.' Even offstage being around Hendrix was a lesson. 'He had this old Epiphone guitar – it was a twelve-string, strung as a six-string – and he used to stand up on a chair backstage and play it.'

He was also impressed with Hendrix's stamina for groupies. 'If you wanted to see some athletic fucking, Jimi was the boy for it. I'd never seen anything like it – there were always lines of chicks going nuts outside his dressing room. It was like, "Take a number and wait."' Did he get to talk to Jimi much? 'Oh yeah. I used to score acid for him. And his dope. I'd get him ten hits of acid and he'd take seven and give me three. They say acid doesn't work two days in a row but we found out if you double the dose it does.'

Thus began Lemmy's next big adventure into the mind-expanding world of psychedelic drugs. On his last trip to America, the LSD evangelist Owsley Stanley III had gifted Hendrix thousands of tabs of super-strength 'Owsley White Lightning', Lemmy recalled. 'They weren't even illegal yet . . .' Back at the flat, before the tour had begun, Neville Chesters had offered Lemmy one of the little owl-faced tabs. 'Neville said one day, "Do you wanna take some acid?" I thought, ha, that's like three or four joints, I know about this. So I said yeah. The tabs were little and white. They looked like a sweetener. So I took it. He turned round and said, "Where's it gone?" I said, "I've eaten it." He looked at me, face like a ghost. "What?" Cos I think you were only meant to take half. But fair play to him, he took one too and came with me. Cos that was the thing in them days. [Acid] was like a fraternal thing. These days it's more like every man for himself, all divorced from each other and having your own experience. Which produces a lot of fucking lunatics. I mean, Neville couldn't do anything either on that first trip but at least he was *with* me.

'Eighteen hours, couldn't move. Patterns and colours and things. You didn't have time to get paranoid. Your head was too busy. Amazing experience. Uncontrollable laughter for hours. If you've ever had your picture taken while you're laughing on acid your face is *different*. Big fucking rings round your eyes! I don't know what it is about acid but I would not have swapped it for any other experience. I would not have *not* done it because I'm sure it made me more aware of everything around me and inside me. I'm sure acid is a good drug but it's abused. And later the abused acid became shit. They put speed in it, strychnine. All sorts. And I'm a great supporter of speed as a drug. Not as a recreational drug as much as a utilitarian drug. To get you places you couldn't make without it.

'But when they put speed in acid it was a bad thing. They shouldn't put the two together. They don't belong together. Acid is a complete experience. You don't need to add anything to it if it's good. And I took a lot of fucking acid, man. I must have taken a thousand trips. I only did it until '75. I stopped then. But I must have taken *a lot* of fucking trips! I mean, ten tabs in a handful. If it fit in your hand and your mouth in them days we just did it. We did the whole [Hendrix] tour all tripped out, every-fucking-body!'

For Lemmy, in the late Sixties, acid wasn't a 'drug'. It was an alternative reality, a creative tool, he said, 'to get you to a certain place. That will improve you, not blot everything out.' Acid, he declared, 'made you hard, mentally. Or it destroyed you. It's hero stuff, acid.'

When the Hendrix tour ended in Glasgow, just before Christmas, Lemmy was bereft. Jimi's next stop was Sweden and Denmark in January, followed by a three-month tour of the US. No need for any English roadies. 'I went to a few radio shows with him in England, *Saturday Club* and all that stuff, but then he didn't need anybody cos he was going to the States. Neville got fired around the same time . . .'

He left Hendrix more determined than ever to get his own band together. 'But I left and I couldn't get a job for a long time. I was dealing dope in Kensington Market for a while.' Dealing dope, he recalled, 'was like selling wine. What side of the hill it grew, and so on. And it was true as well. It was better dope in them days, like meth . . . You could get ten black bombers for a pound and you couldn't give Mandrax away. You could kill yourself real easy in them days. We didn't know how many of us were going to die – it was all new.'

It was at Kenny Market, as it was known to regulars, that Lemmy fell in, briefly, 'With these Irish shadow boxers. They all used to stand in the shadows by the booths. "You want any Mandies, man?" Northern Irish guys. A real brotherhood selling Mandrax and downers.' As a result, he said, 'I spent two years on downers. Seconal, Nembutal, Tuinal, Mandrax . . .'

Lemmy would later write of his downers experience in the

Hawkwind number 'Lost Johnny', where the drug appears in the verse, 'We're all taking Tuinal to murder our young dreams.' Later, when Motörhead performed the song, the verse became 'We're all shooting Tuinal to murder all your dreams.'

'That was the time when Mandrax was getting phased out. I had a script for Mandrax for ages, from Harley Street. I had a Dexedrine Spansules and Mandrax prescription. Then they stopped giving me Mandrax and they gave me Tuinal instead. Which is a really smart move! Suddenly you've got homicidal maniacs where before you had gentle dreamers. Tuinal's a very violent fucking drug. Especially if you take ten in a handful . . . And I still wouldn't go to sleep. Downers accumulate at an incredibly fast rate of tolerance. With Mandrax, if you took one on Monday you'd be taking four by Saturday to get the same effect. It just escalated like hell. So we were doing incredible amounts of downers. You wouldn't even go to sleep. You'd stay up raving all night. And ten Tuinals in one handful is a lot of downers. But you'd be ready to kill. Which is not what they're supposed to do. Eventually the government realised but by then it was far too late and they banned them but you could still get them.'

It was during this period of deep somnambulism that Lemmy – still known professionally as Ian Willis – joined Sam Gopal. Named after its leader, a Malaysian-born tabla and percussion player who had previously made a name for himself in London with Sam Gopal's Dream, an underground psychedelic four-piece who had performed at the 14-hour Technicolor Dream show at Alexandra Palace alongside

Pink Floyd and Soft Machine in 1967. Familiar to London's growing community of squat-dwelling middle-earth 'heads', Jimi Hendrix had sat in with them at the Speakeasy, and the *International Times*, then London's most outré under-ground magazine, had championed them. When the band splintered, Sam merely formed a new outfit, this time with Lemmy on lead vocals and rhythm guitar.

Unlike the Vicars, who gigged non-stop but recorded only rarely, Sam Gopal made few live appearances but immediately recorded an album, *Escalator*. Released on the tiny Stable label – named after the club DJ and hippy aristo-crat scene-maker Simon Stable (real name: Count Simon de la Bedoyere), who would later play bongos on albums by Bridget St John and Ten Years After – the acid-singed, deep-water undulations of *Escalator* were not seen as any-thing out of the ordinary at the time. However, viewed now through the prism of what Lemmy would become known for in Hawkwind and particularly Motörhead, the 11 tracks on *Escalator*, most of which had been written solely by Lemmy, offer a staggering glimpse into a wholly unexpected side of his talents, not least as a singer, where his clear, river-deep voice sounds like a cross between Tim Buckley and Love's Arthur Lee.

Perhaps it's because the only percussion is provided by the tabla and, on one track, finger cymbals, but the songs are mostly floaty invocations of the times – freeform, long distance, completely out there. The only exception, 'Mid-summer's Night Dream', where a session drummer is brought in to depth-charge the ripped off 'You Really Got Me' riff as the band, suddenly fully awake, gallop through something that could have come straight from Love's *Forever Changes*, a big favourite of Lemmy's at the time.

The rest though – the sinister, creeping 'The Dark Lord', the languid, claustrophobic 'You're Not Alone Now' (a forerunner of 'The Watcher', which Lemmy would write for Hawkwind, then revisit yet again in Motörhead), the more-to-life-than-this mission statement 'The Sky is Burning', and the final track, 'Yesterlove', the softest most ethereal moment of Lemmy's career – chimed perfectly, it seems, with the fact that Lemmy was in the middle of his 'heavy downers' phase.

According to Lemmy, though, he actually wrote all the songs in one long, speed-crazed night. Other than that, he always dismissed the album as something of a joke. Embarrassed somewhat, in retrospect, it seemed, by how much it belies the road-warrior image he spent the rest of his professional career fostering. As far as Lemmy was concerned, the label was 'a joke' and the album died a quick and deserved death. 'We did [a] show at the Speakeasy and when we got a standing ovation, we thought, "That's it, we're stars." We played about three other shows in and around London, which were awful, then we went to Munich and played for a week at the Blow Up club, which was even worse, and then we came home and broke up!'

A pity but perhaps inevitable. As Julian Cope later wrote of the album in his compilation of 'lysergic essays and progressive prognosis', *The Book of Seth*: 'All the tracks are about as drugged and unglamorous as the members of Sam Gopal themselves: which, from one look at the cover shot, is an achievement as they all look "street", stoned and pissed off as hell.' You can still find a wonderfully grainy black-and-white video of the band miming to 'The Sky is Burning' on YouTube, Lemmy, looking suitably enigmatic in buckskin jacket and stoner shades, standing on the prow of a boat loping along the Thames, barely moving his whiskered lips.

But after 'two years on downers', he said with a frown, 'I got fed up waking up in other people's vomit. In places I'd never been to before, with my pockets empty and shit.' Instead he weaned himself off – by taking even more speed. 'I never stopped doing speed,' he insisted. Even during his worst times on Mandies, 'I was always a speed freak. The first day I took it I knew this was my music, these were my people [and] well, look at me, you know, I'm still here. All the people who carried on doing downers are dead, man. Gone. And gone some time too.'

He also began tripping in earnest again too. And chasing girls. 'We discovered acid and the pill at the same time! Everyone was fucking like rabbits. If it moves, fondle it, you know?' And at the same time questioning the values of our so-called elders and betters. 'Well, we did. Because we saw that they were the old bastards. They were from the generation before us that had just fought a war. They were in no mood to look at what was going on. As long as they had the car and the fucking TV they were happy.'

Mainly, though, he was into sex and drugs. 'The School for the Dancing Arts and Education in Tring, Hertfordshire, mmm!' He smacked his lips. 'Me and this Scottish guy, we fucked our way through the entire year 1969! Wonderful. Wonderful. All ballet dancers come down to get a bit of rough. Beautiful women, voluptuous, long legs – beautiful naked women pirouetting round the room, with shawls hanging off the ceiling . . . Great stuff . . . But you can't do it nowadays, you can't get the staff. And you don't seem to be able to get the shawls either . . .'

It was also in 1968 that he was busted for the first time. 'I was living in a house just down the road from the Earl's Court police station, where the other guys were dealing a lot of shit around the world. I came home one day and the garden was full of policemen with shovels. I said, "I was just going . . ." And this policeman said, "Don't put your hands in your pockets, son. Let's go inside and see what we can find . . ."'

According to Lemmy, what they found was two pounds of Lebanese cannabis resin soaking in the kitchen sink. 'You soaked them so they weighed five times as much,' he explained, 'and were much more economical. They busted us and took away two pounds of dope and charged us with half an ounce each. What are you gonna do, protest? "No, I had two pounds!"'

Another time, he woke up in hospital after a near-fatal overdose. A girlfriend of a friend who was a nurse had ripped off a bottle of what they assumed from the scratchy label was amphetamine sulphate. What the bottle actually contained was atropine sulphate: Belladonna – pure poison. The ashen-faced doctor informed Lemmy that had he been found an hour later he would have died. An experience Lemmy later described with grim understatement as 'interesting'.

By 1969, Lemmy was a familiar figure at all the regular hippy haunts across London: the Electric Garden, in Covent

Garden and soon to become Middle Earth; the Ship public house in Wardour Street, where the fruit machine became Lemmy's solo domain whenever he was in; the Drugstore, in Chelsea's King's Road, where he frequented the basement record shop and ground floor bar, though never the upstairs restaurant. It was here, in the summer of 1970, that he became acquainted with a lank-haired beanpole with eyes on sticks named Simon King. Simon came from Oxford, played drums like a razor blade tapping a mirror, and was the leader of his own self-consciously stoned, psychedelic outfit, Opal Butterfly. Lemmy later claimed he couldn't really remember how he ended up joining the band. Certainly he wasn't with them very long. He did recall that he didn't like Simon much – not least when King sacked him. An opinion Lemmy felt was later borne out to an even greater degree when they met again in Hawkwind, 'and he tried to get me sacked again'. According to Lemmy, anyway, though it was he who recommended Simon to the band.

In the meantime, the summer of 1971 found Lemmy still out of work, still living off, as he jokingly put it, 'my considerable charm and personality'. Living selling dope and speed, in 'this big squat in Harrington Gardens', in Kensington, he badly needed a gig. He didn't know it yet but there was one waiting for him round the corner. And though it turned out to be exactly what he thought he wasn't looking for, it would be the transforming move that would see 'Lemmy' triumph over Ian Willis and/or Kilmister for ever.

Talking about it with me years later he still seemed confused over how the whole thing went down. 'This huge fucking flat was left to me by the sister of the organ player in Supertramp, Rick Davies. The sister lived up there with three other girls and I used to go up there quite a bit. She told me when she was moving out I could have it and I moved in with a bunch of freaks. So I was in there [the Kensington squat] and there was this girl called Lou who used to live with a friend of mine. She had the most amazing flat in Nevern Square, in Earl's Court. There was wallpaper with a diamond pattern on it, and ceiling with the same wallpaper. And they painted it all in blue and red Day-Glo. The whole lot! And they used to live in it, man. Seriously bad for your health. He was American and he went barmy and went off and she came and moved into the flat in Harrington Gardens. And she brought Dikmik home one night.'

Dikmik was a 27-year-old miscreant named Michael Davis, whom Hawkwind saxist and co-founder Nik Turner would later recall for me as one of several 'chemist robbers and speed dealers' that Nik had first met in his days 'selling psychedelic posters on Margate beach'. Brought in originally, in 1969, as someone to drive the van and hump gear for Hawkwind, within weeks Dikmik had talked his way into the band by building a contraption he called an 'audio generator': made, he liked to claim, from the parts of an old vacuum cleaner – in reality, a customised ring modulator. 'It didn't really do much,' laughed Nik, 'but what he did with it actually contributed an enormous amount to the band's early sound.' According to Lemmy, 'He used to set it up onstage on an old card-table and just sort of make these weird noises with it. If you were tripping, it sounded fucking great . . .'

Lemmy recalled Lou introducing him to Dikmik and

sitting listening to his story. 'He'd left Hawkwind and was going to India to study with the great gurus. But he only got as far as Gloucester Road, which is in the wrong direction anyway. So he came up and we discovered we had this mutual interest in how long the human body could be made to jump about without stopping. So he stayed there for a bit then he ran out of money and he was going back to Hawkwind. He said, "Come with me, I'll get you a job too . . ."'

FOUR

The Captains

Lemmy fixed me with that hard-as-nails stare he'd perfected over the years. The snake eyes of the speed freak, laced with the vicelike focus of the hardcore gambler. He was recalling for me my own memories of seeing Hawkwind live at the Rainbow in 1972. 'You have to admit when you were in that show and they'd been playing ten minutes you were gone. I mean, fucking *gone*, man. I mean, there wasn't no question of shall we go and get some pot while we're listening to these guys.'

In fact, I was only 14 at the time and had never smoked a cigarette let alone pot, but his words had me pinned to my seat and I merely nodded. He leaned in. '*You were fucking gone!* I know you were. Cos I was in the audience at the Roundhouse one time when they played. I'd never seen them before and the entire audience – six hundred people! – stood up and went' – he feigned a long swoon – 'all with the same movements at the same time. I thought, I better join them. I can't watch them.'

Somehow Lemmy and Hawkwind were just meant to be. The most ramshackle, drugged-up guitarist in London, joining the most drugged-up, ramshackle band – on bass. Which he didn't actually play. Not that he let on. No more than they showed that they didn't really care anyway. They were a man down, Lemmy happened to be there. Let's roll . . .

'I remember driving in the van with Dikmik to go and pick him up from this basement flat,' says Doug Smith, the then 25-year-old manager of Hawkwind. 'All we knew was that he was Dikmik's speed freak friend.' Or as Nik Turner would have it, 'One of Dikmik's little drug-orientated loonies that he used to know.' And though Doug's own opinion of Lemmy would go up over the years – 'I was always very fond of Lemmy, even when he was being a shit' – the rest of Hawkwind, with the exception of other equally less-leading lights as Stacia and Dikmik, would never quite accept him into the fold. He was 'tolerated'. And he knew it.

According to Lemmy, 'the band was split into the speed camp and the psychedelic camp. Me and Dikmik were the untouchables because we liked speed.' Speed, Hawkwind leader Dave Brock concurred when we spoke, was regarded as a 'poor show . . . Irksome.' Lemmy shook his head. 'They tolerated it in their scheme of things. They – the band was presented as one unified force. But it wasn't like that. What kept us together was our anarchist thing. Cos we were all for that, depending on what drugs we took. Before that it didn't matter, because it was just for general purpose.'

But then, as Lemmy pointed out, 'People look back now and think of Hawkwind as this sort of hippy peace and love group. But it was never that. They were really unique. For me they were better than the Floyd. They went to far more interesting places, given the Floyd's success, because the Floyd just lapsed into this fucking pop music with lights. Fair enough, acid did the same thing for them. But then it went all laidback. All that Cambridge bullshit, you know? "Wow it's so peaceful out here . . ." We weren't looking for peaceful, we were looking for *horrid*. The spaceship was always broken down with us. We were always on the edge of death and exploding into the atmosphere.'

Hawkwind had begun as they were apparently meant to go on: by accident. Dave Brock, a busker from Feltham, in Middlesex, was already 27 years old and married with a baby son when, in the autumn of 1968, the original line-up of Hawkwind first 'started to sort of congeal around me'. Memorably described once in a magazine as having 'the debonair grace of the first man to swim the Atlantic', Dave Brock always looked like the sort of grumpy, lank-haired, ageing hippy you went to see for a quid-deal in the days when you didn't know anyone else who sold 'stuff'. Short, wiry, and with dark, ominous-looking tattoos on his fore-arms, Dave always looked *heavy*. Whether stripped to the waist or draped in his afghan, onstage he always emanated a different vibe to the others, like he was holding just a little back, some cosmic joke only he would find funny.

Now 74 and more interested in keeping up his sizeable Devonshire plot – replete with livestock, recording studio, rehearsal space and an almost guiltily concealed swimming pool – than he is in dropping acid for breakfast, Dave looks even less changed from his early Hawkwind days than Lemmy did. The grey is there, too, but it's in his face more than his hair that you notice it. Though he became loath to admit it as the years flew by and Motörhead became far more famous than Hawkwind ever were, Dave Brock never really liked Lemmy. A feeling that Lemmy assured me was entirely mutual.

'They hated each other,' says Doug Smith now. At Hawkwind gigs, 'Brock would walk up behind Lemmy and kick him up the arse when he was going too slow cos he'd dropped Mandies that night. Or another night when he'd taken speed and was going too fast, Brock would walk over and go, "Slow down, you cunt!" And he'd do it onstage in front of the audience. I couldn't believe it. And Lem used to hate it, he'd really get angry about it. But because he was so fragile in Hawkwind he wouldn't throw a wobbler. He'd just go, "Ah, fuck", and just disappear.'

As the years went by, though, Lemmy would look back more fondly at his relationship with Brock. 'Dave was one of the only people I ever had complete telepathy with onstage. Playing and singing. We could be facing completely different ways and we'd come up with the same chord. That's really, really rare, you know? It was such fun playing with Dave. I mean, we were diametrical opposites in temperament. He's a Leo, I'm a Capricorn. That's completely the other side of the coin. Didn't get on at all, you know? Yet we were magic onstage together.'

Born on 1 August 1941, the son of a petrol-tank driver for the 7th Armoured Division, Dave Brock was an only child who liked to 'plonk around' on his Uncle Morris's 'old Appalachian banjo', listening to the trad jazz of Bud Johnson and Ken Colyer. Then, when he was 15, his art teacher introduced him to the blues and Dave persuaded his parents to buy him an acoustic guitar, 'playing along to Big Bill Broonzy 78s'. After leaving school, he worked, variously, as an apprentice capstan-setter ('I used to go off in trances on the machine'), potato-picker, junk mail deliverer, and trainee despatch manager. But by night he was hanging out at then fashionable London dives like the Crawdaddy Club and Eel Pie Island, where he remembers playing his first gig and smoking his first joint. 'It tasted like lavender.'

He began busking his way around Europe, and by 1967 was living in Amsterdam, 'reading about the [race] riots' in America and fronting a four-piece 'acoustic psychedelic flower power band' called Doctor Brock's Famous Cure. Despite achieving a small measure of success in Holland, where they got as far as recording a couple of tracks, they were eventually forced to leave 'in a hurry' after one of the band 'got into a bit of trouble'. (What kind of trouble? 'Er, drug trouble.')

After Brock returned to London in 1968, his luck improved when another former busker, Don Partridge, had an unexpected hit with the song 'Rosie', and invited Dave to join him on his own Buskers Tour, sharing a double-decker bus around the country with such 'street legends' as Jumping Jack and Old Meg Aitken. 'We used to sleep on the top deck and quite smelly it was, too!' There was even *The Buskers*, a live album from one of their 'Buskers Happening' shows at London's Royal Albert Hall, to which Dave contributed his folksy version of Willie Dixon's 'Bring It On Home'.

But, by now, 'I'd seen bands like the Floyd, Arthur Brown's Kingdom Come and, of course, Jimi Hendrix, and I wanted to do something new and more . . . electric.' He would sit at home with a reel-to-reel tape recorder and his battered old Harmony Stratotone guitar, 'drop some acid and just plonk away with an echo-unit. I used to make all these weird noises like bowing the guitar with my harmonica and going *weeaannnggg!*'

He took his first trip at the Famous Cure guitarist Mick Slattery's flat in Ladbroke Grove. 'I think I got spiked up round there, actually. But it was not unpleasant because in those days it was more like, er . . . more religious, you know?' Enthralled by a book of Turner's paintings that Slattery had given him to gaze at – 'I was sitting there thinking, "Fucking hell! Now I can *see*!"' – what he wanted to do now, he decided, was 'to create the aural equivalent of an acid trip. That was the idea behind it all. Sitting at home as you go off into your LSD trip, and thinking, "If only I could put this to music . . ."'

Hanging out at the former Bonzo Dog Doo-Dah Band sideman (and future Whoopee Band leader) Bob Kerr's Music Shop, in Putney, where he and Slattery used to jam in the basement, he met John Harrison, a scrap metal dealer from Shepherd's Bush who had once played bass with Joe Loss. John didn't do acid ('John liked golf, actually'), but he could play and Dave soon had him down in the basement, jamming along. The drummer, Terry Ollis, 'a downers freak' who came via an ad in *Melody Maker,* was a self-taught musician who was 'extremely primitive and had his own style'. Which is one way of putting it. Ollis would sweat so much during gigs he took to playing naked. That is, when he wasn't falling off his drum stool too stoned to continue.

The next to join was, perhaps, even more inept, musically, than the bleary-eyed Ollis, but was to prove, indirectly, a far more influential presence in the band during their earliest years: a 28-year-old flute and sax player, Nick (later Nik) Turner. 'I was responsible, to a large degree, for getting people like Barney Bubbles involved in the band, and Robert Calvert,' he would tell me. 'I'd be very accessible to people and I'd try and get the band doing as many benefits and things like that as I could.'

If Hawkwind were *The Young Ones*, who in their most successful, early-Seventies incarnation they seemed to pre-figure, Nik Turner would undoubtedly be the put-upon hippy idealist Neil. (With Brock as the scheming, too-cool-to-fool Mike; Calvert as the theatrically demented Rik; and Lemmy as that dedicated student of medicine, Vivian.) Naïve, idealistic, too easy-going sometimes – all phrases he repeatedly uses to describe himself, particularly when re-calling his days as a 'captain' in Hawkwind – Nik Turner was not just the one who first encouraged Calvert, Dikmik, the sci-fi writer Michael Moorcock, Bubbles and so many others (he even takes the credit for Stacia) into the group: he was the self-appointed conscience of the band; the keeper of the Hawkwind flame.

Nicholas Turner was born in Oxford on 26 August 1940, another war baby whose father worked in an ammunitions factory 'making Centurion tanks'. The rest of the Turner family 'was all very theatrical' and he bought his first rock'n'roll record – Bill Haley's 'Shake Rattle and Roll' – not long after the family moved to Margate, when he was 13. 'I had a quiff, a pair of Levis and a leather jacket. Me and my friends were all heavy into James Dean.'

Leaving school at 17, he took an engineering course at college and joined the Merchant Navy. He lasted just one voyage. 'It was like one big piss-up from beginning to end and shagging as many passengers as you could.' He moved up to London and began 'seeing the Yardbirds and the Stones and discovering that whole scene'. But though he had played alto sax in his older brother Roger's jazz band, The Canterbury Tailgaters, 'I simply didn't consider myself good enough to think seriously about joining a "proper" group.'

Instead, he bought himself a flute – 'easier to carry around than a sax' – and started travelling around Europe. In Berlin, he met 'all these free jazz musicians who used to play with Eric Dolphy, and they convinced me that you didn't need to be technical to express yourself. I decided that what I wanted to do was play free jazz in a rock band. What I was trying to do in Hawkwind, basically.'

Nik first met Dave Brock in Amsterdam, while working as a roadie on something called the Rock'n'Roll Circus. 'A travelling show, basically, with a great big tent with bands playing and light shows and stuff like that.' When he, too, returned to London in 1968, he went to stay with Dave in Putney. At first, he was merely the van driver. 'Then I got my old sax out at one of the rehearsals and everybody seemed to like it so that was that, really.' Hippy idealist that he still is, as far as Nik was concerned, 'We just wanted to do something genuine, with no great aspirations towards success, really. We weren't ambitious at all.'

Dave Brock and Lemmy, however, both had bigger ideas. For Lemmy, Hawkwind were 'one of those incredible bands that flashes and dies, then flashes and dies again'. With 'progressive rock' now taking over in the early Seventies from pure psychedelia, Hawkwind found themselves loosely bracketed in the music press alongside Pink Floyd, Yes, King Crimson . . . The difference was, said Lemmy, 'Hawkwind were dangerous, man. We used to give people epileptic fits. And we had Michael Moorcock and Bob Calvert writing for us, which was very anti-hero shit. We were really anti-heroes.'

Characterised early on, however, as 'the poor man's Pink Floyd', derided for their dearth of recognisable hits and seeming inability to keep a steady line-up (which changed almost album by album), history now tends to overlook the contribution Hawkwind made to the story of rock in the Seventies; the handful of wonderfully evocative and original-sounding albums they made back then almost forgotten now. Dismissed as the cosmic jokers of the psychedelic pack, as Brock said, 'A few times the openings were there. But it's whether you've got a torpedo mechanism to bring it all down and you think, fuck that, you know? Once you do that, you're on the other side. And Hawkwind was always on the other side of everything . . .'

With the luck of a drunk weaving his way unscathed across a busy highway, they actually got noticed with their very first gig: an impromptu 'jam' to which they had invited themselves at the All Saints Hall, in Powis Gardens. It was

Friday, 29 August 1969. 'We hadn't even thought of a name for ourselves so we just called it Group X,' recalled Dave. 'It was this psychedelic club with strobes going and we just turned up and asked if we could play for free.'

Organising the show that night was Clearwater: a Ladbroke Grove-based company fronted by a former 'RAF brat', Doug Smith. 'We were the same age as the bands and it was very eleventh-hour management. Very chaotic,' Doug recalls. 'The only other company that was in touch with the new sort of psychedelic groups was Blackhill, who were managing the Floyd and also later took an office in Notting Hill.' Promoting Friday night shows at All Saints Hall was a useful way of squeezing some of Clearwater's bands onto the bill. 'It was two-and-six entrance [12½p], no booze, just orange squash and sandwiches,' says Doug. 'Suddenly this bunch of complete freaks walked in the door out of their boxes, and said, "Here, we're a band, can we play?" And they just went crazy onstage, lunatics, you know. Afterwards, John Peel, who was there, said, "Douglas, sign 'em. They could be big." We thought, hmmm, if John Peel thinks this is okay, maybe we better get onboard . . .'

Their performance that night had consisted of one 15-minute, largely improvisational onslaught they had dubbed 'The Sunshine Special'. 'We didn't actually *do* songs,' explained Dave. 'It was free-range music, basically. A bit of avant-garde electronics and, er . . . chaos. There's no other way to put it. We had a few basic chords which we could come back to, but no one ever did . . .'

Doug began booking them gigs and the band's activities began to centre around Ladbroke Grove. The singer, writer and underground legend Mick Farren, whose own Ladbroke Grove band, The Deviants, had recently 'collapsed', and who was then writing for *International Times*, was another mentor. 'We were a bit obnoxious to them, at first,' he chuckled when we spoke a few years before he died. 'They were a bunch of country lads coming up to the big city, and we'd already fought the revolution, you know? But it was a whole scene. There was Quintessence, Hawkwind, the Pink Fairies . . . Portobello Road was the focus, playing for free under the arches and along the green.'

'We did a lot of benefits,' remembered Dave. 'And we used to give away copies of *Frendz*, whose office was also in the Grove, and we did things with the Hells Angels, the White Panther Party, the Urban Guerrillas, Greenpeace . . .'

Often they would be accompanied by the Pink Fairies – the Fairies' drummer, Twink, taking over from Terry Ollis when he was 'too far gone' to complete the set – and 'Pink Wind' gigs became a staple of the Saturday afternoon Portobello market scene. 'They really complemented each other,' said Farren. 'Cos one was an incompetent guitar band and the other was an incompetent psychedelic band and they got on the stage and made this huge fucking noise together, and everyone was just extremely happy that the police hadn't been called and we'd all been arrested . . .'

By the start of 1970, the Group X moniker had been replaced by that of Hawkwind Zoo – soon shortened just to Hawkwind. Not, as might be assumed, for any Tolkienesque connotations, but because, 'it made us laugh', said Nik. 'I got this sort of name for flatulence, and clearing my throat – loudly – and spitting, and "Hawkwind" became like my nickname. Then calling the group Hawkwind was sort of a joke on what we were doing – expounding loudly!'

The joke began to be taken seriously when Doug persuaded Andrew Lauder, then A&R chief at United Artists, to actually put the name Hawkwind on a record contract. 'We did the deal with United Artists on the back of Cochise, who we were also managing and who the label wanted badly and paid £4000 for to make an album,' Doug explains. 'Hawkwind, who they didn't give a shit about, signed for £400 to make a single.'

Not having the faintest idea which bit of their now hour-long 'Sunshine Special' might fit onto a single, Dave suggested they record an old busking number he'd knocked up: an upbeat acoustic blues called 'Hurry On Sundown'. An unremarkable and entirely unrepresentative first choice of single, it was released on UA in March 1970 and quickly sank without trace. Undeterred, UA really surprised them by agreeing to pay for them to go into Trident Studios, in Soho, to make an album. For a day. Nik: 'It was produced by the Pretty Things' guitarist, Dick Taylor, who set the equipment up in the studio and told us to simply run through our live set. I think we did it three times all the way through, and that was it.'

Bookended by 'Hurry On Sundown' and the only other 'normal' song on there, another acoustic leftover from Dave's busking days called 'Mirror of Illusion' (with Taylor supplying some tasty lead work), the remainder of the album was a truncated 30-minute version of 'Sunshine Special' which the band now gave five separate titles to. Swathed in a suitably cosmic sleeve – their name spelled out in green marijuana leaves – *Hawkwind* was released in Britain, in August 1970. Never a hit album in the conventional sense, it did, however, 'get the band reviewed seriously for the first time', says Doug. 'Suddenly there were all sorts of strange new people interested in them.'

Then, not for the last time, just as it looked like they were getting somewhere, the band began to flounder. Mick Slattery had left just before the first album – 'He was bored,' said Dave – his place taken by a whey-faced young Welshman named Huw Lloyd Langton. Then John Harrison left – 'because of all the drug taking, basically' – to be replaced by Amon Düül II's former bassist Dave Anderson. Then Huw left abruptly after a particularly 'hectic' performance in Amsterdam, which resulted in him 'finding Jesus', says Nik. 'He took some LSD and . . . never came back, basically.' Then Dikmik arrived on the scene, first, like Nik, as the van driver and all-purpose fellow-freak, then onto the stage itself with his 'audio generator', a typical speed freak's toy turned lethal weapon.

But if these abrupt, often unannounced changes would become a pattern of the band's ill-starred career, they also cleared the way for the arrival of what Dave called 'the captains': noted science fiction author and fellow Ladbroke Grove resident, Michael Moorcock; underground paper *Frendz*'s artistic director and future album-sleeve designer, Barney Bubbles; and, not least, lighting wizard Jonathan Smeaton (aka Liquid Len).

'We were this sort of crazy people's ideal of a band,' chuckled Nik. 'I certainly think Michael Moorcock saw us like that, and he turned Barney Bubbles on to us.' Brock: 'I used to read all his books, *The Jewel in the Skull* and all that series, which I thought was fantastic. For him to actually come along and say, "Is it all right to come and do some poetry?" It was like, fucking hell, what an honour!'

But the most significant addition came with the arrival of a South African-born poet, writer, mimic, singer, actor, comedian and serial manic-depressive named Robert Calvert, then working in a tyre shop in Portobello Road and writing 'surreal' short stories for *Frendz*. 'Immediately [Bob] was interested in being involved we invited him to be in it,' said Nik. 'Because he had such great ideas. Being into science fiction and inner states and outer states and all that sort of thing.' Nik, who had known him since they were both teenagers in Margate, also knew that Bob's mental disturbances went far deeper than the occasional 'bum trip' the others might experience. 'Bob used to have like a nervous breakdown every eighteen months. He would vary between hyper-activity and depression. When he was hyper he would talk non-stop and be absolutely exhausting to be with. And then there'd be a period of depression when he didn't speak to anybody.'

For all his personal dilemmas, it was Calvert who first successfully conceptualised what Hawkwind were doing, beginning with the 22-page 'Hawkwind Log' which he authored for their second album, *In Search of Space*, released the same month Lemmy joined – an impenetrable hippy spiel full of Burroughsian sci-fi argot and mushroom mysticism that Barney Bubbles embellished with appropriately lysergic images of aliens, space storms, Stonehenge and naked breasts. 'Much as Michael Moorcock was the typical science fantasy-type guru that they would all look up to,' says Doug, 'Calvert was something else. Calvert was like John Updike. He wrote stories that were far more real, with a little bit of horror attached to them as well, because of his own mind.'

And then there was Stacia, the 22-year-old statuesque beauty whose incongruously feminine presence always looked terribly vulnerable before the Bacchanalian uproar of a typically male Hawkwind audience. 'We were doing a gig in Exeter,' Dave remembered, 'and she came and asked if she could dance, and we said yes, and then she took all her clothes off!' When Stacia also turned up the following night at a gig in Redruth and got up and danced naked again, 'We decided to keep her.'

And, finally, there was Lemmy. The last of Brock's 'captains' to arrive, yet the one who most people now re-member best from those days, again his appointment was haphazard. When Dave Anderson left abruptly, said Nik, 'after one too many arguments with Dave Brock', Dikmik immediately suggested Lemmy, not bothering to point out to the band that Lemmy didn't actually play bass. 'It didn't matter,' shrugged Lemmy. 'I really needed the gig and the last guy had left his bass behind so I just picked that up and started playing it like a rhythm guitar. And that's the way I've played bass ever since.'

Offered £15 a week, just a fiver more than he'd earned as a roadie for Hendrix, and more than ten times less than what he'd been used to earning in the Rockin' Vicars, Lemmy accepted without any argument. 'With the Vicars we were making money but we were safe. With Hawkwind we weren't safe. We didn't mind. Nobody made a lot of money out of Hawkwind except possibly Doug Smith. But even he couldn't have made that much because we were buying so much shit for the show. We had eighteen projectors on a gantry at one time. And they weren't cheap, you know? And we would play for three hours. Without stopping, I might add. Because we had bridges between songs, never stopped playing.'

For Lemmy, it really wasn't about the money, not in 1971. It was about the scene. 'The whole thing was Ladbroke Grove . . . Me and Nik and Dikmik, for a while we all lived in one house. Then we all split and lived in different places. Simon used to live in Kensington, on the hill there. I used to live in Ladbroke Grove in a variety of places with Dikmik. One of the first things I did with Hawkwind was a concert on the green up there underneath the arches, by the Mountain Grill café.' On those days when they actually sought food, the latter would become the band's unofficial headquarters, even lending its name to the title of their 1974 album, *Hall of the Mountain Grill*.

'Hawkwind were a fuck-up in the fabric of time,' said Lemmy. 'Whenever we had a new out-front soundman, Dave used to go up to him and say: "When Nik starts playing solos"' – makes cutthroat gesture – '"Out!" Cos he used to just play. He didn't know where we were [in the song]. The one that stands out is "Brainstorm". We'd be playing away, playing away. Next thing Nik would pipe up on the sax, toodle-oo-toodle-oo. Dave got so sick of it. "You cunt! *Vocals*, you cunt!" That's why the song was nineteen

'I still get kids going, "Hey, Lemmy! 'Ace of Spades', man!" I say, "You're not old enough to fucking remember it!"' Lemmy onstage with Motörhead at the Download Festival, Donington Park, June 12th 2005. (Getty Images)

'I would never have left Hawkwind if they hadn't sacked me.' Lemmy, at the height of his 'Silver Machine' fame, London, May 17th 1973. (Getty Images)

'Me and Dikmik were The
Unacceptables – we took speed.'
Hawkwind at Rockfield Studios,
September 1972. L-R: Nik
Turner, Dikmik, Del Dettmar,
Simon King, Dave Brock,
Lemmy. (Getty Images)

'I loved Lemmy but we were
born two days apart so we could
never have been together.' The
beautiful Stacia, onstage with
Hawkwind, Copenhagen, 1972.
(Getty Images)

Top left: The Three Amigos – drummer Phil 'Philthy Animal', Lemmy, and guitarist 'Fast' Eddie Clarke – shooting up, London 1978 (Getty Images); top right: Ace of Spades tour, London, 1980 (Getty Images); bottom: Performing 'Overkill' on *Top of The Pops*, 1979 (Andre Csillag/REX/Shutterstock).

Ozzy Osbourne, 'Fast' Eddie and Lemmy, just before Motörhead go on to top the bill at the Heavy Metal Holocaust festival, Port Vale football ground, August 3rd 1981. (Local World/REX/Shutterstock)

White line fever: Sid Vicious with Nancy Spungen and Sid's bass teacher, having a quiet night out on the town, January 1977. (Getty Images)

'No sleep till I say so!' Lemmy takes aim, London, 1980. (Getty Images)

Promoting the *St Valentine's Day Massacre* EP with Girlschool in 1982. (Andre Csillag/REX/ Shutterstock)

Lemmy frightens the geese. Onstage at the Music Hall, Canada, May 1981. (Getty Images)

Below left: Backstage, Newcastle City Hall, March 1982. Eddie and Lemmy putting on a show for the cameras. In reality they were now constantly rowing. (Getty Images)

Below right: Wendy O. Williams of the Plasmatics, who in 1982 Lemmy recorded 'Stand By Your Man' with. 'Utter shit,' according to Eddie, who walked out in protest. (Getty Images)

New gunslinger in town. Former Thin Lizzy guitarist Brian 'Robbo' Robertson replaced Eddie in what Lemmy later described as 'a complete disaster.' London, 1983. (Sunshine/REX/Shutterstock)

The band on Channel Four's flagship Friday night TV show, *The Tube*, later the same year. Robbo fell off the stage. (ITV/REX/Shutterstock) minutes long. He just would not stop playing sax. I mean, he was singing as well in that song. So he didn't mind. It was his song.'

The upside to this, said Lemmy, was that musically 'We did whatever we wanted. We didn't give a fuck. And that is the secret. Because if you start trying to please people you will fuck up. Cos they don't know what they want, how should you know? Also, when you're doing a lot of acid, it's hard. We did a *lot* of jamming.' This would be, let's jam, and drop acid? 'No. No, no. If we'd begun the set the acid would already be done. Acid wasn't recreation with us. Acid was more interesting than that. Food for the brain. All the other drugs were recreational.'

Many of their gigs would be free. 'We got to know a lot of shit through doing lots of benefits. We did a lot for Friends of the Earth. I remember going down to Cornwall, they were all in a commune on this old farm, and they showed us this sonic facility down there. All the sheep for ten miles around were dead. Lying on their backs in the fields with their feet in the air dead. There's something going there that was bad news. Bringing electricity to the nation, silent, strong and beautiful. All them dead animals. Turned out some of the conspiracy theories were rubbish, and some of them weren't.'

There wasn't anywhere that Hawkwind didn't consider a good place to trip – the stage, the studio, the street. Lemmy recalled they did have one particular spot they liked to go, though, and drop acid when they weren't working. They would pile into the band van and drive out to this spot in the countryside specifically to commune together with the 'sacred sacrament' of the most powerful LSD they could get their web-fingered hands on.

'It was this old ruined house,' Lemmy remembered, 'with these huge gardens all run wild. All little patios and things and little ponds and stuff. We used to go over the wall and walk around this garden and take acid. It was fucking amazing. Beautiful, you know, sit there at sunset, this old, ruined house on the side. A magical time. That's what I re-member about acid. It could make the really mundane into something untouchable. It was fantastic.'

Being an acidhead also had its darker side for Lemmy. 'I'm a Capricorn,' he explained to *NME*'s famed writer Chris Salewicz. 'It's very attractive to Capricorns, all that magic stuff. I used to fuck about with it when I was doing a lot of acid. Me and this friend used to scrape the floor clean and draw pentacles on it, but we were wasted on acid all the time so,' he laughed, 'I can't really vouch for the hallucin-ations that came up, whether there was actually anything there or whether it was just the acid. But I did quite a lot of it. You know, the Capricorn thing is that there's a lot more under the earth than there is above it.'

It was also now that the Hawkship readied itself to leave Earth orbit and head for the stars. Their second album, *In Search of Space*, had gone Top 20 and picked up glowing reviews. 'The band's claim that it is specifically aimed at dope freaks certainly seems to be valid,' reckoned *Melody Maker*. Recorded at Olympic Studios in Barnes, *In Search of Space* was the first Hawkwind collection to feature not just stage favourites like the opening 16-minute acid-jam 'You Shouldn't Do That', but also the band's first (almost) cohesive attempts at actual songs in 'Master of the Universe' (with suitably 'spacey lyrics' by Nik) and 'We Took the Wrong Step Years Ago', another of Dave's old busking songs, but baked under the hydroponic lights of the band in full frenzied flow. 'I always used to take LSD to mix an album and we used to actually spike the engineers up, too,' Dave would tell me. 'People used to be dead wary of us.'

Or as Lemmy put it, 'It was astounding, you know? And powerful. *Jing-jing-jing-jing-jing-jing-jing.* You knew the train was coming. Don't get in the way!' But the line-up was still shape-shifting. One-time Cochise roadie Del Dettmar had joined on synthesiser. Then Lemmy, tired of Terry Ollis 'falling off his drum stool', introduced the band to Simon King, a 'proper' drummer. 'Terry just couldn't do the drugs and play at the same time,' said Dave, deadpan. 'It was unfortunate . . .'

It was the Brock–Calvert–Turner–Lemmy–King–Dikmik–Dettmar (plus Stacia) line-up of Hawkwind that recorded 'Silver Machine', live at the Roundhouse, on 13 February 1972, at a benefit show for the self-styled Greasy Truckers, an alternative Notting Hill Gate community organisation. The vocals were originally sung-spoken by Bob Calvert, with Lemmy's lead vocal only added later in the studio. But that is perhaps just as well as Lemmy was in no condition to speak, let alone sing, on the night.

He explained to me, while coughing with laughter, that on the afternoon of the show, a Sunday, 'Me and Dikmik had been up for four days, right, on Dexedrine Spansules, so we're pretty well bent by now anyway. But we had this gig at the Roundhouse so we had a couple of Mandrax each to calm us down. Then it got a bit boring so we had two black bombers [speed] each. And then we got in the car and Dikmik wasn't enjoying driving but he wouldn't let you do it and so we were following the kerb up there, you know, *very slowly*. He said things kept sticking in his eyes from the right . . .

'We get to the Roundhouse and somebody comes in with a lot of bombers and we take ten bombers each. That's a lot of bombers. Then someone comes up with some Mandrax and we were getting very twisted up by now and so we had at least three Mandrax each to calm us down again. Then somebody came up with some cocaine, fucking big bags of it and so we thought we'd have some of that. And all this time in the dressing room there is constant smoking, you know. So we were all blasted out of our heads from smoking dope as well. And acid. People were producing acid and mescaline. So we all had some of that.

'By the time we came to go onstage, me and Dikmik were stiff as boards. I said, "I can't move, Dikmik, can you?" He went, "No. It's great, isn't it?" I said, "What are we gonna do when we've got to play?" He said, "They'll think of something . . ." It was like Gene Vincent, they just got us up by the heels of our boots and pushed us onto the stage. Then someone hung my bass on me. I said, "Which way's the audience?" They went, "That way." I said, "How far?" They said, "About 10 feet" and I walked five. I said, "Okay, hit it!" and we recorded that and you can't tell. And that's where the backing track to "Silver Machine" comes from.'

'The gig itself was incredible,' says Doug Smith now, still shaking his head in disbelief more than 40 years later. 'But that was the thing about Hawkwind. You never really knew how out of it they were because they were like that *all* the time. I mean, it was insane! In fact, I think we were insane for a long time . . .'

But then, who wasn't bent, twisted and possibly insane back in 1972? Certainly, no one Lemmy or Hawkwind knew. Even Doug Smith, who they relied on for sage business counsel, considered dope-smoking almost mandatory in his office, and would enjoy his own coke and even occasionally acid. Doug had an Old English sheepdog that would carry his dope in his collar. Indeed, it was Hawkwind, arguably, who embodied the self-mythologising, over-indulgent, permanently fucked-up Seventies better than any other band in Britain until the Sex Pistols came along. (Indeed, it was no coincidence that the Pistols kicked-off their 2002 reunion tour each night with 'Silver Machine'.)

The gig was mixed straight off the desk by future Stiff Records supremo Dave Robinson, and two tracks – 'Master of the Universe' and 'Born to Go', 18 minutes of propulsive lysergic power that spread like a disease over the whole of one side of the original vinyl – were later included in the live double album, *Greasy Truckers Party*, released two months later.

It was Doug Smith who shrewdly kept the recording of 'Silver Machine' back, taking it into Morgan Studios to remix it himself, where he wiped Calvert's portentous vocals from the track and encouraged Lemmy to rerecord them. 'Lemmy just had the best voice for it,' explained Doug. 'But, of course, Bob was *not* pleased when he found out.' In fact, Bob, who had actually been sectioned for 28 days, had no say in the matter. 'My decision, I'm afraid,' said Doug. Lemmy, meanwhile, was cock-a-hoop. 'Calvert sang the original version. It was abysmal, in his terrible upper-class accent. Stacia dancing all round him, Nik playing sax all over the words. They tried *everybody* else in the band before me. Nik, Bob, Dave . . . there was only me and the drummer left. So they tried me and I sang it very, very well first time. And they fucking couldn't stand it!'

Indeed, the whole provenance of the song has always been cloaked somewhat in shadow. Written by Calvert (words) and Brock (music), though the latter used his then wife Sylvia Macmanus' maiden name as an alias, thus triggering a separate publishing deal for himself, along with a handy advance. 'Dave was always doing deals none of the others knew about it,' laughs Doug Smith now. The riff itself was a basic, chugging eight-bar boogie as heard on dozens of early rock'n'roll records, enlivened in this context by the raspberry-blowing squalls of Del Dettmar's primitive synthesiser and the battering-ram drums of Simon King, who later admitted, 'I didn't know what I was doing.' The Roundhouse show was only his third gig with Hawkwind and 'I thought that "Silver Machine" was a Chuck Berry number – really.'

The lyrics, which revolve almost entirely around the three-line verse, '*I just took a ride, in a silver machine, and I'm still feeling mean*', were inspired by Calvert's reading of 'How to Construct a Time Machine', by the French nineteenth-century symbolist Alfred Jarry, an essay on what Jarry described as 'pataphysical' travel – that is, not through three dimensions but via imaginary phenomena beyond metaphysics. Calvert divined something else in the work that no one else had: that it was about how to build a bicycle.

As Calvert later explained, '[Jarry] was the kind of bloke who'd think it was a good joke to write this very informed-sounding piece, full of really good physics (and it has got some proper physics in it), describing how to build a time machine, which is actually about how to build a bicycle, buried under this smokescreen of physics that sounds authentic.' Which may or may not have been so. Only Bob Calvert, though, would then consider it 'a great idea for a song'. He went on: 'At that time there were a lot of songs about space travel, and it was the time when NASA was actually, really doing it. They'd put a man on the moon and were planning to put parking lots and hamburger stalls and everything up there. I thought that it was about time to come up with a song that actually sent this all up, which was "Silver Machine". "Silver Machine" was just to say, I've got a silver bicycle, and nobody got it. I didn't think they would. I thought that what they would think we were singing about was some sort of cosmic space travel machine. I did actually have a silver racing bike when I was a boy.' When I mentioned this to Lemmy, he growled with pleasure. 'Yeah, they don't write 'em like that any more.'

Almost everybody with the exception of Doug and Lemmy admitted they were stunned when 'Silver Machine' actually became a hit, reaching No. 3 in the UK charts in July 1972. 'It just reverberated everywhere and we had a hit in virtually every country in the world,' Doug recalled, 'only you didn't realise it until twenty-five years later.' According to Lemmy, though, despite the huge upturn in the band's fortunes engendered by the global success of the single, the rest of Hawkwind 'hated it', he insisted, when 'Silver Machine' became a hit with his vocals. 'Because I was the only one that could sing it. And then it [was a hit] and they *really* couldn't stand it! My picture on the front of the *NME* without them – the one who took them filthy speed drugs . . .' (Although, intriguingly, Del Dettmar somehow managed to get a picture of himself alone on the cover of *Frendz*, reading the *Dandy*, next to a strapline for a William Burroughs interview.)

As Lemmy suggested, if the arrival of their first (and last) big hit may have spurred Hawkwind on to some of their best work with their next two albums, *Doremi Fasol Latido* (1972) and the live double *Space Ritual Alive* (1973), 'Silver Machine' was also a turning point in other ways, too. 'Everybody became very serious suddenly.' They had added a second drummer, Alan Powell (ex-Vinegar Joe) to 'the Hawkestra', as they now unofficially dubbed themselves, and 'we were doing big places', remembered Dave. 'Things like the Oval with Frank Zappa, but suddenly there were egos and yes-men everywhere. Even Nik used to have an entourage. All these weird characters – a right fucking pain in the arse. You'd say, "For Christ's sake, Nik, don't bring 'em down here."'

With Lemmy and Simon King in the band Hawkwind now had real rhythmic muscle to go with their sonic perambulations. *Doremi Fasol Latido* tracks like Turner's 'Brainstorm', replete with Lemmy's whiskey-ghost backing vocals, was destined to become a cornerstone of the Hawkwind live show, where it remains to this day. While

Brock was coming up with still greater meditations on the inter-dimensional worlds he continued to explore on his countless acid trips, in 'Space is Deep' (sample lyrics: *'It is so big, it is so small, why does man try to act so tall'*) and 'Time We Left This World Today', a wonderfully paranoid nine-minute war dance on which Brock warns that *'the brain police are not far behind'*. Lemmy is again featured on counterpoint backing vocals and a beautifully twisted bass solo, riffing on the Jimmy Edwards catchphrase 'oompah! oompah! stick-it-up-your-jumpah', considered quite risqué when the comedian used it in the Fifties, then purloined into something actually subversive by the Beatles on 'I Am the Walrus'. It might be nice to suggest that Lemmy was being postmodernist in his revival of the phrase here but the truth is, it's actually just the self-hypnosis of a speed freak tripping on acid while drinking whiskey and smoking endless joints. And Lemmy was right, they really don't write them like that any more. He did, however, score a sole writing credit on the closing track, 'The Watcher', which he also sang lead on, morbidly intoning the words, *'This is the end now . . .'*

Released in November 1972, in the commercial comet trail left by 'Silver Machine', *Doremi Fasol Latido* became their biggest hit yet, barging into the charts at No. 14. Hawkwind's live show, as celebrated on the double live opus released the following summer and their first Top 10 hit, *Space Ritual Alive,* was now a full-blown multimedia event. Beyond the pulsing green and purple orbs, the montage of back-projections, Weimar eagles, Eastern religious symbols, zodiac signs and in-joke drug references cooked up by Barney Bubbles and Liquid Len, there were the band themselves; a veritable circus of characters – Brock wearing First World War aviator goggles as though they were sunglasses, Turner in tricorn hat and dressed as a frog, Stacia dressed in not very much at all, and of course the manic-mechanic himself, Bob Calvert, whom Mick Farren accurately described, in 1973, as being 'like a cross between Biggles and Lawrence of Arabia'.

Calvert it was who helped turn Hawkwind's simple psychedelia into authentic rock theatre; whether in blackface, top hat and long black overcoat for 'Steppenwolf', stripped to the waist and wielding a broadsword for 'Hassan I Sahba', or dressed simply as Valentino in leather jodhpurs for 'Born to Go', he was always more of an orator than a singer, the ascetic Mr Spock to Brock's nervy Captain Kirk and Lemmy's snarling Dr Bones. As Calvert explained at the time, 'It all works up to a nice piece of spontaneous theatre. It's great to be able to improvise something like that at the drop of a hat. Rock is a very theatrical thing, what with body language, gesture, movement, mime and the like.'

Or as Lemmy puts it now, 'Hawkwind were dangerous, man. We used to give people epileptic fits. We used to lock all the doors in the hall. And we used to have the strobes pointed *out* at the crowd. Five strobes from the stage all slow – wocka-wocka-wocka. And Dikmik had these two knobs on a card table and we used to call it an audio generator. It was a ring modulator. It used to go out of human hearing in both ways. If you put it out that way it fucks your balance up and you fall to the ground in a vomiting frenzy. The other way it makes you shit your pants. Shakes up your inner workings, you know? And that isn't Pink Floyd, is it? We used to fuck people up good, man. I remember in Torquay once this kid ran into the hall where everybody was sitting like hippies on the floor. And this kid took refuge in the middle of the crowd and the cops came and they couldn't get at him. Every time they got near him the crowd would rise up and block them. They couldn't arrest everybody.'

Certainly, that was the feeling one got when they played the Rainbow in 1972 and the crowd broke down the doors to allow the ticketless in. The police arrived but there was nothing they could do and the crowd cheered as the out-numbered 'pigs' were forced to withdraw, realising they would have a riot on their hands if they tried to throw even one person out.

But if the 'Space Ritual' – Calvert's idea for a sprawl-ing cinematic stage show designed by Barney Bubbles and brought to eerie life by Liquid Len's eye-reddening light show – was Hawkwind at their zenith, 'Urban Guerrilla', their next single, found them at a commercial nadir. With London then experiencing its first wave of IRA bombings, the BBC objected to lines like, *'I'm an urban guerrilla / I make bombs in my cellar . . .'* and promptly banned it. Radio Luxembourg took up the baton and pointedly made a big show of playing it on the hour every hour. It was perched at No. 39 in the UK charts when UA, under heavy manners from government officials, withdrew the single from shops. 'It was silly, really, cos the words are fantastic,' insisted Dave, when we spoke. 'It *was* a political statement. But not about the IRA. And probably that did actually change things. Because if that had been another hit, that would have been another successful album . . .'

For his part, Lemmy never liked the track anyway. 'Bad choice, eh? Coincided with a string of IRA bombings across England. They made us withdraw it. The establishment stopped us. They stopped us promoting it.' Was that them really reading into it, though? Or was that where the song was really at? Lemmy scoffed. 'Well, obviously the song wasn't that. But Bob Calvert thought of himself as something of a radical – which is just about the furthest from radical you could hope to find. You know, "I'm an urban guerrilla . . . I'm a tormented killer" or something. It came out at exactly the wrong moment. *Exactly*. It was a terrible record anyway. I mean, we played it very badly and of course the first take was cheaper so they used it.'

In stark contrast to the previous summer, when he had found himself on *Top of the Pops* with Hawkwind, singing 'Silver Machine' (actually a bowdlerised live clip filmed by the BBC two weeks before at a gig in Dunstable, and mainly featuring Stacia), the summer of 1973 brought Lemmy the first really tragic event of his adult life, when Susan Bennett, who he had begun seeing again in London, died of a drugs overdose.

'My old lady died on heroin,' he told me, just like that, nearly a quarter of a century later. 'There's a passion killer for you.'

He was concerned not to unnecessarily derail the bonhomie of another interview, as if obliged to mention it, as I was researching his life, but in no hurry to elaborate in case it made me unduly uncomfortable. Lemmy, the gentleman, who, despite his pugnacious exterior, was always deeply sensitive to the feelings of others.

'Yeah, yeah,' he continued hurriedly. 'Susie. Black Susie. First black girl I ever went out with. She died in '73. Drowned in her own bathtub. Stupid way to die, eh?' He paused, looked at me, puffed out more smoke. He gave me the rest of the story in dribs and drabs. How he and Susie had gradually reconnected after he arrived in London, where she was still working at the Speakeasy. How neither of them had been 'faithful' but how they really were in love. And how it had all finally gone wrong for Susie when she'd returned from some sort of 'hostess gig' in the Lebanon. How she'd been out there for several months, and come back completely strung-out on smack. How she'd try to clean up but always slid back into the abyss. Until.

'So I'm over it now, you know,' he said, eager to move on. 'It was a long time ago. But all my fucking friends went. Heroin cut a terrible swathe through my generation. All kinds of fucking people died. I got to the stage where you just don't fucking care.'

Clearly, though, he still did. He may not have enjoyed talking about Susie much any more, but he would rail for hours against the 'sheer stupidity' of heroin. Unlike speed or LSD, he said, with heroin, 'You don't have to worry about anything. You can just cower in the corner with your heroin and your syringe. Just shut off from everything. An entirely negative experience. Throw up until you get used to it. Then nod out all the time, your face in your food. I never saw that as much of an alternative to anything.'

In reality, Lemmy did what he could to 'blot out' the death of Susie in the best way he knew how. With speed, with whiskey, with dope, by having sex with other women.

Though he began to lay off the acid for now. Acid, he said, 'was the truth serum', and Lemmy needed to lay off that, too, for a while.

The only woman close to him that he never tried to bed was Stacia. 'No, they were never lovers,' says Doug, 'They were close friends. Really, really close friends. Stacia would be there for Lemmy when the others didn't want to know.' Something Stacia acknowledges, though she insists her friendship with Lemmy was always a two-way street. 'We could never have been together, no. We were too much alike. My birthday was two days after his. No, but as friends we were great.' She tells of one particular time when she was broke and Lemmy offered her money. 'He acted like it was my money. Like, "Oh, here's that money I owe you." I'd say, "You don't owe me money!" But he would insist. "No, you've forgotten. I owe you this so just take it." He was lovely like that, very sensitive and very intelligent. People talk now about him partying or whatever, but my memory of him on the bus was that he was always reading, books on the war and stuff like that.'

By the end of the year, Lemmy and the rest of the Hawkship's captains were headed at warp speed for America, where word had now spread of the new 'space rock' band from Britain. In April '74, they headlined the 7000-seater Auditorium in Chicago. Stevie Wonder and Alice Cooper attended their show at Stein's Academy of Music, in New York. And Joanna Leary – wife of the acid guru, Timothy Leary, then serving time for miscellaneous drug offences – invited the band to be her guests when they played at the Zellerbach Auditorium, in San Francisco. 'They picked us up at the airport in this fantastic cavalcade of old Forties gangster-like cars,' Dave recalled. 'Then on stage that night, they rigged up a telephone link to Leary in his jail cell and he gave this speech. The police in the hall went fucking bananas.'

But it wasn't just America's famous that were drawn to the group. In common with their cultural cousins, the Grateful Dead, Hawkwind became a magnet for, as Lemmy put it, 'every acid casualty in town'. Brock: 'They still have a few Hawkwind Farms over there, with all the words of the songs written down in a leather bound book, like their prayer book . . .'

And, of course, America was also the home of more mundane pastimes. 'Acid everywhere,' Lemmy recalled. 'Cocaine everywhere.' And some new drugs even Lemmy had never come across before. 'We got spiked once by two separate bunches of hippies with angel dust, in Cleveland. We went on stage, I'm holding this piece of wood – what's this? A guitar? What's a guitar? What a long strange trip it's been, as Jerry Garcia, who was one of the least strange people I've seen in my life, said. Funny he turned into a junkie, eh? All that Grateful Dead shit, all those people out there studiously not taking heroin and there he is, spaced out on smack up on the stage.'

Then in Nashville when Nik Turner snorted what he presumed was coke only to discover it was angel dust, it had an even more bizarre effect. 'He went back to age four and demanded that Stacia bath him and take care of him,' remembers Doug Smith. 'He was only a little baby and he had to be taken care of.'

In Hammond, Indiana, they found themselves placed under house arrest at their hotel accused of not paying their holding tax on the tour. 'It was utter bullshit,' says Doug, 'because we had paid it. It was just a shakedown.' Nevertheless, the IRS busted them and confiscated all their equipment until Doug paid up – again. When he argued, one of the agents opened his jacket revealing a huge handgun holstered. They were stuck the whole weekend. Just then someone gave Doug a line of coke, which also turned out to be angel dust. 'But I got through it,' he says, 'somehow . . .'

And so things might have continued had the band not been . . . well, Hawkwind. Bob Calvert had bailed out of the band before they'd left for America, nominally to pursue a solo career but, in reality, says Doug, 'because Bob was fairly off the rails by this point. He was completely mad. He'd ring up in a complete state, telling me he's Christ and pinned to a wall. I'd have to spend hours talking him down . . .' Dikmik had also somehow fallen over the ship's rails again, and Del Dettmar liked touring Canada so much he and his wife decided to stay there. In came Notts-born violinist, keyboardist and synth player Simon House, the first classically trained musician in the band, followed by a second drummer in Alan Powell, who Lemmy took an instant dislike to. And regular onstage appearances by Michael Moorcock, whom Lemmy adored. 'He gave us T-shirts with characters out of his books. Brock was the Baron Meliadus. I was the Finnish mercenary, whose name I forget. Got killed quite early in the book, though. Nik was someone else. Then years later Mike dedicated a compendium issue of his *Hawkmoon* books to me, which was very nice of him.'

The new line-up recorded two of their most focused and direct Hawkwind albums of their career, 1974's *Hall of the Mountain Grill* (a pun on Edvard Grieg's 'In the Hall of the Mountain King' and the Mountain Grill café in Portobello Road) and the following year's *Warrior on the Edge of Time*, both of which again reached the Top 20. With Calvert out of the picture, Lemmy came more to the fore on *Mountain Grill*, trading lead vocals with Brock on an album that was a far more straightforward proposition for the rock market than any previously. The synths and jams were still all there, but the riffs had tightened and there was cohesion to their tripped out musical sensibilities, as evidenced on the hit-single-that-should-have-been, 'The Psychedelic Warlords (Disappear in Smoke)', and Lemmy's co-write with Mick Farren, 'Lost Johnny', a startlingly bitter reflection on 'cancelling the dream', on which he sounds lost himself, the helpless if knowing victim, an echo of his own very real feelings about losing Susie. About never really having her back in the first place. Not while the spectre of the ultimate downer, heroin, still hung over her.

Warrior on the Edge of Time, released in May 1975, was an entirely different proposition, with Brock now leaning on the lyrical input of Michael Moorcock to fill the imagination gap left by Calvert's departure. Lemmy, despite putting in his usual sterling performance on bass, is supplanted as even backing vocalist by Brock, Turner and Moorcock. That and the inclusion much higher in the mix of Simon House's violin, and the doubled-up drums and percussion of King and Powell, greatly diffuse Lemmy's presence. A sign of things to come, as the new powerbase of the group

– Brock and Turner as always, but joined now by King and Powell – began to turn against their recalcitrant bassist.

'Speed was the main thing in the band that pissed Brock off,' says Doug Smith now. 'That and the fact they were jealous of him.' Because he'd been the one who'd sung 'Silver Machine'? 'Not because of "Silver Machine", because he was Lemmy! Lemmy and Nik were the front of the band and Dave wasn't – and it used to piss Dave off like mad.'

So much so, says Doug, that Brock and the others now began to actively discourage Lemmy from writing songs. 'They wouldn't let him write. They didn't like his songs, cos his songs were much rockier than anything Dave Brock liked. Lemmy always tried to see if one of his songs could be used. But they weren't interested. They wanted hippy-dippy stuff.'

Lemmy did manage, however, to foist one new song onto the *Warrior* line-up. A clever ditty he'd knocked up on tour in America – where he'd first heard the phrase, used to describe speed freaks like himself – titled 'Motorhead'. Beginning with a stomach-rumbling bass part, followed by a punchy two-chord guitar riff, Lemmy laying it all out like a big fat white line, the story of his life in a nutshell: '*Sunrise, wrong side of another day / Sky high six thousand miles away / Don't know how long I've been awake . . .*' It was hyper-tense and brilliant, speedy and uncompromising. If you wanted to hear Lemmy's true story, here it was. '*I should be tired / All I am is wired . . . Motorhead, all right!*' You either got the joke, man, or you didn't. What was plain was that Lemmy didn't seem to care either way.

Frankly appalled at the thought of including this musical

nosebleed into the Hawkwind show, not only did Brock refuse to allow Hawkwind to play it live, but he blocked it from inclusion on the *Warrior* album. Instead, 'Motorhead', the song that carved Lemmy's mission statement *and* epitaph into one delightfully deranged three-minute masterpiece, was relegated to the B-side of the next Hawkwind single. Written by Brock and Moorcock and titled – oh, the irony! – 'Kings of Speed'.

FIVE

The Three Amigos

'I should have seen it coming,' Lemmy would tell me years later. 'The writing was on the wall.' But he didn't see it coming and when Hawkwind – that is, Dave Brock and Nik Turner – sacked him on tour in America in the summer of 1975, Lemmy was devastated. 'He rang me in tears,' says Doug Smith. 'He cried throughout the entire call. Because, in his own way, Lemmy's a free spirit. Life came and life went for Lemmy. You didn't question the fact that sometimes he was a pain in the arse, and sometimes he was late, or rude, or wicked, or just a nuisance. Everybody had their own foibles that were just appalling on some occasions. He didn't deserve to be booted out of the band. It wasn't like they weren't taking fucking loads of drugs as well.'

The story is now a well-told one in Hawkwind-lore. How the band had been travelling from Detroit to Toronto when Lemmy was busted by cops on the Canadian border for possession of cocaine: a felony later downgraded to a fine when it turned out it wasn't coke Lemmy was carrying but amphetamine sulphate – not then actually illegal in Canada. But causing ructions in the group anyway as it meant they almost missed a gig. They didn't, Lemmy being let out of jail just in time to get to the show. But they sacked him later that night anyway.

The real story, of course, is somewhat more complicated. Despite the lifelong protestations that followed from Lemmy, he was not fired from Hawkwind for 'the wrong drugs'. He was fired, says Doug Smith, 'for being Lemmy'. A conglomeration of some wildly out of control personalities, the ego had only really landed in Hawkwind after 'Silver Machine' had been such a hit. The entrancing Stacia may have been the focus for *Top of the Pops* and – certainly picture-wise – the music press. Robert Calvert may have been the poet laureate of the hippy underground, and Nik Turner the embodiment of the eternal 'loon'. But it was Lemmy who represented the real street-level, squat-dwelling, hog-riding edge that Hawkwind always exuded at their live performances. A favourite of the Hells Angels, Lemmy was the one everybody wanted to be – or to be seen with. The one who got the really crazy chicks and plainly hadn't been to sleep since 1965.

What neither Brock nor Turner – nor Simon King, nor Alan Powell, who Lemmy insisted had also conspired to get him out of the band – understood was just how fiercely proud of and loyal to the Hawkwind cause Lemmy always was. When Lemmy sang of having 'an electric line' to 'your Zodiac sign', he *meant* it.

'The problem was they were jealous of him. But also pissed off because Lemmy was a law unto himself. Him and Dikmik. Then Dikmik wasn't around any more and that left Lemmy alone, except for Stacia, who always looked out for him. Then Stacia was gone too and so I suppose it was only a matter of time before Lemmy also came a cropper.' In the early days when Lemmy and Dikmik would sometimes disappear on tour in their endless search for speed and good times, Doug recalls, 'I didn't mind so much because at the end of the day whatever Hawkwind did onstage it didn't matter whether Lemmy was there or Stacia was there or anybody was there because the lights just covered it up. You couldn't *see* much.'

The vibes had been getting heavier though since Stacia had gone. 'She got married,' says Doug. 'We had a leaving party that Brock didn't even come to and he was very angry with me spending the money on having a party for her.' Brock, the grumpy hippy who had once revelled in being surrounded by the most far-out gang in town, now had his eyes fixed more firmly on the prize. By 1975, Pink Floyd, once considered secondary to Hawkwind by the more serious 'heads' of the London scene, now presided over two albums, *The Dark Side of the Moon* and *Wish You Were Here*, that had sold tens of millions worldwide. Yes and Genesis were also enjoying chart albums at home and in America. Hawkwind, while still producing Top 20 albums in Britain, had settled into becoming a niche act, almost a psychedelic novelty. Brock, who had started the band to make 'the aural equivalent of going off into your own acid trip', was now breaking the cardinal rule of the psychic dope freak jester: he was taking himself too seriously.

Lemmy, meanwhile, seemed not to care at all. At least not to Dave Brock and Nik Turner, the most earnest of Hawklords. Leading up to his sacking they had been doing a gig in Chicago where Lemmy hooked up with 'this rather beautiful, either half-Chinese or half-Korean American girl', Doug recalls. 'She had crystal meth.' Their next show in Detroit was scheduled for three days later. Nevertheless, it was decided to use the day after Chicago to take the tour bus to Detroit, and have a day off before the next show there.

Lemmy, still entranced by his new Asian-American girl-friend – and her crystal meth – went to Doug to try and persuade the band to spend an extra day in Chicago, but they didn't want to know. Plans had been made, everyone else was happy to leave. So Lemmy asked Doug if he could stay an extra day in Chicago on his own. Doug again said no. 'I told him, "Lem, you'll never make your own way to Detroit and I just don't trust you." In the end he'd left birds in various ports many times. It was the crystal meth he was really after.'

The next day, en route to Detroit, when the bus stopped at a truck stop, Lemmy suddenly disappeared. It was an-other two days before Doug or the band saw him again – at the hotel in Detroit. Doug shakes his head. 'He actually told us he'd gone to the toilet at the truck stop, which was on the other side of the street and that he'd been knocked out and his camera was stolen. And that when he woke up we'd gone.' He laughs. 'What a load of bollocks. In those days Lemmy could not have afforded any more than a cheap fucking camera because he spent everything else on drugs and drink. So why anybody would knock him on the head at a truck stop and steal it is beyond me.' Doug's theory is that Lemmy went across the street, got a ride with a truck driver back to Chicago, spent the night with the girl with the meth, then she organised for him to get to the gig in Detroit the following night.

Brock, says Doug, 'was well pissed off when Lemmy arrived [in Detroit] with this cock and bull story. "Fucking bastard's arrived. Go and sort him out, Doug." So I went to do my managerial thing. I went down to his room and he was lying there flat out on the bed crashed out. I said, "Where the fuck have you been?" He went, "Fuck off." So I fucked off and just let him sleep. He played the gig. There were no problems. But that's what he did. He would stay up for four or five nights running then sleep one night.'

There was a short break in the schedule before the band left for a show in Cleveland, followed the next day by that fateful drive to Toronto. 'They were still in a self-righteous froth about [Lemmy's disappearance],' says Doug. 'He'd been warned many times before about his behaviour.'

'Then we were going through [on the tour bus] to Canada and I got busted in the tunnel,' Lemmy told me. Lemmy knew though that the bust 'was just an excuse to get rid of me'. Lemmy claims now that the only reason the band even put up the money for his bail was because 'they couldn't get [Pink Fairies bassist] Paul Rudolph over quick enough to do the show in Toronto. So I did the show and at 4.30 in the morning I was fired.'

Intriguingly, while Dave Brock later told me it was he who told Lemmy, Nik Turner insisted he was the one who delivered the news personally. Dave: 'It was awful, I'll never forget it, man . . . knocked on his door, went in there and said, "Look, I've got something really awful to tell you but the band has decided that you're sacked." Lemmy said, "No, I don't believe it!" He said, "But everything revolves around this! This is my life!" I always remember him saying that . . .'

According to Nik though, 'Nobody wanted to tell him. So I sort of undertook to tell him. I said, "We've had a meeting, Lemmy, and we just find it really hard to work with you and have decided that we'd like you to leave the band." I think he was probably quite shocked, because he probably thought that this situation could go on for ever.'

For Lemmy, though, the 'situation' had never changed. As he saw it, he said, he was the victim of maliciousness. Things had been going fine, he insisted when we spoke, 'But then I made the mistake of introducing Simon King into the band, and he was the reason I got fired. He was the one who introduced Alan, the second drummer, the three of them worked the feeling of the band against me, until they got to where they got me sacked in Canada after being arrested. They fired me for getting busted. The most cosmic band in the cosmos fucking fired me for being busted for the wrong drug.'

To add insult to injury, 'They left me in there [jail] for two days and then they found out Paul Rudolph couldn't get there quick enough [so] they rushed me onto a plane, got to the gig for soundcheck at five p.m., did the show, great show, then at four a.m. they fired me . . .' If Rudolph had been able to get there in time for the first gig, 'I'd probably still be in jail now . . .' He laughed bitterly. 'So much for hippies . . . So much for peace and love. I think I was probably the only one who believed in that, in the whole band. The rest of them were all fucking jockeying for power.'

By his own admission, Lemmy returned to London angry and bitter – feeling shat on. 'Then I got my revenge,' he said, scowling. 'I came home and fucked all their old ladies. Cos they used to like me. I made sure of Simon King's and Alan Powell's first. Alan Powell has still never forgiven me. And I hope he never will, cos there was a lot of malice involved, and I really meant every fucking minute of it. I actually liked her anyway. She was a nice girl. She left him soon afterwards.' He said all this with a wicked glint in his eye. 'More of an educational experience, you might say. Eat that, you bastards.'

Whatever their reasons, firing Lemmy became the high-tide mark in Hawkwind's career: the moment their luck began to run out and, finally, it seemed, the drugs just didn't work any more. With Lemmy gone, observed Mick Farren, 'I think a lot was lost. They could have gone on and been the Grateful Dead if they'd managed to hold it together. But it schismed and . . . I didn't lose interest, because they were all mates. But certainly round about '78, '79, I thought Lemmy was actually making a greater contribution to music [with Motörhead] than whatever was going on with Brock.'

Or as Doug put it, simply, this was 'the magic band. They were the key to it all. And as soon as you took one of those elements away – which turned out to be Lemmy – you lost it all.' Not that Lemmy saw things like that at the time. 'I immediately urged him to form his own band,' says Doug. 'But he moped around for a long time, still hoping the others would have him back.' Weeks trickled by as Lemmy, still being paid a weekly stipend by Doug and his then business partner Richard Ogden, tried to figure out what to do next. 'In the end, Richard said to me, "Look, this is ridiculous. We can't go on like this." And so we decided to put out a press release saying Lemmy had formed his own band.' They decided to do it without telling Lemmy 'because we knew he'd only come up with more excuses why he wasn't ready'.

It was also Doug that chose the name for Lemmy's new band – Motorhead. (Originally, without the umlaut.) 'I'd already discussed it with him and Lemmy was insistent he wanted to call the band Bastard. I pleaded with him. 'Come on, Lem. You'll never get on the radio or *Top of the Pops* with a name like that.' But he wasn't having it. In the end, I just went ahead and did it.'

The day the press release reached the news desks of the London music papers, Doug's and Richard's phones began ringing. 'Everyone wanted to speak to him straight away, to find out what was going on,' says Doug. 'I thought, shit, I better phone him and let him know what we'd done. I remember it was early in the morning – or early for Lemmy anyway – which was probably just as well because he was still groggy. He sort of went, "Oh . . . all right. And what did you call the band?" I said, Motorhead, after the last song he'd written for Hawkwind. He went, "Oh

... but I wanted to call it Bastard." I went, "Come on, Lem . . .""

As the years went by, Lemmy would swear blind it was he and he alone who had come up with the name Motörhead. In fact, all he did was add the umlaut. 'To make it look mean,' he said. 'No other reason. Like when Paul Newman in *Slap Shots* asks the bus driver why he's hitting the bus with a hockey stick, and the bus driver says, "To make it look mean."'

He was also always insistent that he knew exactly what he was going to do after being unceremoniously dumped by Hawkwind. 'I had a very clear vision of what I wanted to play,' he told me, 'and the only way I could do it was to form a band that did it. I didn't want to be a singer or nothing. I was gonna be just the bass player. I tried to get a singer but of course we couldn't get one.' So at rehearsals to fill the gap Lemmy would sing. 'We wanted to get a proper singer in but they're very hard to find – good ones, anyway – and by the time we came to the first rehearsal we still hadn't got one so I did it, just to fill in so we could rehearse. Plus it was cheaper, cos I was already there. And that's how I got stuck with it.'

He had sung with Hawkwind, of course, 'when they could bear to let me near the spotlight'. Remarkably, considering the gravelly roar he would become better known for in Motörhead, he always did the high notes in the backing vocal harmonies with Hawkwind. 'I can still do it, too. When we haven't been on tour for a bit. I can still hit the high notes. My voice is very high actually, it's just rough so it sounds like it's deep but it isn't.'

He said that the original idea behind Motörhead was: 'I wanted to be the MC5, that's all. Nothing to do with Hawkwind or anything else. I wanted to do the British version of the MC5, that simple. If I could have joined the MC5 I'd have joined them. But they were in Detroit so I couldn't, so I formed my own version instead. I wanted it to be a five-piece band, fast and vicious, like them. I wanted to be that. Instead I got something that sounded like Blue Cheer,' he joked. It wasn't a bad comparison, actually. Blue Cheer, named after a batch of Owsley acid, had built their bottom-heavy sound on the same three-piece configuration Motörhead would, with founder Dickie Peterson playing a similar-sound 'rhythm' bass and sneering out the vocals, while the drummer, Paul Whaley, beat the shit out of his drums in a style also very close to the early Motörhead sound. In truth, however, Lemmy, who didn't yet see himself as an accomplished songwriter, was happy to be making any sort of noise with a band that put up with him.

Originally, that dubious honour fell to the Pink Fairies' guitarist, Larry Wallis, and drummer, Lucas Fox. Larry was already a veteran of several low-rent London outfits such as Steve Took's Shagrat, Blodwyn Pig and UFO, and had a pleasingly low-slung style that came fully formed. Larry also wrote songs and brought with him a heavy presence in all situations. 'I remember the first time I met him he walked into rehearsals with his own roadie,' says Eddie Clarke. 'Ooh, I thought, a proper rock star.' Mainly, it was a front to disguise the guitarist's unease. 'Larry worries,' Lemmy said at the time. 'As soon as he gets hold of anything, he drops it on his toe.'

The drummer was another Notting Hill urchin named Lucas Fox, short, dark-haired, intense. Lucas had never played in a 'name' band before, but what he lacked in experience he did his best to make up for in nervous energy. Still tinkering with the idea of making the band a four-piece, Luther Grosvenor – aka Ariel Bender, recently of Mott the Hoople – also auditioned for the band. But while Lemmy dug his playing, 'He wasn't the sort of bloke I fancied being stuck on a tour bus with.' In Mott, Grosvenor had developed a spotlight-seeking persona that saw him jostling frontman Ian Hunter for position onstage. That was something else Lemmy didn't fancy about him.

Rehearsing on an ad hoc basis in the basement of a furniture store in Chelsea, where a friend of Lemmy's named Aeroplane Gaye worked and would let the band in whenever the place was empty, things got off to a shaky start for the new band when their first gig was opening for Greenslade at the Roundhouse. Greenslade played whimsical, keyboard-driven progressive rock. Music that was the polar opposite of what Motörhead was supposed to be about. On the night, though, the comparisons all went in Greenslade's favour, whose elevated musicianship stood in stark contrast to their support act's apparent inability to even stay in tune. 'Awful' was how Lemmy described the performance. 'We were doing a lot of covers and I had this blue-painted skull on my amp. It didn't help. It was terrible.'

Nine more dates around the country followed, with the band, still billed as Lemmy's Motörhead to help sell tickets, leaning heavily on covers like Chuck Berry's 'Bye Bye Johnny', the Yardbirds' 'Train Kept A-Rollin'' and Eddie Holland's

Motown classic 'Leaving Here', alongside all three of the tracks Lemmy had written and recorded with Hawkwind, and a handful of Larry Wallis originals. The run ended in October with what was hoped would be a high-profile spot opening for Blue Öyster Cult at London's Hammersmith Odeon. BÖC, with their sci-fi metal and flaming guitars, were thought to be a better fit for Motörhead than Green-slade. In fact, the only thing the two bands had in common was their umlauts. Reviewing the show for *NME*, Nick Kent described Motörhead's performance as 'shocking', and having 'all the panache of a butcher stripping meat from an overripe carcass'.

But at least Lemmy's new band was working, getting reviewed, being talked about. Even if it was something of a joke among the media cognoscenti. Nevertheless, Doug Smith was somehow able to parlay this into a deal with his friend Andrew Lauder at United Artists. The advance was modest, enough to buy the band some equipment, keep them fed, and record an album.

Welsh singer-songwriter, Dave Edmunds, was hired to produce, something that delighted Lemmy, as, according to Doug Smith, he 'was Lemmy's favourite musician at the time', and sessions were booked at the Edmunds-owned Rockfield Studios in Monmouth, South Wales. Again, though, the band was having trouble 'getting it together'. Lemmy eventually lost patience with Lucas Fox and fired him because, he later explained, 'he was trying to keep up with my habit. He was doing all this speed, and the veins were standing out on his head, and he was going off on his own and standing against the wall looking intense and telling me things . . . so I had to let him go, to coin a phrase.'

He did, however, already have a replacement in mind: a 21-year-old tearaway from Leeds named Phil Taylor. Phil also took speed – and everything else – but he already had his own craziness going on and saw no need to try and emulate Lemmy, who at 30 he saw as 'an old man'.

'I met Lemmy through speed really,' Taylor later claimed. 'You know, dealing and scoring. I wasn't actually playing in a band at the time.' In fact, Taylor was a former skinhead and Leeds United football hooligan, whose father had bought him a drum-kit and told him in desperation, 'If you wanna beat something up, beat this up.' Taylor was born in Hasland, a suburb of Chesterfield, Derbyshire, but when he was 14 the Taylor family moved up to Leeds, where Phil's father worked as a commercial photographer. He was 19 when he made his way down to London, not long after, as he once told me, 'escaping from school'. He'd been trying unsuccessfully to form bands for years, he said. 'The only people I could get to play with were students who weren't at all serious about being musicians. They'd all piss off when the holidays started.' Hardly academic, an admitted 'hot head', but with a lot more going on beneath his 'half-punk, half-rock' haircut than most people gave him credit for, Phil had become acquainted with Lemmy via the Hells Angels, who they both enjoyed the hospitality of, living in various squats around West London, as he said, 'dealing and scoring'.

Having stayed up for several days together just before Christmas 1975, Lemmy talked Phil, who had a car, into giving him a lift back to Rockfield, where sessions were due to continue. When Phil told Lemmy he also played the drums Lemmy told him to bring them with him. Reluctantly, not seeing the need, he did so, and the two took off up the M4 for Wales. 'I remember the windshield was smashed,' Lemmy later recalled, 'but I had this bird in a fur coat sit on my lap so I was okay, I was warm.'

When they arrived at the studio, they stayed up together for another night, 'skating on the ice', as Lemmy put it. Early the next morning, Taylor ran outside into the garden, completely naked, and began bouncing around bashing at things, making a terrible row. When he noticed the curtains twitching in several nearby houses, he looked up at them and screamed, 'It's all right! I'm on drugs!' Later that day, Lemmy suggested Phil take a turn at the drums. Just to hear what he could do. Larry Wallis was there and the three of them rattled along together through a couple of numbers. At the end of which, Larry turned to Lemmy and gave his verdict. 'What a horrible little cunt. He's perfect.'

In fact, Phil Taylor was a far more accomplished drummer than either man had given him credit for. When it was suggested he try and rerecord Lucas Fox's drums, not rerecord the tracks, but actually just 'drop in' his own performances where Fox's performances had now been wiped from the finished tapes – something even highly paid session players might baulk at – Phil did so effortlessly. He was in. To underline the fact, Lemmy bestowed upon him the nickname that he would be known by for the rest of his life: 'Philthy Animal'.

The only track Taylor didn't replace Fox on was 'Lost Johnny', prevented by an arrest in London for drunk and disorderly behaviour that meant he wasn't able to get back to Rockfield in time. But by then the sessions in Wales were taking their toll. Doug Smith recalls taking Tony Tyler, then of the *NME*, to Rockfield to visit the band. 'The first thing we saw was Dave Edmunds, his head was flat on the mixing desk. He'd been sick. Phil Taylor is at the back doing lines of speed. And nothing's happening. They'd been down there for weeks. It was chaos. They'd recorded a few tracks. But they were having more fun than working, just trying to see how far they could wipe out poor old Dave. Lemmy was bouncing around as usual being Lemmy. "I can handle it no problem at all. Those fuckers can't."'

Listening back to the album in London at the start of 1976, Andrew Lauder and other executives at UA were unsure of what they were supposed to be hearing. *On Parole*, as Lemmy had now titled the album after one of its better tracks, a barrelhouse Larry Wallis original, was hard to figure in the context of the times. Listening to it now, it's easy to see it as a proto-punk tour-de-force of ill-intentioned lyrics and back-to-basics rock'n'roll. Yet punk was another year away and the album's speedy, ramshackle mien was at odds with the presiding fashion for overblown, epically proportioned rock as evinced by 1975's biggest stars like Bruce Springsteen, Pink Floyd, Led Zeppelin and Queen. The nearest musical equivalent to what Motörhead had recorded was perhaps Dr Feelgood – and UA already had them on their roster. By comparison, it's easy to see why *On Parole* sounded like an awful hodgepodge to UA. Only three Lemmy numbers – all of them from his Hawkwind days: 'Motorhead', 'The Watcher' and 'Lost Johnny', albeit

delivered with twice the speed and aggression of the originals. Four Larry Wallis songs, including two on which he
sang lead – the cheerless 'Vibrator' and the Stonesey 'Fools'.
And one by Phil Taylor with help from one of the band's
Hells Angel friends, Tramp, and probably the best track on
the album, 'Iron Horse/Born to Lose'.

A decision was taken to put the album 'on hold.' Indefi-
nitely. Someone would have to pay, Lemmy decided. When
he then phoned Doug asking for another cut from the original UA advance, to keep the band going, 'I told him there
wasn't any. The money had all gone. He said, "Oh, well,
fuck it, Doug, I'll find another manager." And he put the
phone down on me. I thought, thank god. Never again!'

In the meantime, the band staggered on as best they could.
Still on the lookout for a second guitarist to augment the
live line-up, it was Phil who found the man for the job this
time, when he took a temporary job working on a houseboat in Battersea. His boss was a part-time TV repairman
named Eddie Clarke. He played a mean guitar, but despite
gigs backing Curtis Knight in the band Zeus, co-fronting
his own boogie outfit, Blue Goose, and a short-lived 'super'
group called Continuous Performance with Be-Bop Deluxe's
bassist, Charlie Tumahai, Eddie had never made it. At 25 he
was beginning to wonder if perhaps his time had passed.

Then he met Phil, 'this kid who was speeding out of his
box the first time I met him, his eyes all sticking out. He was
a hard worker, though, probably because of all the speed,
and I liked him.' When Phil told Eddie he was in Motörhead, Eddie was intrigued. To him, Motörhead was already

'a name band. I'd read about them in the music papers and that meant something to me back then.'

When Phil decided Eddie should come and audition, he forgot to mention it to Lemmy. 'I turn up and Lemmy obviously has no clue what I'm doing there. But he was always very good at waffling through stuff like that. He adjusts very well, Lemmy. You'd never know quite that he didn't have a clue, or whether he did or not. He covered his tracks well.'

Still Eddie didn't quite know what he was letting himself in for. Not even when he discovered he would be expected to pay for the rehearsal room too that day. 'I actually paid for my own audition, which was quite funny.' Less funny was the non-appearance of Larry Wallis. When he finally showed up after three hours, Eddie was getting on so well jamming with Lemmy and Phil, Larry seemed to pick up on the atmosphere, plugged in to play just one number, and walked out again. That's more or less how Eddie remembers it anyway. Speaking to Lemmy years later, his memory was slightly different. 'Larry always said he wanted a four-piece, so we arranged a rehearsal with this other guitarist, Eddie Clarke. Then we had one rehearsal as a four-piece, which went well – and Larry split immediately. It was just as well, really. Larry's a great guy to talk to but he's not a great guy to work with. There's a lot of people like that around.'

Whatever the truth, Eddie left the rehearsals that day convinced he hadn't got the gig. 'I thought, oh, well, that's it,' he says. 'Then the following Saturday, about eight o'clock in the morning, I'm lying in bed comatose and there's suddenly this banging on my front door. I go downstairs in my underpants thinking, 'Who the bloody hell is this, waking me at this time of day?' It was Lemmy. Standing there with a leather jacket and a bullet belt in his hand. He just gave them to me, said, 'You've got the job', and walked off again. I just stood there in my underpants looking after him.'

It wasn't just the clobber that went with the job. As with 'Philthy Animal', Lemmy would now add a sobriquet to the new guitarist's name, making him for ever more 'Fast' Eddie Clarke. And so was born the most famous line-up of Motörhead, the Three Amigos, as they jokingly became known. The Motörhead that over the next five years would record all the band's classic hits, beginning with practically the first thing they ever wrote together, the supremely aptly titled 'White Line Fever'.

'After we got Eddie and Phil in I knew we had something special,' Lemmy later told Dave Ling. 'That was an excellent band from day one. I'd only written three songs for Hawkwind and I wasn't too good at it yet. But this band has always been the eternal underdog, and we're good at it.' While Clarke confided that, 'It wasn't until after three or four auditions that I realised we didn't sound normal. There was Lemmy playing his bass as a rhythm guitar, and Phil and I were struggling to find out what we should be doing. For the first year, everyone thought we were fucking mad, because it hadn't quite gelled.'

Indeed, for their first year together the band stumbled from one disaster to another. Bad gigs, bad record deals, bad reviews . . . Eddie recalls their first ten-date tour. 'First ever show I couldn't get my guitar working. We did the Lyceum with Stray. Then we went up to the Wigan Casino and headlined. Then we came back down and we supported either The Damned or Edgar Broughton. And my guitar didn't work. The roadie had plugged me wah-wah pedal and me guitar in the wrong way round.' A subsequent review in *Melody Maker* was suitably mocking. Eddie was downcast.

'Lemmy was so great about it, though. We were in the Transit van on the road, a mattress and all the gear in the back. We were in Plymouth when the review came out. We'd parked on the edge of a cliff and Lemmy put his arm around me and said, "You're going to get a lot of these. You're gonna have to get used to it. But don't worry, it happens to all of us." That was the beauty of Lem. He had a way with words that was spot on. And he meant it. The nice thing about Lemmy was he did mean it.'

It was a side to Lemmy that most people didn't see and for good reason. Lemmy had a lot of love in his heart, says Eddie, 'but he kept it in his fist, and he never let it out. How could he? Cos there's no doubt these things really do ya. People don't realise how much these things do ya.' There would be barely 30 Motörhead shows in 1976, and still no sign of *On Parole* ever being released. Eddie, who hadn't played on it, was nonetheless perplexed. 'I thought it was all right. It sounded like a band, you know. It wasn't quite as mad as it became a bit later, though . . .'

Lemmy, of course, found other ways to keep himself busy. 'I walked into this chick's fucking house in Notting Hill,' he told me, speaking of those days, 'in Pembridge Terrace, around where the flats were all connected and the police could never bust you cos you'd run across the walkway to the next block. I went up to this girl's flat and she goes,

"Argh!" I said, "What the fuck's the matter with you?" She said, "You're dead!" I said, "I assure you I'm not." That was a rumour. I heard that one twice. From the time I stayed up for two weeks solid on Methedrine. You used to get it in glass amps. They used to put it in with hydrochloride BP with a skull and crossbones underneath it. You were supposed to inject it but we didn't inject it. We used to put five in a glass of orange juice and drink it – and go and talk to everybody in Hyde Park within half an hour! Zzzz! Ahhhh! Buzz-saw mouth, you know?'

He narrowed his eyes. 'That was the *real* speed. I mean, that was dangerous. All that "Speed Kills" stuff came from that, not the powders. Powder and pills are nothing compared to that shit. That shit is lethal. Thirty bob [£1.50] for a box of five and that was fucking terrifying shit. But good fun, you know?' By the time he'd run out, 'All me teeth had gone . . .'

It was around this time that a newly hired reporter from *Melody Maker* came to interview Lemmy. An eager young Welshman named Allan Jones. He recalls that first meeting with Lemmy as 'a mess of warts, whiskers and loudly creaking leather'. Lemmy, he recalls, was wearing a Second World War German helmet, sprayed silver, 'which he promptly turns upside down on the table between us. Inside the helmet, there's a bag full of amphetamine sulphate . . . He then produces a knife, and plunges it into the toot. With an astonishingly steady hand for someone who looks like he hasn't slept since before the earth cooled, he lifts the knife blade towards me, a miniature Matterhorn of sulphate at its end. "Not too early for you, I hope," he says.'

For a while, they were managed by a well-meaning friend of Eddie's named 'English' Frank, whose father owned a duplication shop in Putney. Frank bankrolled the band because he wanted to get into the music business. He set up and paid for a tour. But the tour made no money. In desperation, Frank gave Doug the accounts to see what he could do. Doug chuckles as he recalls. 'Frank was a good guy. He'd done his best. But all through the accounts there was "plumbing", "plumbing", "plumbing" . . . I said, "What's plumbing?" "You know what plumbing is, man!" That was the drugs.'

By the start of 1977, however, things were beginning to look bleak for Motörhead. They had so little money that they were living on speed and porridge, says Eddie. 'Lemmy would come round and if there was any fat in the frying pan he would grab a piece of bread and run it around the fucking pan, put salt on it, and that would be a meal for him.' Not that Lemmy ever ate much. 'He was a sandwich kid, really.' Speeding for days, with little else to do, Lemmy and Eddie would take machines apart and put them back together. 'I had a room in a flat and one end of it was all these bits of things that Lemmy had brought round . . .'

Meanwhile, band management had been taken over, briefly, by someone called Ludo, whom Doug Smith now refers to as 'this mad Belgian promoter who turned up in London with sacks of coke'. Doug gave him an office downstairs at his place. Meanwhile, Ludo paid for some rehearsal time for Lemmy and the band in Putney. 'Then they began to suss out that Ludo was a waste of space. So that lasted five minutes and then they came back to me *again*.'

After it became clear UA had permanently shelved their album, the last straw came when Stiff Records, who'd agreed to release a single, 'Leaving Home' b/w 'White Line Fever', also reneged on the deal – only for the latter to appear on a Stiff compilation, *A Bunch of Stiffs*, released in April. Doug Smith recalls taking Stiff owner Jake Riviera to watch the band rehearse. 'We went to talk about releasing the first single. But they never paid us for it, they never gave us a contract. They just released it out of the blue, in the box set.' He frowns. 'It went a bit cold after that.'

'The Stiff thing really pissed us off,' says Eddie. 'Cos we really had a following by then. Some great fans. They were the only things that kept us going.' Furious, Lemmy, Eddie, Phil and Bobs, their new tour manager, went to Stiff's offices to confront Jake. Eddie: 'And guess what, he gave us thirty quid! Between the four of us! So we had £7.50 each . . . Lemmy fucking hated them for what they did to us. They're supposed to be for the music and the band. But they was just the fucking same as all the others. Cunts, you know? We really were bitter. It nearly finished the band. That's why we found ourselves in this situation in April 1977 of breaking up.'

Eddie says that Phil was the first to want to throw the towel in, complaining, 'This is shit, it ain't going nowhere.' Lemmy merely turned to him and said, 'All right, so where you gonna go? It wasn't like there was anywhere else for him to go.' Then Eddie got down too and eventually it was decided to break up the band. First, though, bright idea, they would record a live album, as a farewell gift for the fans. They had a show coming up at the Marquee – then the most famous club venue in London – that surely would be the place to bow out. But when they looked into the cost, they knew they had no chance. Hiring a mobile studio to do the job would cost £500. Where to turn for that kind of money?

Doug Smith recalls Lemmy coming to see him. 'He sat in front of my desk and told me how Ted Carroll at Chiswick Records had said he would front half the money for them to record the Marquee show, if I would come up with the other half of the £500. I absolutely refused. I didn't even know Ted at that point. But Lemmy sat there and kept on and on and on. He just wouldn't leave. So in the end I said, "Okay, if Ted's willing to risk his money, I'll come in with the other half", thinking nothing would happen. Then Lemmy immediately picked up the phone on my desk and rang Ted and said, "Look, Ted, Doug Smith says he'll put up half the £500 to hire Ronnie Lane's mobile studio to record the last gig if you'll put up the other half." I thought, here we go again . . .'

Ted Carroll was an Irish promoter who had been one of the original managers of Thin Lizzy, whom he'd relocated to London with in 1970. Since quitting Lizzy in 1974, he'd built a second-hand record stall on Portobello Road named Rock On, where he first met Lemmy, into his own independent record label, Chiswick Records, run with his business partner and fellow Irishman, Roger Armstrong. 'I'd known Lemmy since he was in Hawkwind and always had a soft spot for him,' Ted says now. 'When he came to me about making a live album out of what was supposed to be Motörhead's farewell performance at the Marquee,

I admit I was sceptical. But then we talked and I thought, well, maybe.'

But when the Marquee found out what was going on and demanded £500 for the right to record there, the idea bit the dust. 'In those days £500 was a king's ransom,' Eddie explains. 'So we thought, fuck, fuck, fuck.' Ted came to the rescue though when he offered to pay for the band to record a 'farewell' single instead. The Marquee show was 'one of the best we ever did', according to Eddie. 'Lemmy said the sweat was climbing up the walls trying to get out. It was packed!' After that, any thoughts about it being their last were quickly forgotten about. Two weeks later they all piled into the Transit van for the drive down to Escape Studios in Kent.

Unlike the Rockfield session 18 months before, which had dragged on for weeks, the Escape sessions were completed in just 48 hours. At the end of it, the band had more than a single to play to Ted and Roger. They had the bones of 13 tracks, eight of which would become the album *Motörhead*. Essentially, a rerecorded *On Parole*, minus three of the Larry Wallis tracks and the cover of 'Leaving Here'. Their replacements, two new Lemmy–Clarke–Taylor originals in 'White Line Fever' (itself a rerecording of the Stiff track) and 'Keep Us on the Road', written with the help of Mick Farren. And, finally, an absolutely steamrolling cover of 'Train Kept A-Rollin''.

The sessions had been produced by Speedy Keen, another old mate of Eddie's, who'd been the multi-instrumentalist whizz-kid behind Thunderclap Newman's international smash, 'Something in the Air', and who had just come straight from producing *L.A.M.F.* for Johnny Thunders & The Heartbreakers, now considered one of the seminal punk albums of the era.

'Roger and I worked out that it would cost us £3500 to finish recording and mixing the album at Olympic Studios, in Barnes,' recalls Ted Carroll, 'and that we'd be able to advance the band £1500 on the album.' Plans were also made to release a single ahead of the album, which would be the new, much tighter three-amigos version of 'Motorhead'. Released on the Chiswick label on 10 June, Ted and Roger brought all their indie-nous to bear, presenting it in a 'limited edition of 10,000' 12-inch format, the first time such extravagance had been lavished on a rock record. Ted says that pre-orders were so strong Chiswick upped the initial run to 12,500. They also ordered 7000 seven-inch singles.

Roger Armstrong later recalled the band turning up at Trident Studios for the cut along with an entourage of Hells Angels, plus Motorcycle Irene, who was then Phil's girlfriend, and who had provided the label with the photos they would use on the single and album sleeves. 'The place was awash with black leather jackets. In Irene's case, she appeared to be wearing little else. As each track played and engineer Ray Staff nervously worked on it, Irene would punch the air and yell out her approval. One by one the band members would lean forward and politely ask if maybe a bit more top, middle or bass could be added, favouring their particular instrument. The end result was that all the faders were up full on all frequencies, and so Ray politely explained that this was much the same as having them all down. At one point Speedy Keen joined us and slumped down between two massive speakers in the control room. Now and then he would lean over, put his head in a speaker and say, "More bass."'

When 'Motorhead' was released it astonished everybody by jumping into the UK Top 75. Well, almost everybody. Doug laughingly recalls he and his wife, Eve, scouring the chart-return shops in London (from whence the UK charts were compiled, based on the weekly sales figures from these shops), buying up three or four copies of the single at a time. 'Everybody used to do that in those days,' says Doug, 'and it would only get the record so high in the charts, but the thought was, if you could get it into the Top 75, radio would be more inclined to play it and you might even get on TV.'

What else helped the single's sales was that for once reviews in the all-powerful music press had been good. Roy Carr in the *NME* warned listeners to check for structural damage in their homes after playing the record. While Pete Makowski, star writer at *Sounds*, declared: 'Lemmy is the Lee Marvin of megadeath rock.' To aid the record further, Doug even talked Dave Brock into letting Motörhead open for Hawkwind as 'special guests' on a two-week tour. When Phil had a fight the day before the tour started with a junkie who refused to leave Lemmy's flat, he managed to dislocate a knuckle. Undeterred, he simply had the band's faithful roadie Bobs gaffer-tape a drumstick to his hand for the shows. As a result, the Chiswick single stayed in the Top 75 for seven weeks, peaking at No. 51, selling the sorts of quantities that would have placed it firmly in the Top 10 by today's standards. Then with the album, also titled

Motörhead, but with an umlaut added to the name for the first time, also reaching No. 43 in the charts, Motörhead, it seemed, was finally on its way.

Along the way, the band had also found the logo that was to become a crucial part of all their record artwork and merchandise for the rest of their career. Designed by an American expat sci-fi artist, Joe Petagno, whose main claim to fame at the time was his stunning cover illustrations for the Corgi SF Collector's Library edition of Ray Bradbury's *The Silver Locusts*, now better known as *The Martian Chronicles*, Joe had originally brought his work to Doug Smith to see if he might be considered for any future Hawkwind record sleeves.

Doug explains: 'Joe Petagno had wanted to design for Hawkwind but Barney Bubbles was already in there. So I suggested Lemmy's new band. Joe went and came back later with what looked like a very sci-fi scenario. It looked like a space soldier – with that head on it. But the head didn't look like that. The head was much more manicured and very neat and tidy. It was just as *Star Wars* came out and I'd been really impressed with Luke Skywalker's spaceship compared to the rest of them. It was a beaten-up old spaceship. So I told Joe to get rid of the sci-fi psychedelic aspect to the design and come back with something more like what Lemmy's about – rock'n'roll. "I like the mask," I told him. "Forget the body. Take it away and do something around that."'

When it came back, they had the prototype for what soon became known as Motörhead's War Pig: a snarling boar's head with huge tusks from which hangs a heavy chain, a tiny Iron Cross dangling from one side. Doug loved it. But at their next gig, the promoter, John Curd, 'wasn't crazy about the lettering so he changed the Motörhead lettering by just thickening it. It was in very thin Germanic lettering originally. And then Lemmy added the umlaut. He liked the image of it. It was something that he and I had talked about many years before.' Following a Hawkwind gig in Berlin some years before, Doug and Nik discovered 'all these German words on the wall of this girl's flat. She had big cut-out words with umlauts over them.' When they told Lemmy the story Doug mentioned how powerful the Germanic script looked. 'I didn't know what they meant, they just looked great. And Lemmy must have picked up on it.' But the story didn't end there. Later, when Ted Carroll was given the new logo to use on the album sleeve, by accident his printers had reversed the image. 'So they used the negative as opposed to the positive and that turned it into this very powerful image, a white War Pig on top of a black background, as opposed to a black War Pig on white. It was a pure accident. And from then on it stayed like that.'

Also known down the years as Snaggletooth, The Iron Boar, The Bastard, and The Little Bastard, the Motörhead War Pig would become one of the most iconic symbols of rebelliousness in rock'n'roll, up there with the Rolling Stones' sticking out tongue or the Hells Angels' skull and angel wings. According to Petagno, he got the idea after studying the skulls of wild boars, gorillas and dogs. For Lemmy, though, it only ever looked like one thing, he told me: 'What your face looks like if you stare in the mirror when you're tripping. Insane!'

Another tour was launched to promote the album, with Motörhead headlining this time, which they promoted as the Beyond the Threshold of Pain tour. It turned out to be a horribly prophetic title. First though they decided to fire Doug Smith – again. 'The Chiswick single had been a hit of sorts,' Doug recalls, 'and I thought, this is good. Then the next day they walked in with Bobs and told me they were leaving me to go with Tony Secunda. Lemmy said Bobs, their roadie, couldn't afford shoes so Tony Secunda was going to buy him shoes, and give them money. So that seemed like a good idea to Lemmy . . .'

Doug told Lemmy he never wanted to see him again. After all he'd done for him. Tony Secunda, meanwhile, had bigger things in mind for Lemmy, he said, than recording for a tiny label like Chiswick. Tony had been the manager of The Move during their late-Sixties heyday, had overseen the career of T. Rex and even taken po-faced folk rockers Steeleye Span into the pop charts for the first time. Doug was good for the underground networks, he told Lemmy, but Tony had the razzle-dazzle Motörhead now needed to get them to the top. And for a while Lemmy believed him. Mainly, it seems, because Tony always had money.

Things got off to an inauspicious start, however, when Phil and Bobs got into a fight after just a few shows of the next tour – Bobs had apparently said something Phil didn't like about Motorcycle Irene, but the two had been digging at each other for weeks – and Phil injured himself again. This, literally, beyond the threshold of pain when he broke his wrist, something no amount of gaffer tape would fix. The rest of the tour had to be cancelled.

Secunda was furious and fired Bobs on the spot. So now Lemmy was unhappy, too. Bobs had become to Lemmy somewhat as Nodder had been to Ciggy in the Rockin' Vicars: a trusted retainer. Losing Bobs was almost as bad as losing a member of the band, Lemmy complained. Secunda told him not to be ridiculous and carry on. But there was little else to do. There would be a 'comeback' show at the Marquee in November and half a dozen regional dates leading up to Christmas, but after that Motörhead ground to a halt. Secunda had approached every major label in London about securing a deal for Motörhead but nobody was interested. Some still thought of them as a joke. Others were simply put off by the band's biker image and association with the Hells Angels. Secunda's attentions had begun to drift, first towards Marianne Faithfull, whom he also managed for a short spell, then later to a young American wannabe named Chrissie Hynde, whom he placed on a weekly wage while she began writing the songs that would later make her garage band The Pretenders world-famous.

Secunda had told them he was out and with no money coming in Lemmy began to fret that Motörhead really were coming to an end this time. By the start of 1978, there was so little going for Motörhead – just eight gigs in the first six months – that Phil and Eddie had begun playing in a new band with Speedy Keen called The Muggers. Lemmy saw it as another nail in the Motörhead coffin. But, if anything, playing with another group only strengthened Phil and Eddie's resolve to make something again for the band. Speedy was a brilliantly gifted artist, and the bass player they had hooked up with, Billy Rath, had been in bands with The Heartbreakers and Iggy Pop. But it simply wasn't the same as playing with Lemmy. As Phil said at the time, 'You hear a lot of good things and a lot of bad things about Lemmy, and most of them are true. He is a cunt, he is a bastard, he does knock other people's chicks off. But he's also incredibly funny. Every time you go out with him it's a memorable experience.'

Eddie had decided he wasn't going anywhere, either. 'Me and Phil were especially close because Lemmy was a bit of a loner. I can't imagine being any closer to anyone else than those two, and it never even entered my mind whether I even liked Lemmy or not, because it wasn't even an issue. We felt almost indestructible because we'd had so much shit thrown at us and we'd decided that no matter what happened, we were gonna fuckin' carry on.'

They had decided to make another demo, shop it around. Lemmy's idea had been to do 'Bye Bye Johnny', the old Chuck Berry number they'd been playing live for years. Eddie had a better idea, though, how about 'Louie Louie', a Top 10 American hit for The Kingsmen in 1963. Lemmy wasn't so sure but the first time he listened to the cheap one-take tape they'd done with Alvin Lee producing, he knew they had something. What, though, to do with it? Who could they possibly turn to in their hour of need?

Doug Smith was sitting in his office one summer's afternoon in 1978 when he got a phone call from a friend named Karen. Doug still owed Karen a tenner from weeks before when he'd scored some coke from her. 'It was no big deal, we were good friends, she knew I'd give it back to her when I next saw her.' When she called out of the blue asking if he could drop it off he was surprised, thought it must be urgent, and went over. There waiting for him was Lemmy. 'I thought, "Oh no, absolutely no fucking way."'

'Here, Doug,' said Lemmy, 'sit down. Listen to this.'

Doug did so and Lemmy played him the demo of 'Louie Louie'. When it was over Lemmy asked Doug what he thought of it. 'I said, "It's a bit sweet, not very heavy, is it? Not like you were."' Lemmy said, he thought so too. Then he played Doug another song they'd recorded with Alvin, an original this time called 'Tear Ya Down'. Fast and furious, this was more like it, Doug decided. 'At which point, Eddie and Phil jump out of the back bedroom. They go, "Surprise! You wouldn't want to work with us again, would you?"

'I was like, "You must be fucking joking!" But they kept talking over me, then all three disappeared back into the bedroom. Then they came out again and asked me to come into the bedroom with them. I said, "Don't wanna know." But they kept pestering me. In the end I said, "Okay, but you do it my way." And they did. For about five minutes . . .'

Knowing that Lemmy was out of luck with the majors, and that they'd burned their bridges with Chiswick, Doug shrewdly hit on the idea of paying for a proper recording of 'Louie Louie' and 'Tear Ya Down' himself. 'A friend of mine, Neil Richmond, owned a studio opposite the Roundhouse and so I took them in there and rerecorded the "Louie Louie" single with Neil.' After that, he took it to Dave Betteridge at Bronze Records, another 'old mate'.

Bronze was another independent label, but one with serious clout, akin to that of Chris Blackwell's supercool Island Records or Richard Branson's newly opened Virgin

Records. Bronze had already had hit albums with rock acts like Uriah Heep and Manfred Mann's Earth Band. Doug knew he'd have to go in with more than just a good demo in his hands. He'd need to sit down and offer them a proposition. Which he duly did. 'I told Dave, "Let's do a single. It's already recorded so you don't have to pay for it. And if it charts we'll do a deal with you."'

Still unsure, Betteridge played the single to his boss, Bronze's founder, Gerry Bron, who later admitted he thought 'Louie Louie' was 'about the worst record I'd ever heard'. But Doug had been scheming again and persuaded the booking agent Neil Warnock to put together a ten-date tour for the band. When Neil rang Gerry to ask him to put the single out to help sell the tour, Gerry relented. 'Neil Warnock had said, "I've got a twelve-date tour lined up for this band called Motörhead. But the promoter says that unless we get a single out to promote it, he's gonna pull the plug."' Released on 30 September 1978, 'purely as a favour to Neil', once again everyone involved was rewarded by seeing the single jump straight into the UK charts at No. 75. And this time without the benefit of Doug and Eve running around buying copies of their own record from the chart-return shops.

'There was no need,' says Doug simply. 'Bronze was a bloody fucking great record company, let me tell you.' They even parlayed the success of the single into Motörhead's first ever appearance on *Top of the Pops*. Recorded on 25 October, as was usual for the show on a Wednesday evening, Eddie was 'doing a painting and decorating job to bring a bit of cash in' when the show aired the following night. 'I had to ask the punters if we could watch their telly, because I was on in a minute! I was standing there in my overalls with a paintbrush in my hand . . .'

The limited chart success of 'Louie Louie' also garnered Motörhead their first John Peel session, on which they played four numbers: the single, plus 'Tear Ya Down' and two more new numbers, 'Keep Us on the Road' and 'I'll Be Your Sister'. Suddenly, Motörhead were in danger of actually becoming cool. A situation unhindered by Lemmy's growing presence on the London punk scene, appearing onstage for a one-off show at the Music Machine with The Dammed – billed as The Doomed – and being photographed with Sid Vicious, who let it be known that Lemmy 'was the one what taught me the bass'. Lemmy laughed when I once reminded him. 'I liked Sid, thought he was great, and it was true he lived in the same squat as me for a while and did ask me to show him how to play. But he just couldn't get the hang of it at all. I told him to give up.'

With momentum now building beneath them the autumn '78 British tour was extended by Neil Warnock into a full-blown extravaganza, culminating in November with Motörhead's first headline show in their own right at the Hammersmith Odeon, the venue that was about to become part of their growing mythology.

Motörhead's signing to a long-term contract with Bronze now seemed like a formality, but, just to be sure, Doug made sure Gerry Bron was at the Odeon in order to gauge the reaction of the crowd for himself. 'I knew it was going to be full and that the fans would go mad,' says Doug, 'the hard part was making sure people like Gerry and Dave and

Neil were all there to see it.' Doug needn't have worried. As Gerry Bron later told Dave Ling, 'I went to see them at Hammersmith Odeon and it was packed to the rafters with people going absolutely crazy.' That was when he knew, he said, 'We had to sign them right away.'

There was no sleep in Hammersmith that night.

SIX

Don't Forget the Joker

So began a four-year period in which virtually everything Lemmy and Motörhead touched turned to gold – or, at the very least, silver. Four Top 20 singles, three of which went Top 10. Six Top 30 albums, including two that went Top 10 and one all the way to No. 1. It was also now that Lemmy (words) and Eddie (riffs) co-wrote all the songs that would make Motörhead a legend. 'Lemmy was still finding his feet as a lyricist, and I'm not a virtuoso, I'm a journeyman. But Clapton never came up with "Ace of Spades" or "Bomber". My job was giving Lemmy something to sing over. And we were a great team like that.' The trick, he says, was, 'You're bombing along having a fucking ball then as you're having a ball you put a couple of little changes in and next thing you've got a song.'

Phil was always credited as an equal co-writer on the albums because, said Eddie, 'We knew if we did make it that we didn't want Lemmy and I coming to work in Rolls-Royces and Phil on a pushbike.' Yet it was Phil who came up with the musical motif that turned Motörhead from a street-level punk-metal band into something far more transcendent, when he began, to test out a new kit, pounding out the outrageous double-time rhythm to what became 'Overkill'. 'That was the big turning point song-wise,' says Eddie. 'It was fantastic! Blimey, we loved that!'

They were rehearsing in Notting Hill and Phil had just taken possession of a new kit fitted, unusually for the times, with two double-kick drums. 'Phil goes, "Why can't we do a song like this?" And starts going mental cos Phil's got these two bass drums and he doesn't know what to fucking do with them. Lemmy goes, "All right then", he starts playing in E, as he usually did, and I jumped in. Ten minutes later we had "Overkill". We were all grinning going, "Yeah, that was a bit of all right. Let's do it again . . ."'

Lemmy's lyrics reflected the speed and sheer exuberance of the track: '*On your feet you feel the beat, it goes straight to your spine / Shake your head, you must be dead if it don't make you fly!*' The band were so delighted they made it the title track of their first Bronze album, and insisted it be the first single released from it. It was Phil Taylor's over the top drums, though, that would leave the most lasting impression, not least on the coming wave of thrash- and speed-metal bands. As the renowned metal musicologist Joel McIver puts it, 'The double-kick drum was what gave thrash its intensity, its relentlessness: it was what makes thrash sound like the end of the world, rather than merely a riot.' Or as Metallica's drummer-founder and former president of the US Motörhead fan club, Lars Ulrich, once told me, 'Phil Taylor was the first drummer I ever heard play that double-bass type of thing. The first time I heard "Overkill" it fucking blew my head off. I could not believe what I was hearing. Of course, then I wanted to play like that too.'

For his part, Taylor seemed supremely unaware of the revolution he had helped create, admitting that when Metallica later supported Motörhead on an early tour, he barely understood what was going on, they played so damn fast. It's worth mentioning at this juncture, though, that there was far more to the Philthy Animal's playing than mere speed and power. McIver points to the example of 'Ace of Spades', another classic Motörhead song built around Taylor's ferocious double-kick drums. 'Taylor lifts the song after the second chorus with a series of almost jazzy rim shots. You might think that song is all blood and thunder, but it's really not.'

Eddie recalls how Lemmy used to get exasperated at first at Phil's habit of playing in double-time, yelling at him: 'Fucking hell! Can't you play a straight four!' But then, as Eddie points out, Lemmy's bass could also be 'fucking difficult' to play along with. 'It was fucking difficult because there was no bottom end. Especially in those days, a bottom end on the bass was how it was played. Well, we didn't have any. So that made life very, very tricky. That's why the very first album was quite difficult. Just trying to get that fucking sound down on tape, it was almost impossible, to be honest.'

In fact, Lemmy's skill on the bass – much like Phil's on

drums and Eddie's on guitar – was totally underrated. As Joel McIver, now author and editor of *Bass Guitar Magazine*, explains, 'Lemmy's bass style, at least while he was in Hawkwind, was based on drones and power chords, with the latter coming into play more prominently in Motörhead. This was partly out of convenience. As any bassist will tell you, making a two-string power chord from the root note plus a fifth and strumming at it with a pick is a damn sight easier than picking individual strings, especially when your head is pointed upwards at an unnatural angle, and you're shouting into a microphone and unable to see the fret board. Distort the tone and it's even easier, because no one can hear it when you mess up. Interestingly, at least from a bass guitar geek's point of view, Lemmy didn't use an overdrive pedal, simply rolling off the low end from his Marshall rig and pushing the cones to create natural distortion. The naturally mids-heavy tone from his Rickenbackers enabled the wall of noise still further. But none of this is meant to imply that Lemmy wasn't a skilled bass player: check out any of his bass solos for evidence of that. Instead, he believed in a less-is-more approach, hence the broadly similar bass parts in tracks like "Overkill" and "Ace of Spades", to name just the two best-known, which basically consisted of a single note with an approach note added a couple of times per bar. "I like to see the whole road, not just individual bricks," he once told me. Technique be damned, Lemmy had a unique bass style and tone, and that's what matters.'

With the £30,000 advance from Bronze that Doug Smith had negotiated for them, Motörhead were now able to afford to hire the legendary former Rolling Stones producer Jimmy Miller to oversee two months at Roundhouse studios making what would be their breakthrough album. With the single and album released two weeks apart in March 1979, and a 20-date UK headline tour to coincide, *Overkill* became the first Motörhead album to go Top 30, reaching No. 24, while the single performed a similar feat, giving them their first Top 40 hit, reaching No. 39. There was another *Top of the Pops* appearance to go with it, Lemmy's gap-toothed smile devouring the camera, the front cover of *Sounds* magazine, and a half-hour live broadcast on Radio 1 in May of a concert from London's Paris Theatre. The day after that they played their first show abroad, before a curious and mostly stunned audience in France at the Palais d'Hiver in Lyons.

A second single was released from the album, 'No Class' – a three-amigos 'original' that was essentially a rewrite of ZZ Top's 'Tush', itself essentially a rewrite of every 12-bar blues boogie ever invented – but was not a significant hit. Lemmy didn't care though, he was too busy revelling in his newfound success. The drugs and drinking, however, were a given come rain or shine. What increased now, he said, was the sudden uptake in new female admirers. Not that he was choosy. On the road, at the end of another long night of not sleeping, 'That's when everybody becomes good-looking, or at least manageable. But sometimes, it's like there's the last chicken in the shop and you don't seem to be able to help yourself. It's like having an out-of-body experience. You see yourself chatting up this dragon, and you know you're doing it, but you still do it . . .'

What Lemmy was less inclined to talk about was how he had tried more than one close relationship with a woman, only to run a mile when things got too serious. 'No, it wasn't him, being with the same girl for ever,' says Eddie confirming the impression of Lemmy the eternal loner. 'When I was in the band he'd already made up his mind. He had his son, we knew about Paul. But he hated Tracey for fucking doing it to him. He was angry about that. Then he had a girl called Jeanette who was giving him an awful lot of trouble.'

Lemmy had been living with Jeanette in a squat in Battersea. According to Eddie, though, 'They had some terrible fights. I think she just used to wind him up. As women do, you know? And he just got fucked off with it in the end. He nearly fucking strangled her once. And I think he thought, that's enough of this, you know? He got so angry! I remember being there. He got so fucking angry with her, I thought fucking hell! Women have the ability to do this. He said, "I ain't fucking doing that no more." And Phil was no different. To be honest, the three of us. It's why we were so perfect. Apart from him having Paul Inder, none of us had any kids or anything. We never settled down. We were what we were. That's why we were so right for each other. That's the joke. We were so right for each other, how it got broken I don't fucking know. I've asked myself the question so many times . . .'

At the same time as Motörhead were being heralded as one of the coming men of what *Sounds* had recently dubbed the 'New Wave of British Heavy Metal', Lemmy was becoming equally familiar to the real new wave crowd, who also ate speed for breakfast and detected in Motörhead a no-shit gang of do-badders not a million miles from themselves. The punk association came about, Lemmy said, because 'we did actually hang out and play together. I saw an old advert from one of the music papers that the fan club had reprinted, and it was for a gig at the Roundhouse in about 1979 and the bill is The Damned, Motörhead and The Adverts. The Damned would get bottles thrown at them by our fans, we got bottles thrown at us by their fans, and The Adverts got bottles thrown at them by everybody . . . It was a good bill. But it also showed what we were up for. I always thought we had more in common with The Damned than Judas Priest. The only reason we were thought of as a heavy metal band was because of our hair. Though I never thought much of The Jam, actually,' he adds as an aside. 'I always thought Paul Weller was a boring little shit, as he still is today. Just a more influential boring little shit.' He recalled trying to talk to Weller at the Music Machine one night 'sitting on one of those pool tables at the back. Two or three minutes into it and I thought, fucking hell, I can't talk to this guy for long. He was having "such a hard time" and "Ooh, it's so tough . . ." Fucking miserable little creep. I'd much rather talk to [Captain] Sensible.'

In fact, Lemmy did more than just talk to the Captain. With The Damned now signed to Chiswick, a plan was hatched with Bronze to release a double-A side Motörhead–Damned single. Studio time was booked but it all came to nought when Lemmy baulked at the idea of recording a cover of the Sweet hit 'The Ballroom Blitz' for their side of the single. (The Damned were to have recorded a Motörhead song for their side.) 'So in the end we just had to trash the place,' Eddie said and shrugged. 'Lemmy smashed something in the toilet and they sent us a bill for a hundred quid.'

In August, the same month Motörhead made their first appearance on the bill at the Reading Festival, a mammoth, groundbreaking article on the band appeared in *NME*. Written by one of the paper's alumni, and fellow knight of Notting Hill, Chris Salewicz, it was the first really serious in-depth look into what made the now 34-year-old, suddenly budding rock star tick. This was a substantial piece, far from the 'worst band in the world' taunt made by Nick Kent in the same paper just two years before. As Chris explains, he'd first met Lemmy back in 1975. 'He was a good mate of Mick Farren. I first met him there, at Mick's place, lying on the floor behind Mick's stuffed armadillo with a Bali-an mask on his face that turned out to be an elaborate hash pipe: he was holding it by handles on each side.'

In the *NME* article, Chris also mentioned another time a couple of years later when he visited a mutual friend at a somewhat palatial squat in Kensington. 'One of the other squatters was Lemmy, and during the course of the evening we were shown his room (he was out at the time). In one corner, as though underlining the bassist's angelic outlaw image was a pile of weighty tomes on the Third Reich. I remember smiling, though, when I glanced at the open book next to Lemmy's bed. What Lemmy was really reading was a novel by P. G. Wodehouse. "That," I recall thinking, "says it all."'

Sent to cover the band at a festival appearance in Helsinki, in June, Salewicz told how Lemmy had begun the show by offering the sizeable crowd 'Peace and Good Vibes' in Finnish, only to end the day by destroying all the equipment on the stage. 'I don't know why I've got this terrible reputation,' Lemmy had told Salewicz previously. 'I mean, you never see me completely fucking out of it. You never see me falling all over the floor, puking up over everyone, being totally obnoxious, having to be carried home. I never get like that. How can I? I'm a speed freak. I'm up twenty-four hours a day.'

When Chris, who has always believed in the sacramental value of the finest herbs, suggested that speed was, well, 'Bad for your head, man', Lemmy, naturally, begged to differ. 'It doesn't kill your soul, though, does it? Hopefully not, anyway, but it doesn't half kill your body.' The clincher for Lemmy, he added, was that 'It's the only drug I've found that I can work on, and it's helped me to be good. Not made me good – it doesn't do that – but it's helped sustain me being good when ordinarily I'd have been knackered and below par.' But wouldn't Lemmy at least agree, Chris pushed, 'that it basically disorders your nervous system?' Again, Lemmy demurred. 'Well, it does a lot of people. I seem to be lucky. I've got a nervous system that just eats it and goes, "Waahhh, give me some more!" So far I've got a mental and physical constitution like a rock – touch wood.'

He also tackled Lemmy about why the Hells Angels, which he accurately described as 'part of Lemmy's Hawkwind inheritance', had so readily adopted the band. Again Lemmy was proud of the connection. 'It's a very rigidly organised set-up. It's a full-time occupation, really. It can be a very violent career for a young man. Sure, it can be very negative in some ways, but it can be very positive in others. They're good lads, you know. I get on with all of them. As an alternative to disco-dancing you must admit it has its merits.'

At a time when it had become normal for sections of the more fashion-conscious punk crowd to sport swastikas, Chris quizzed Lemmy on his own Iron Cross fetish (Lemmy's collecting of Nazi regalia had not yet kicked in), asking the obvious and most important question: why?

'Because it's obviously a joke,' Lemmy laughed, almost astonished at the question. It can confuse people, though, Chris responded. 'Confusion's good for the soul sometimes. Actually, what it is, is that I was given this leather jacket in 1973. It just arrived in a mystery parcel with no note or anything. And I just thought, "Well, what're you gonna wear on a leather jacket?" Nik Turner had ceramic flowers but I figured it should be something – heavy. It's just like the Hells Angels, really – into shock. If there was Nazis around today I'd be in the concentration camp immediately.' As far as Lemmy was concerned, he told Chris, his only real rule of the road was: 'Treat me alright, I'll treat you alright. I don't care who you are – Jews, blacks, Arabs, Italians. If they're okay to me I'll be okay to them. It's the only way to really work it, isn't it?' The only thing Lemmy was genuinely prejudiced against, he said with a dry chuckle, was the record business. 'And the police, of course.'

Musically, however, Salewicz was prepared to meet Lemmy halfway. Astutely pointing out that 'as a pure hard-rock outfit Motörhead are in a league of their own and a whole different scene to such contemptible contemporary heavy metal contenders as Ted Nugent or Judas Priest; the M-heads show that Heavy Metal does not have to be the crypto-fascist music it generally is.' Adding: 'I don't think it's just because Lemmy's a bit of an old hippy that Motörhead evince such a positive spirit. Rather, it's because within the band there dwells an unblemished rock'n'roll understanding and spirit that makes me think of them as something like a *Daily Mirror* version of The Clash. If you're a rock fan who's a sheet metal worker from Stoke or on the dole in Glasgow or Barrow you'll know what I mean. You'll have sympathy with what Eddie's talking about when he says that, in the really bad old days of '76, they were sharing ten pounds a week between them, and that now they earn £45 a week they feel they "can conquer the world on that".'

In retrospect, there was one other point of note that Lemmy made to Salewicz, when he confided, 'I'd really quite like to move out of this country. I'd really like to move to America, because America may be completely crazed but at least it enjoys being crazed. I mean, you can get busted by a cop and if you give him the right rap and spiel he'll actually let you go, and maybe he'll even blow a joint with you first.' Lemmy's romantic view of America would alter drastically over time. But he never gave up on the idea of how much better his life would be if he lived there.

Chris also went on to describe how the band were arrested at Helsinki airport, following complaints to the police by the festival promoters horrified at the damage done to their stage. They were thrown in jail, where they languished for the next three days. Although Chris had mentioned the tree Phil Taylor had lobbed into the dressing room – via a window pane Lemmy had put his fist through – and of course the extensive damage to the stage, he had missed the moment, Lemmy later recalled, when the band had given said tree 'a Viking funeral. We set fire to it and pushed it out on the lake, and it looked really great, you know, it was dusk. Then, of course, we got on the bus going back to the airport and the driver made the terrible mistake of saying, "You will not make a mess on my bus." Immediate food fight . . . When we got to customs, the official said, "Step into this room, please . . ."'

After finally being released, Lemmy told Joel McIver, the pilot of their homebound flight came storming down the aisle to inform them, 'I've heard about you. You guys are a disgrace to society! If you do anything on my plane, I'll have the police waiting for you at Heathrow.' As soon as the plane took off though, Eddie somehow managed to pour a very large vodka and orange down the neck of the female passenger in the seat in front of him. 'We didn't think that was too bad, though,' said Lemmy, 'but as soon as we got to Heathrow we saw all these police lined up on the tarmac! We thought, "Oh no, we're fucked here!" But then they arrested the captain – he was drunk! Talk about poetic irony!'

The rest of the summer was taken up with trying as fast as possible to make a follow-up to *Overkill*. It was the 1970s and bands could still be forgotten in a matter of months if they didn't keep pumping out product. Particularly bands like Motörhead, who despite their hot streak no one was ever really sure would last for long. As if not to jinx it, recording was once again arranged at the Roundhouse with Jimmy Miller at the controls. Only, this time Jimmy, whose heroin habit had already seen him fired by the Stones, was so out of it Lemmy complained of finding him nodded off in his chair during playbacks. 'We used to think that we were bad at being late,' Phil later recalled, 'but he would be, like, *half a day late*, or even more late, you know, and his excuses were marvellous.' Lemmy, who'd taken to yelling at the producer before takes, 'Is everything louder than everything else?', said he always knew something was up whenever the hapless producer failed to answer.

Despite these drawbacks, the subsequent album, *Bomber*, remains one of the best Motörhead would ever make. Built around more soon-to-be Motörhead classics like the ballistic opener, 'Dead Men Tell No Tales', the slash-and-burn groove of the marvellous 'Stone Dead Forever', or, best of all, the anthemic title track, inspired by Len Deighton's novel *Bomber*, with its fire-engine riff and double-fisted drums, Lemmy gargling with nails over the top: *'Ain't a hope in hell / Nothin' gonna bring us down . . .'*

The rest of the tracks were nearly as good, Lemmy now beginning to aim his barbs directly at real-life targets: his hatred of the police on 'Lawman', his anger still at the way his father left his mother on 'Poison', his disgust with television on 'Talking Head'. The album also featured one track, 'Step Down', with Eddie on lead vocals. In his memoir, Lemmy recalled how Eddie 'had been bitching that I was getting all the limelight, but he wouldn't do anything about it. I got sick of him complaining, so I said, "Right, you're gonna fucking sing one on this album." He hated it, but really, he was a good singer, Eddie.'

'The way Lemmy's lyrics improved,' says Eddie now, shaking his head. 'For fuck's sake, he was improving all the time. Once we'd cracked the little formula of how to really work together on *Overkill* then we really started to take off. Then *Bomber* was fucking . . . some of the stuff on *Bomber* is fucking . . . I mean, "Stone Dead Forever", fucking hell! Did I *really* play that guitar?'

He did and the fans loved him for it, sending *Bomber* to No. 12 in the UK, and the single, along with another *Top of the Pops* showdown, to No. 34. The tour that accompanied the album's release was also a huge step up for the band, featuring as it now did the famous 'Bomber' lightshow – a specially built lighting rig suspended high above the stage made up to look like the nose and wings on a Lancaster bomber, its guns firing as it swooped upon the stage as though about to crash into the audience.

Eddie says it was he who came up with the idea. They were sitting in the office, across from Doug. 'Talking about a way of incorporating plane wings into the stage set. But it was really a bit far-fetched.' Then their lighting guy, Peter Barnes, came up with the truss idea. 'Why don't we put the lights on a fucking bomber truss. And then, put it on chains and move it up and down. I thought, steady fucking on! But we tried it and it worked, really worked!' The *Bomber* set was a step up, no doubt.

In today's world of computerised stage productions, where dancers and video screens provide as much entertainment

– often more – than the music itself, it's hard to imagine the excitement and astonishment that greeted Motörhead's relatively simple new *Bomber* stage show. But the photographs that now peppered music magazines all over the world and the column inches it also helped generate meant the *Bomber* show really helped spread the message that Motörhead were now far beyond the usual punk-metal bash. That what they were doing now was on another level. Still of the street, but looking up from the gutter at the sky, or at least the bombs dropping from it. Class in a distinctly no-class way. 'If you were having a bit of a bad one,' says Eddie, 'you'd think, "Thank god the bomber's coming next number." You knew damn well that once that thing come down it killed everybody!'

Again, the music press lapped the new album up. *Zig-Zag*'s editor, Kris Needs, summed it up thus: 'Motörhead needn't be taboo if you're a punk or whatever other uniform you choose. They simply pack more punch, sheer mania and represent the ecstasy of excess more than anyone around in any of the enclosures.' But then, as Lemmy said, 'Every liner has its tug.' And suddenly United Artists woke up to the fact they still had an unreleased Motörhead album in their vaults. Typically, in such a situation, UA gave no mind to the fact the band had already released a far superior version of *On Parole*, nor the fact that Larry Wallis was no longer in Motörhead, but went ahead and released *On Parole* in time for Christmas 1979. 'Another valuable lesson learned about record companies,' Lemmy sneered. 'Also proving that I was right all along and the album should have come out when we'd recorded it in the first place.' It reached No. 65, and, ironically, is now considered a treasured collector's item in their back catalogue – assuming you can find the original vinyl pressing.

Chiswick Records also got in on the act, releasing *Beer Drinkers and Hell Raisers*, a four-track EP comprising the four tracks from the original Escape sessions that had not been included on *Motörhead*: the Wallis-less version of 'On Parole', two covers, including the eponymous ZZ Top of the EP's title, and an instrumental, essentially an unfinished track credited to the band and titled 'Instro'. This, though, did rather better than UA's cash-in release, climbing to a very respectable No. 43 – and bringing in some much-needed income for Ted Carroll's label. 'I didn't like it but I could hardly begrudge Ted,' Lemmy said. 'After all he'd done for us.'

The first few months of 1980 would find Motörhead bringing their ungodly row to concerts in France, Germany, Holland and Italy. Bronze were having a hard time persuading European labels to license any of the Motörhead catalogue. 'We always seemed to have a problem with Motörhead,' Gerry Bron later recalled. 'Nobody liked them, not on a professional level. They had a fantastic following, but licensees around the world absolutely hated them. We had a terrible job getting them to work with the band.' Live though, they were picking up new fans wherever Lemmy plonked his white cowboy boots. Though the idea of 'stage clothes' was not a concept Lemmy recognised, nevertheless the band's image was now consistently based around the same look for all but Philthy, who wore whatever he liked when he liked. For Eddie, this meant a black shirt, done up to the collar, with long dark jeans studded along the seams with metal stars. For Lemmy it meant a black shirt open to the navel, showing off his hairy chest and Iron Cross dangling from his neck, dark blue jeans, and always but always those white cowboy boots.

All those TV appearances and magazine covers had turned Lemmy, Eddie and Phil into stars back home. With their weekly wages now upped to £200 a week, the band was also starting to see some real money for their efforts. Suddenly their lives were changing. Doug was determined that it should all be for the good; at the same time, as he says, 'This was Motörhead we're talking about, not the Three Degrees.'

Lemmy, in particular, says Doug, 'was very easy to work with in those days. Lemmy was never a problem working with. He just made me angry because he felt that he didn't need to do anything. So he'd get people in the office to go and buy his boots for him. I said, "Lem, you've got to try them on." "No, no, they know my size down the market!" The white boots. He always wore those silly white boots. Everybody in the office had to do something. Go and buy Jack Daniel's for him or whatever he was drinking at the time. He wouldn't bother to look for a flat so somebody had to go and look for a flat for him.'

Doug recalls organising a £10,000 publishing advance for each member. 'They were all going to buy a house with it. Once they'd found a place, we'd give them the ten grand each so it didn't go anywhere else. Eventually, Eddie bought a place in Chiswick. Phil bought a place in Lots Road, Chelsea. And Lemmy still hadn't looked for anything.' Then when Doug arranged some appointments for him, 'The first one he went to, the woman opened the door, screamed and slammed the door in his face. That was the last time Lemmy looked for a place to live.'

In the end, after they'd returned from Europe, Lemmy simply moved into another hotel near Little Venice. 'He was there about four weeks. Then one of the merchandising girls, Jane, had a friend who owned a hotel near Maida Vale, right on Edgware Road. Big house turned into single-room "studio apartments". Mostly let out to Arabs. Lemmy got a room there with a bathroom and little kitchenette in it. That was his place for about nine months. That was very expensive.' It was also near enough to Doug's office for Lemmy to visit most days. Or when he wasn't there to phone Doug and ask him to come over. Doug remembers one such call, when Lemmy phoned and demanded Doug come over quick! 'I got there and he'd set the kitchenette on fire. "What am I gonna do?" He'd burned it cooking chips and a toasted cheese sandwich. A big meal for Lemmy. I never really saw him eat more than a sandwich . . . Whenever the band would be taken out for a meal on the road he wouldn't go. He'd wander off on his own somewhere.'

Back in the rehearsal room, in the summer of 1980, working on new material for their next album, the band had developed a familiar ritual. Before starting work, Eddie recalls, 'We'd have a little toot. But once it becomes normal you're not out your nuts any more . . . In the early days that was sometimes a problem. Because you didn't have any money sometimes there wasn't any speed. That would make terrible problems, particularly for Lemmy. Me and Phil were not so bad. Me, I could live without. Phil could manage. But Lemmy couldn't. He used to get flu and all sorts. Trying to get him down to rehearsals or to do a gig was very difficult. It wasn't his fault, he was just on a downer. So sometimes it was very hard to get him fucking motivated. And a lot of arguments came out of that. It did create bad blood at times, with Phil in particular. Phil was very hot-headed at times. But I got pretty angry as well at times. We'd begin rehearsals and Lemmy wouldn't be there.'

In May, Bronze released a live four-track EP, *The Golden Years*, comprising cheaply recorded live versions of 'Leaving Here', 'Stone Dead Forever', 'Dead Men Tell No Tales' and 'Too Late, Too Late'. It immediately leapt into the charts at No. 8 and the band were back again on *Top of the Pops*, miming along convincingly to 'Leaving Here'. Radio 1 refused to play any of the EP's tracks, though. Complaining Lemmy's vocal was mixed too low. So Bronze hurriedly remixed 'Leaving Here', bringing up the vocal track, and reissued it to the station as a special seven-inch single. They still refused to play it.

Recording at producer Vic Maile's Jackson's Studios in Rickmansworth, a few miles outside London, this next album would, for many long-term fans at least, be the last of the true Motörhead masterpieces. The sound was better than on *Bomber* or *Overkill* – Maile had worked in the past with such giants as Jimi Hendrix, Led Zeppelin and The Who and knew exactly how to get a great live band to replicate their best work in a studio – and the 12 tracks, again, were built around three truly colossal Motörhead moments:

the title track, 'Ace of Spades', '(We Are) The Road Crew', and 'The Chase Is Better Than the Catch'.

The former, of course, would go on to become the band's signature song, like 'Satisfaction' for the Stones or 'All Right Now' for Free. By the time of Lemmy's death 35 years later, 'Ace of Spades' was still the one song everybody knew him by. The one song no Motörhead show would ever be complete without. With its rumbling thunder bass, lightning-fast drums and speedy, corner-hugging guitar riff, overlaid by a thrilling lyric in which gambling metaphors become code for how to live your life to the full, Lemmy outdid himself this time – although, as he was always quick to point out, he was never much of a poker player in real life, always preferring the swinging arm of the fruit machines (one of which he now had installed in the dressing room on tour each night). Thus we hear about 'snake eyes' – double one on gambling dice – and the 'dead man's hand, aces and eights', 'Wild Bill Hickok's hand when he got shot,' he explained.

And, of course, it's immortal pay-off line, about being born to lose, and how gambling's for fools, *But that's the way I like it baby, I don't want to live forever!'* One of the greatest kiss-offs in rock history, followed by the final twist of the absurdist knife, *'And don't forget the joker!'* Cue: that fearfully cackling, gloriously insane solo. How true was it, though, I asked him. Wouldn't it come back to haunt him? The way Pete Townshend's famous line in 'My Generation' – *Hope I die before I get old* – eventually did? 'Of course!' he laughed. 'See, I cover a lot more ground than Townshend. 'I don't want to live for ever is a long time. You could be 294 and not reach "for ever". But I think you'd be sick of it by then. I think anybody would be sick of it by then. Even me. And I like to stay up late, you know? Actually, I'd like to die the year *before* for ever. To avoid the rush . . .'

The other major cornerstones of the album also embraced tenets of Lemmy's personal philosophy. The most affecting, '(We Are) The Road Crew'. Having once been a roadie himself, Lemmy always felt an affinity for the hard-working roadies and crew that gave their all on tour for Motörhead. Lemmy recalls in his memoir how when one of the roadies, Ian 'Eagle' Dobbie, heard the song, 'he had a tear in his eye'. More rowdy and to the point was 'The Chase Is Better Than the Catch', which drew bile from several female rock writers, but Eddie couldn't see what the fuss was about. 'It's about the true life experience of what it's like being in a band like this,' he says now. 'Cos when you haven't got a pot to piss in and slogging around the country and having a fucking laugh, you haven't got time for thinking. If you got a drink and a joint and toot you figure your fucking life's sweet, man, and a bird's fucking sucking you off, what more do I ever want?'

When 'Ace of Spades' was released as the lead-off single from the album in October, despite little or no airplay again, it rocketed into the charts at No. 15, triggering yet another *Top of the Pops* appearance and yet more front covers on *Sounds* and *Melody Maker*. What really hit home for Lemmy, though, was when the *Ace of Spades* album went straight into the charts at No. 4!

'That was it, really,' Lemmy would tell me years later. 'We thought we'd made it, and actually we had. And that's when we started to fuck up. Not all at once, but that was probably the start.' Eddie concurs. Pinpointing the next 12 months as both 'the height of our success and the moment really when it started to go wrong'. At first it was little things, Eddie says. 'Phil always had this thing about everybody being equal. Phil always used to get the hump about Lemmy sitting in the front of the car. But I never gave a flying fuck. I never minded Lemmy having his edge. That was fine with me. He was Lemmy and that was okay with me. But it used to get up Phil's nose a fair bit. These things don't happen until you get successful. But what happens when you start to become famous, and suddenly you get a bit arsey or something pisses you off, you think: I don't have to put up with this. I'm famous! I never felt like that but I think Phil and Lemmy did a tad.'

Suddenly there were 'business hassles, too', all of which Eddie now took upon himself to try and resolve. 'Anything tricky, Doug wouldn't go to Lemmy,' he recalls, 'cos Lemmy would never do anything about it anyway. So he would come to me and I would pass the info on.' Most glaringly, when Doug rang Eddie, he says, 'on the eve of the *Ace of Spades* tour to say the promoter couldn't come up with the £118,000 we'd agreed to do the tour. That the tour would have to be cancelled unless we agreed to lower the price to £108,000. I went and told the boys and at first we were all like, 'Fuck that!' But we would have done anything rather than cancel a tour. Our attitude was, 'We can't do this to the fans. Doug knows this, so he's got us over a barrel. This is two days before the tour is supposed to kick off.'

Even once the tour had started, the band still found

themselves the victims of bad luck when Phil either fell or was thrown, depending on which speed freak you believe, down the stairs of his hotel at an early show and landed on his head. He was forced to get through the rest of a tour playing with a neck brace on. At first, they feared he'd broken his silly neck. But it turned out to only be his vertebrae he had damaged. Something, nevertheless, that left him with an unsightly calcium deposit on the back of his neck – which he nicknamed 'the knob'.

Things only got harder when between April and July 1981 they took off for their first major US tour: 42 dates across North America and Canada, some opening for Ozzy Osbourne in arenas, others headlining their own smaller club and theatre shows, that would test the band's resolve to its limits. Neither Eddie nor Phil had ever been to America and so viewed the start of the tour as the beginning of a great new adventure. Mercury Records in New York had agreed a deal with Bronze in London to release *Ace of Spades* and hopes were high for a repeat of the success they were now enjoying in the UK.

But the novelty soon wore off as they found themselves either being roundly ignored or worse still catcalled and booed by Ozzy's boisterous crowd, or playing to largely empty rooms at their own shows. 'The Americans,' says Eddie, 'were not ready for Motörhead. We didn't get a single encore for about the first four weeks.' He admits that he and Phil would suffer, where Lemmy, ever the road warrior, would 'just kind of muscle to it. Cos he was an old soldier, you know?'

The band began to pick at each other. Especially Eddie

and Phil, who spent most of the tour permanently at each other's throats. 'The fights between me and Phil were legendary,' says Eddie. 'We'd really try to hurt each other.' The tour became so stressful Doug considered calling it off at one point. 'I once thought Phil Taylor was dead of an overdose in New York,' he later confessed to Dave Ling. 'And in America the police arrive whenever you call an ambulance, so I'd been going around his room hiding every drug I could find, hoping they'd think he'd just collapsed. It was life-threatening all the time, for all of them – even Lemmy, who I once thought was gonna have a heart attack when we got to a gig in Canada and there was no speed around.'

What made it harder in America was the knowledge that they were now big stars back home in Britain. So much so that in February, when Bronze released a three-track EP featuring both Motörhead and Doug's latest signings, Girlschool – titled *St Valentine's Day Massacre* – it became the band's biggest ever selling record, reaching No. 5 and shifting more than 200,000 copies. Lemmy, who it was whispered was 'very close' to Girlschool's blonde bombshell guitarist, Kelly Johnson, was delighted. The result: yet another appearance on *Top of the Pops* – this time with Girlschool alongside them, the two bands billed as Headgirl – playing the lead track, a cover of 'Please Don't Touch' by Johnny Kidd & The Pirates, one of Lemmy's favourites. (The other two tracks featured Motörhead covering the Girlschool original 'Emergency' and Girlschool covering 'Bomber'.)

It wasn't just *Top of the Pops* Motörhead were now regular guests of. They were being invited onto children's shows, too, most memorably the blissfully anarchic *Tiswas*, where they were interviewed by Sally James, thoroughly 'flanned' by the Phantom Flan Flinger, then hosed down with water by various members of the cast, including Chris Tarrant and Lenny Henry. At the time, appearing on *Tiswas* had become the mark of cool for any self-respecting rock band and Motörhead would return there for several appearances, blasting out bits of 'Bomber' and 'Ace of Spades' as the kids in the studio frantically bounced around them. 'Doing that show probably brought in more fans than if we'd done a gig in Birmingham [where the show was made],' Lemmy would later tell me.

The best – and worst, Lemmy would always insist for years after – was yet to come, though. Motörhead were in Los Angeles, at the end of June, getting ready to open for Ozzy at the cavernous Long Beach arena, when Doug phoned Lemmy with the news. Their new album – a long-planned-for live album, that they'd jokingly titled, *No Sleep 'til Hammersmith* – had just gone into the UK charts, first week of release, at No. 1!

Even Paul Morley, then the most outspoken of the *NME*'s new, spikier generation of all-out warfare punk apostles, couldn't resist its illicit charms, ending his review with the words, almost choked out: '*No Sleep 'til Hammersmith* is disgusting, bleeding, gruesome magnificence and Motörhead are one of the Great Popular Groups. The LP represents the limitations, absurdity and rare glory of HM rock so comprehensively and madly it has to be considered a major work. It tells you everything you need to know about the stinking sin of rock'n'roll.'

Quite so, dear boy. What no one could have guessed at yet though was how the very title, *No Sleep 'til Hammersmith*, would become so imbued into the vernacular over the coming years. To the point here in the twenty-first century where 'No Sleep' is a common prefix to any number of sayings in any number of ways. The Beastie Boys were the first to co-opt it in their 1987 hit 'No Sleep 'til Brooklyn'. Now, though, it crops up all over the place. 'No Sleep 'til Bedtime'. 'No Sleep 'til Holloway'. 'No Sleep ''til I Get Paid'. Other bands use it. YouTubers use it. Comedians use it. You use it. Even Motörhead eventually used it again in their next live album, released seven years later, *No Sleep at All*.

One of the most regrettable moments of my friendship with Lemmy was the night when he took me to one side at some gig we were both at, and asked me what I thought of *No Sleep at All*. 'I like it,' I told him. 'But I don't like it as much as *No Sleep 'til Hammersmith*.' 'No,' he grimaced. 'Don't say that. Why?'

I didn't know why. Now I do. I just didn't like the title as much as the original. It was and remains unbeatable. Hence all the copycat versions over the years.

The phrase itself, he told me, came from one of the truck drivers on the 1980 *Ace of Spades* tour. 'We had it painted on the front of one of the trucks. One of the truck drivers painted it there: "No Sleep 'til Hammersmith". Because we had fifty-two gigs on that tour and only two days off. "No Sleep 'til Hammersmith" – it became the trucker's motto.'

And is that how it felt, to be on tour with Motörhead in those days? 'Yeah, I suppose. We didn't care, though, there was plenty of speed. Everybody was doing it, you know. Poor old Saxon [the support act on the tour who didn't do drugs] trying to keep up! Tea-junkies, they were. Two of them were on coffee if you ask me,' he chortles. 'All these maniacs from Sheffield suddenly surrounded by drug loonies.'

And still it wasn't quite time to put the band to bed just yet. But it was coming, and faster than even Lemmy, who liked to know everything, realised.

SEVEN

Nobody's Perfect

For the rest of his life, Lemmy would look back on the aftermath of Motörhead's crowning success with the *No Sleep* album, and protest that it wasn't his fault they could never follow it up. Lemmy: 'The trouble is, you can't follow a live album that went straight in at No. 1,' he told me with a straight face. 'I mean, what do you do? You can't put out another live album. And you can't follow it with a studio album because that's been the live album people have been waiting for, for five years, right? So we were fucked whatever we did. We could have done the best studio album in the world and we would have been fucked. Except we didn't, we did *Iron Fist* instead . . .'

In reality, no one wanted or was expecting another live album. What their fans did expect was another studio album at least as good as the previous three. Instead what they got was *Iron Fist*, 12 tracks light on inspiration or spirit, and overloaded with arrogance and disaffection. Exactly the kind of ill-starred, done-quick, out-of-control album, in fact, that events leading up to its creation all but guaranteed.

As Eddie Clarke now relates, 'Iron Fist was the toughest because we were getting a bit low on ideas and things were getting quite strained. We were all getting quite famous and Phil was affected by it all. Lemmy was not himself, either . . .'

Indeed, Lemmy, that man of the people and virulent anti-star, had begun to delight his ego just a tad too much of late, breaking his own golden rule about 'being as out of it as you like as long as you don't blow the gig'. Playing the biggest show of their career so far, headlining a six-band line-up billed as the Heavy Metal Barndance at the massive Bingley Hall, in Stafford, Lemmy collapsed halfway through the set, causing the rest of the show to be cancelled. 'Lemmy's been up for three days drinking vodka,' Eddie recalled to the writer Sylvie Simmons. 'He's been fucking chicks all day [and] we've got 12,000 kids crammed in there waiting for us. All day, people have been offering me lines of coke and everything, and I've [only] had one fucking Heineken because I want to be together for this show. Fifty-five minutes into the set, right, Lemmy disappears backwards, collapses on the stage. So me and Phil are furious at the end of it. We're going, "You let us down, you cunt." And he was saying, "Me being up for three nights has nothing to do with it." The fact that he was up for three days, getting blowjobs or whatever, had nothing to do with the fact that he collapsed onstage. Of course not!'

The irony was that the show itself received an ecstatic review in *Melody Maker*, who seemed to view the whole thing as the most marvellous theatre. 'I said to Phil, "Now suddenly we're the definitive live band, they were calling us cunts last week."' Lemmy was in true form though for another festival appearance, this time billed as the Heavy Metal Holocaust, at Port Vale football ground, in the summer of 1981. 'I'll always remember Pete Townshend, after the Port Vale show, late, late, late at night after everybody else had gone, dancing with Eric Clapton,' he reminisced. 'The waltz, to the radio, amidst all this debris, both in long coats. Pete and Eric dancing, very slowly. Magic . . .'

Nevertheless, the fact was none of Motörhead were quite themselves over the latter half of 1981, as dark storm clouds seemed to hover ominously over everything they did. Lemmy could see it coming, he told me, but was far too busy 'doing more interesting things' to do anything about it. He still believed that the key to the palace of wisdom lay in obliterating himself as much and as often as possible. A belief, you might say, he carried with him to the grave. Mick Farren, who'd known Lemmy well since Hawkwind days, co-writing songs with him, and, as he put it, 'logged many thousands of flying hours in the Ladbroke Grove Air Circus' with him, looked back on this period with greater sympathy than anyone else, but then Mick probably knew him better than either of his two band mates. As he later said, 'We were all exceedingly badly behaved. We all took far too many drugs. We all drank too much. Lemmy took more speed than any human being I've ever seen, which could be great fun but which could also cause problems when you were trying to sleep. We probably deserved to go to jail many times over . . .'

In fact, they very nearly did when the band suffered a series of busts. The first and most serious, after a four-night run at Hammersmith Odeon, when all three had their homes raided by the drugs squad. Doug and Eve Smith were also the subject of a horrendous dawn raid the same night, as were the band's roadies ensconced in a West London hotel. 'Turned out the cops had been at the gig every night of the Hammersmith run,' Doug recalls. 'They even bought T-shirts from the stall, to look like punters. Then at six a.m. the morning after the final show twenty-six officers came through my door. Rammed open the door, took it off its hinges. Another seventy of them went to the hotel where the crew were. And they did Lemmy's flat but Lemmy wasn't there. As usual he got away with it, because he was out in the West End snorting and drinking, out in the St Moritz club, pulling the machine. Next morning, he goes, "Oh, I didn't know this all happened, Doug."'

Eddie had also been out but Phil had been at home. The police didn't discover much there, though, and his subsequent arrest for possession of 2.2 grammes of cannabis resulted only in a fine. Doug was similarly arrested after being escorted to his office, where they found some grass. 'Fortunately, I'd managed to hide a packet of coke in a bookshelf on my way downstairs at home.'

Another time, on their way to do a special gig organised by the Hells Angels, the band bus was pulled over by police by the roundabout at Shepherd's Bush. 'They were in a van. Got pulled over. Phil was driving his Camaro behind them,' explains Doug. 'It might have been speed they were busted for that time, it might have been coke. By then Eddie had given up speed and was doing coke. But they were eventually released and they did the gig.'

Away from the stage there were now growing disputes over money. As far as Lemmy and the band were concerned, they'd just had a No. 1 album and should be rich. Yet they were all still on a weekly wage of £250. Moreover, Eddie maintains that their weekly wages 'were purely from the publishing. So there's the gig, the records and the T-shirts, which we sold thousands of, there's all that money that we've never seen a penny from. And yet the crew aren't getting paid and there's people chasing us for money. I remember it like it was yesterday. We went in and said, "What's going on, Doug?" So the three of us are sitting in front of Doug and in the end he lost his temper. "All right then, go and get your own fucking lawyer and accountant!" So we stood up, the three of us together, and said, "All right we will!" And off we went.'

According to Doug, though, the management company was covering all the band's expenses too, along with the costs of touring. 'I never talked to them about money, only from the point of view that they kept spending it. I always warned them, "You're spending money." Eddie kept a roadie on for six months doing nothing. "Cos I wanna make sure he's here when we go on the road again, Doug." I said, "Don't do that. Just book him. He can find work in between." "No, man." They had their roadies employed all the time. They burned money like you cannot believe.'

Despite sold-out concert halls in Britain and parts of

Europe, Doug points out, 'The majority of the tours didn't make a lot of money. The merchandising made a lot of money. On many occasions the merchandising had to subsidise the tour.' He says that 'when the band really got into problems, the merchandising company lent the band £36,000, which they never saw again. To this day, Eddie goes, "So where did all the merchandising money go, Doug?" Eddie, you had it. "Well, we never saw any of it." No, you never saw any of it. We just paid your fucking bills. That was a lesson I learned, never to touch a band's money. If they wanna blow it, give it to them, fuck off, just blow your money.' As far as Doug is concerned, he 'protected' Motörhead. 'They always had money to go on the road.' Which, finally, was all Lemmy ever really cared about, according to Eve Smith. 'Lemmy wasn't really interested in money. He was just interested in what was in his pocket. He wasn't interested in accumulating or buying property or anything like that. As long as he had an unlimited amount to spend on machines or whatever . . .'

Eddie, though, was having none of it and, as the self-appointed spokesman in matters related to non-musical business, he began to rail against what he increasingly saw as the second-rate way the band's career was being managed. On more than one occasion he threatened to walk out of the band and quit if he didn't get what he wanted. Lemmy recalled Eddie 'leaving' once on tour in France. 'Gerry Bron and Douglas flew over in a charter plane to talk him out of it. You know, cos there was big bucks in it.' Eventually, Eddie was talked out of it. 'Much against his better nature and all that shit. The only thing they didn't do was promise him more money. If he'd had any sense he would have held out for that.'

Doug tells of another occasion when he was in Canada with Girlschool and Motörhead were in LA. He had just received a phone call informing him that Eve, who was pregnant with their first child in London, had gone into labour, and was frantically making arrangements to get the first flight home, when Eddie rang him in a furious mood. 'I pick up the phone in my hotel room and it's Eddie ranting and raving. "The fucking band left the gig without me, I had no fucking car to get back to the hotel, I had to get a fucking taxi and the driver tried to kidnap me and take me to Mexico. I'm leaving the band!" I stopped and very calmly said, "Eddie, I understand all that but I am just about to fly back to London. Eve has gone into labour." He went, "Oh, I'll leave the band next week then . . ."'

Eddie doesn't deny any of this. 'Oh yeah, of course I did. I was highly strung. Plus I was under a lot of pressure . . . But between the three of us I thought we could get through it.'

Phil was also becoming impossible to deal with some days. 'Eddie and Phil were always having fistfights,' Lemmy remembered. 'At one point, even on their way to the stage. I've separated them cos it's time to go onstage and on the way down the stairs from the stage Phil Taylor's hit Eddie round the head with a fucking drum stick and it's started again. In Glasgow they rolled off a seat into the elevator. There's people keeping out and they rolled in, the doors shut and they're still fighting.'

Lemmy professed not to know why Eddie threw so many wobblers. 'Who knows, man? Things that we would know about that he thought was bad, you know? A band is closer than family, because in a family you can go to your room. And part of the family is from a different generation and you can blame it on that. Or your siblings are older or younger than you and you can blame it on that. In a band you can only blame it on each other. And if you blame each other, in a three-piece band that's a pretty long [bus ride].'

He went on. 'Bands are very fragile things . . . If they're not getting enough money there's not much to hold a band together except trust, and very few bands trust each other after about the first year. They're all in it for themselves and that's what I tried to fight in Motörhead. I never wanted it to be like that. I wanted it to be a band that believed in what we do and believed that we're valid. Whatever people say it doesn't matter, because every great band goes through that shit. We just did it for longer but it's still the same thing.'

Much more concerning to Lemmy and the band was the murder in the winter of 1981 of Lemmy's then flatmate, Andrew Ellsmore. 'He was a bit of a sleazebag,' Doug recalls. 'Lemmy wasn't a friend. He just sort of moved in.' It was later reported that Ellsmore was an actor. However, an old friend of Ellsmore's, Malcolm Edwards, now recalls how 'In the mid- to late 1970s he was one of the buyers at Compendium Books in Camden High Street. His area, I think, was the section of "head" books, and he also built up their selection of sci-fi imports. He was a very keen fan of the kind of sci-fi *New Worlds* published, and of Philip K. Dick. He managed to get the funds together to publish two issues of a magazine, *Other Times*, which was modelled on *New Worlds*. I recall Andy describing himself as "a little pervert", but I think he was what later became known as "polymorphous perverse" rather than straightforwardly gay. Basically, he'd do anything with anybody. But he was very amiable, and while "sleazebag" might be one way of describing him, there was more to him than that. He was also a very little fellow – maybe 5 feet 5 inches – slightly cross-eyed and very shortsighted, with very long hair.'

Doug Smith: 'There was a shop on the Harrow Road. If you walked through the back of the shop there was a little cinema. It was a porn studio. And he ran that. And the people that hung out in that place were the Hells Angels.' Which was how Lemmy probably got to know him, he presumes. Motörhead was away on tour in Sweden when news broke of his ghastly death. 'He was very viciously murdered,' says Doug. 'They stabbed him up the arse and cut his balls. Everything. Lemmy wasn't there. Lemmy was in Sweden. But he shared a flat with him.' As Malcolm Edwards, who visited the premises, now recalls: 'It was in Colville Houses, off Talbot Road . . . Lemmy had the one bedroom; Andy's bed was on a kind of makeshift mezzanine in the big front room.'

The first Doug knew of it was when he got a phone call from Scotland Yard. He had to go to the house. 'Thank god they'd removed the body. Nothing they could do as far as Lemmy was concerned because he had an alibi, but it was awful.' The killers had tried to burn the body but then an upstairs neighbour – John McVicar, the convicted armed robber now turned journalist and book writer – smelled smoke and called the emergency services.

When the redtop newspapers got hold of the story they

had a field day, and suddenly the name Motörhead was twinned with 'drug slaying' in certain tabloid headlines. In Lemmy's memoir he puts the murder down to 'some gay hate killing'. Doug, though, has his own highly plausible theories about who was responsible but refuses to go on the record about them. While Malcolm Edwards attests, 'Everyone I knew assumed it was a drug deal gone very wrong, and assumed that Lemmy knew all about the reasons but was keeping quiet.'

The upshot would have a strange knock-on effect for the group when Doug decided they would all be safer living in the same shared house. Doug set about arranging a large house on the Fulham Road for them. 'But once that murder hit the papers,' said Lemmy, 'they didn't want us to live there no more.'

Plan B was a three-storey building on Eland Road near Clapham Junction. But this also caused unforeseen problems. With the band still away on tour, Eddie's then girlfriend was the first to inspect the property – and bagged the best room in the house, a large spacious loft extension with en suite facilities. As Eddie recalls, 'My bird's gone in there and got the best room. I said to Phil, "I don't feel comfortable with this." He said, "If you don't want it give it to me, I'll have it!"'

Considering Lemmy rarely used a bed to sleep in, he was surprisingly tetchy about this latest development. But then, as Eddie points out, 'He thought he should have it cos he was Lemmy, and Motörhead was his band. I didn't have a problem with that but Phil would have done his nut if I'd given up the room and not given it to him. And if I'd given the room to Phil, Lemmy would have gone fucking mental too. So I was stuck.'

Lemmy also later claimed that it was during the spell in Clapham that Eddie 'stole one of my birds'. When I remind him, Eddie guffaws. 'I'm thinking, which bird was that then?' According to Doug, 'Lemmy didn't really have relationships . . . He had a girl who was only a friend. She may have been an affair at one time, or a girlfriend or someone he hung out with. But girls were just something Lemmy shagged. There was very little love there.'

Even when Lemmy did take to someone and begin to develop a relationship beyond the merely physical, it never lasted. 'I think the only one that he had a long-time relationship with was the bass player in Girlschool – Gil Weston. She'd been the girlfriend of Kevin Rowland previously.'

Lemmy had met Gil when she was the bassist in The Killjoys. When Girlschool's original bassist, Enid Williams, left in 1982, Lemmy urged them to hire Gil. They did, by which time Lemmy had invited Gil to move in with him. At least, for a little while. 'I got Lemmy a houseboat on the Thames and Gil was living with him,' Doug recalls. 'Gil and Lemmy were an item, which was a surprise because Lemmy had never really had any items. Not that I can remember. He had girlfriends probably I didn't know about. But she came home one night and he kept her locked out while he was busily servicing someone else. And that was the end of it, I think.'

Whatever Lemmy was really brooding about now at the house in Clapham, he began calling Eddie 'Fancy Bollocks'. 'Lemmy had a problem with me,' says Eddie. 'But I still don't really know what.' When Fancy Bollocks then took up an offer to produce an album for a new powerhouse trio called Tank, which had supported Motörhead on their most recent tour, Lemmy refused to talk about it. A situation that became even more tense when Phil suggested Fancy Bollocks then produce the next Motörhead album.

Originally, the plan had been to repeat the process that culminated in *Ace of Spades*, working with Vic Maile again at his Rickmansworth studios. But the vibe was all wrong from the beginning. Phil had an almighty row with the producer over a new drum-kit, which he didn't like the sound of. 'So Phil, who was getting a bit carried away then,' says Eddie ruefully, 'refused to work with Vic Maile any more.' The star got his way and Vic was fired.

Doug immediately approached Chris Tsangarides, who had produced the Gary Moore and Phil Lynott hit, 'Parisienne Walkways', but, according to Eddie, Tsangarides wanted £10,000 plus £500 per track. Another producer Doug approached asked for a flat fee of £20,000. 'The band was only earning £250 a week at the time. So we said no to both. Vic only had £300 a track, I think. In the end, because I'd done the Tank album previously, Phil said, "Why don't you do it? You done the Tank album, sounds all right." I said I don't think I could do that and play on it. But of course once Douglas got wind of it he said, "Oh, that would be fantastic." Because it wouldn't cost him any money.'

Then Lemmy weighed in: 'Let Fancy Bollocks produce it then.'

Time was hurriedly booked at Morgan Studios in

Willesden. To assist him, Eddie brought in Will Reid-Dick, a budding engineer-producer Eddie had met when Saxon toured with the band – Will had been the engineer on Saxon's chart album, *Wheels of Steel*. But, again, it was an uphill process. 'Phil started to do the wrong sort of drugs at one point for *Iron Fist*. I know he was smoking a bit of the bad stuff [heroin] and we were an anti-fucking bad stuff band. I don't mind getting busted but only for things I would associate with and I don't want to be labelled with that shit. But first Phil slid into it, then road crew slid into it as well. Me and Lemmy didn't know. They were fucking doing it behind our backs.'

Meanwhile, Lemmy seemed to have lost heart in the band. 'Not only were we struggling to find material – we were running out of riffs – we needed a break. I remember one particular incident about his bass. He'd done a wrong note. I said, "Look, Lem, can we straighten that note out." He said, "Oh, man, I ain't got time. I gotta go." Cos there was some bird sitting there with her legs in the air and he wanted to go to the Speakeasy or wherever.' Eddie was left with no option but to try and cut in a bass note that he played himself, using strips of razored tape in those pre-computerised analogue days. 'That's how much he didn't want to be there.'

Doug recalls Lemmy being very lackadaisical about the album: 'When he wrote the "Iron Fist" lyrics he sat and wrote them in the catering room at the studio at Morgan. There was a girl there that served behind the counter and he would refer the lyrics to her. Never met her before. He would write these lyrics then go, "What do you think? What do you think?" She just sort of smiled at him and went, "Yeah, very good." Then on another occasion he sat on the loo and wrote the lyrics as he was having a shit.'

Speaking 20 years later to Dave Ling, Lemmy admitted, 'The *Iron Fist* album was bad, inferior to anything else we've ever done. There are at least three songs on there that were completely unfinished. But there you go. We were arrogant. When you're successful that's what you become, you think it'll go on for ever.'

When *Iron Fist* was eventually released, in April 1982, it jumped into the charts at No. 6 – then a week later began sliding sharply down the charts again. Even the single, the title track and the best thing on the album, struggled to get into the Top 30 (peaking at No. 29) whereas their previous single, a live, in-your-face 'Motorhead' from *No Sleep*, had reached No. 6. Panned by the same critics who had been singing their praises for the past two years, unable to forgive the obvious staleness of the album, the subsequent *Iron Fist* tour was another sell-out – three nights at Newcastle's City Hall, three nights in Birmingham and four at the Hammersmith Odeon – but the feeling backstage was no longer one of outlandish fun and overindulgence. Or rather, the over-indulgence was still much in evidence but the old fun and games, the filthy banter, the brotherly bullshit – was now decidedly thin on the ground.

'Lemmy was such a great frontman,' says Eddie. 'He'd get up and sing into that mike and whatever state he was in, man, he would deliver. Every fucking night. Man, the pool of sweat on the floor around Lemmy every night, there was a bucket of it. One of my fondest memories is of Lemmy sweating his fucking bollocks off in that black silk shirt he used to wear. I get memories of that and it makes me almost choke a bit. I fill up, cos we were at the height of our fame and we were really tanking.'

Not that you'd have known it from the outside looking in. Lemmy was now a regular face in music paper gossip columns, as recognisable as any other major rock star. When he turned up unexpectedly on *Top of the Pops* alongside his new friends the Nolan Sisters, as joint guest stars of a one-off single from the Young & Moody band, titled 'Don't Do That', everyone was expected to laugh along at Lemmy in his white waiter's jacket and moody mirrored sunglasses. Was Lemmy the dangerous one really turning into Lemmy the all-round entertainer?

Meanwhile, the British tabloid press was having a field day. The *Sun* ran pictures of Lemmy cuddling 16-year-old Coleen Nolan with a suitably lascivious story beneath. Gossip spread that Lemmy was doing his best to corrupt the youngest, prettiest Nolan. Something she was happy to confirm years later when she told the *Huffington Post*: 'When I was younger, Lemmy from Motörhead had a bit of a thing for my breasts. I turned him down, mainly because I knew I wouldn't be able to take him home to my mother! He was lovely though.' Speaking on her TV show, *Loose Women*, in the wake of his death, Coleen, now 50, recalled how 'Lemmy was the nicest, most intelligent, philosophical person you could ever meet.' Before adding, 'I remember how much he loved women and big boobs. He was certainly fascinated with mine. He used to say: "Great tits!" but he was never being lecherous, he was just saying, "Be proud of yourself." It wasn't creepy, Lemmy actually made me feel good about being a woman.'

As for Lemmy, he insisted there had been nothing untoward, although, he admitted, 'it wasn't for the want of trying. They are awesome chicks. People forget those girls were onstage with Frank Sinatra at the age of twelve. They've seen most things twice. We were on *Top of the Pops* at the same time as them and our manager was trying to chat up Linda: the one with the bouffant hair and the nice boobs. He dropped his lighter and bent down to pick it up. Linda said to him, "While you're down there, why don't you give me a ..." It blew him away. We didn't expect that from a Nolan sister. None of us did. We were supposed to be the smelliest, loudest motherfuckers in the building but we more than met our match. We were in awe. You couldn't mess with the Nolan sisters.'

Phil affected not to give a shit about such shenanigans, deriding such efforts to friends while secretly wondering why he hadn't been invited along to the party. Eddie, though, quietly seethed. When Lemmy then announced plans for Motörhead to collude with The Plasmatics' singer Wendy O. Williams in a roughed-up version of the old Tammy Wynette chestnut, 'Stand by Your Man', Eddie lost it.

The way Lemmy saw it, the EP with Girlschool had given the band its biggest-selling hit. Maybe this would work out that way too. For a start, Wendy was a good deal tougher than those girls. Leaving home at 16, she'd worked as a stripper, done live sex shows and starred in a porn movie, *Candy Goes to Hollywood*. With The Plasmatics – a hardcore American punk band with a stage act that included blowing up speaker cabinets, sledgehammering television sets, even blowing up cars – Wendy performed onstage almost completely naked, long metal spikes covering her nipples, the rest of her squeezed into tiny bikini briefs. She also had a Mohican, was a fitness freak and came from New York, where trading insults with passers-by had been turned into an art. Lemmy thought she was the baddest, coolest chick on the scene and that a joint record with her would be a gas, gas, gas, and another potential big hit for the band – maybe even open up the doors for them in America. As Doug says, 'Lemmy knew bloody well that if he did certain things he was going to make it bigger. And it was fun, good for a laugh, and Lemmy was up for it.'

The way Eddie saw it though was as a joke, and a very bad one at that. 'I thought it was absolute shit!' he spits. 'The idea had come up in a meeting at Bronze. Lemmy had been pictured in one of the music papers that week with Wendy [*Sounds*] at the Marquee. Everybody went, "Wow, yes!" Except me.' But Eddie's objections were treated as a downer. Typical Eddie. Always moaning. He'd stop in a minute. Only he didn't.

The argument was still going on after they'd flown to Toronto for the start of their next North American tour in May 1982. A meeting was held to discuss plans to record the track at Eastern Sound in Toronto. Everyone – Phil, Doug, even members of the road crew present, but especially Lemmy – were enthusiastic about making the record with Wendy, who was waiting in the next room with her manager, Rod Swenson. Eddie couldn't believe what he was hearing. Standing his ground, he argued that instead

of wasting time on such 'crap' they should go into Eastern and lay down the backing tracks for a handful of blues
and R&B covers, one of which he says now was 'Hoochie
Coochie Man', 'and a couple of others we'd been pottering
about with'. Eddie suggested doing that, sending the tapes
back to London for Will Reid to mix, 'then we could have
Motörhead Plays the Blues'.

In retrospect, it might have been the saner move. With the
band out of ideas for the time being, it could have plugged
a gap and brought them some real kudos. But Lemmy,
who was an avid reader of the music press, which was then
entirely in thrall to punk, felt it would be better to make
a more high-profile record with Wendy. He also liked the
idea of appealing to a wider audience than the largely heavy
metal crowd that followed them. He identified with the
more basic rock'n'roll sound of punk. It returned him to the
1950s. Metal was something else. Metal was about guitar
virtuosos and elongated epics. Even Hawkwind were more
punk than that.

Lemmy was furious with Eddie. Eddie hated the idea of
working with Wendy. Lemmy hated Eddie for hating the
idea. In the end they agreed to compromise – and do the
track with Wendy. Come the actual session the next day,
hearing the track unfold, Eddie was even more adamant
that this was a terrible idea. In the end he simply downed
tools, announced he would have no part of it, and walked.
The session ended up being produced by Swenson. 'She was
a nice enough girl and I tried hard on those tracks but they
just weren't working,' says Eddie.

Lemmy was having none of it. Lemmy loved the record.

Lemmy loved Wendy. What else was there to discuss? But still Eddie wouldn't let it go. Finally, Lemmy told him: 'All right, I'll tell you what we'll do. We'll put on the cover: THIS RECORD HAS NOTHING TO DO WITH EDDIE CLARKE.'

'I said, but Lem, hang on. It's my band. You can't do that. You're destroying the credibility of the band.' He pauses, his voice still angry. The trouble is, he says, 'you get to a certain level of fame and it starts to affect the way you're thinking. The nice thing about not having a pot to piss in, you don't think. You just get on and do it. I said, "I'll have to leave the band then." They said okay.'

Eddie offered to do the tour then leave after that. But things quickly escalated. On the drive to their next gig at the Palladium in New York, instead of defusing the situation, Lemmy deliberately mocked Eddie by playing the rough cassette mix of the 'Stand by Your Man' track on the tour bus – over and over and over. And over. 'He threw fucking fuel on the fire,' says Eddie. 'And they were all wearing Plasmatics T-shirts. It was fucking awful. I was fucking freaked.'

Another meeting was convened at the hotel in New York, the day before the Palladium show. But Eddie knew he was outnumbered. A furious row broke out instead, which ended with Eddie storming out and checking into a different hotel. Worried that Eddie might be about to book the next flight home, a roadie was sent over to stand guard outside Eddie's room with strict instructions not to let him out until the following morning. By now Eddie was fearful more than angry. The following afternoon he was driven down to the venue to soundcheck – alone. Lemmy and Phil had already done theirs and gone back to their hotel.

That night, before the show, he was taken down some stairs away from the band dressing room and shown into a small boiler room. This was to be Eddie's dressing room for the night. 'You've no idea how fantastic the two superstars thought they were at this time,' he says now. 'They'd gone right up their own arses. By the table there was a bottle of vodka and a little pile of speed. And that's it, I'm on me own.' He got his own back in a minor way, he says, when later on he was joined in his little room 'by a couple of cracking-looking birds. I always had the best-looking birds so I think that might have pissed Lemmy off too.'

The show that night was strange. Lemmy didn't even feign interaction with Eddie. Phil avoided eye contact. After the gig, 'which was difficult, cos obviously there was a lot of angst on stage', Eddie summoned his courage and decided to go up to the band's dressing room. 'Opened the door and it was full of people and smoke.' Spotting him, Lemmy and Phil came over. 'I said, "Look, guys, I know this has got a bit out of hand. Come on and let's do the gig and carry on, you know?" And [Lemmy] said, "No, man. Fuck off." I said, "Are you sure?" They said, "Fuck off." In a way they deserved Brian Robertson after what they done to me . . .'

Speaking with me years later, Lemmy recalled bumping into Eddie on the street in New York a few days later and 'we just stood there looking over our shoulders at each other for about a minute. And that was when I knew he'd left. Because we had nothing to say. Not "good luck" or "why don't you stay" or anything. Just nothing . . . I knew he'd gone then.'

That isn't how Eddie remembers it though. For Eddie, 'It was like losing a brother. Two brothers.' The real problem, he says, could be summed up in one of the best songs he and Lemmy wrote together, 'The Chase Is Better Than the Catch'. 'All that happened with the Wendy O. Williams stuff was because the chase was over. And of course that's when the shit hits the fan.' Still, he confesses, he never got over it. Lemmy could be challenging to work with, to live with, to put up with. But Eddie still loved him, he says, 'Cos Lemmy's Lemmy! Fuck sake, man! Don't get me wrong. Lemmy's Lemmy! He's a wonderful man to sit down with and have a fucking [laugh with]. He's a good man! But I never got over it, being pushed out of the band by him. Never.'

Doug, for his part, says he felt powerless to do anything about it either. Lemmy had made up his mind. Which was a great pity, because without 'Fast' Eddie Clarke Motörhead would never be the same. Did Lemmy know what he was doing at the time? How could he? That said, he was probably the only one who didn't. When news broke back home, fans were distraught. One of the most appealing aspects of Motörhead had been the perception of them as a gang, desperados, gunslingers, the band of whom Lemmy had in the early days famously vowed, 'If we move next door to you your lawn will die.' The three amigos. Now down to two. What the fuck?

'Why does anything fuck up?' Lemmy told me irritably when I later pushed him on the subject. 'You get sick of each other and you end up losing the will to live. When Eddie left, we'd been going round and round in circles, arguing forever about the same things. Then he walked out and if we'd been bothered to sit up all night trying to talk him round he would probably have stayed. But we'd been through it all so many times by then I just couldn't be bothered any more. None of us could. Even if we had talked him back, he would just have left again later.'

Nevertheless, 'When Eddie left it went downhill rapidly,' admits Doug now. 'Once Eddie walked out of the band it's amazing how quickly the press stopped. Really quite staggering, actually. Had Eddie not have walked I think they would have been bigger than Metallica now.'

Instead they did something that even Lemmy, who was rarely ever wrong about anything, ask anybody, later came to see as 'one of my big regrets'. At the urging of Phil Taylor, they got Doug to go and look for Thin Lizzy's former guitarist Brian Robertson, last seen bloviating about being sacked from his own band, Wild Horses, while sinking quadruple tequilas and snorting coke in any number of expensive London niteries which, in truth, he could no longer afford to be in. 'We brought in Brian because Phil loved Thin Lizzy,' said Lemmy. 'I did too but Phil was fanatical, you know.'

Robbo, as he came to be known, was a 26-year-old firebrand who'd grown up in Glasgow, where belying his tough guy image he'd spent eight years studying cello and classical piano before switching in his teens to guitar and drums, gigging around town with a local band, Dream Police, who later evolved into the Average White Band. Robbo was 18 when he caught the train to London to audition as one of two new guitarists in the Irish rock band Thin Lizzy. Over the next four years Robbo's brilliantly swaggering lead guitar helped transform Thin Lizzy from a one-hit-wonder novelty act (their only hit previously had been an electric version of an old Irish folk tune, 'Whiskey in the Jar') into one of the coolest, most successful rock bands of the Seventies, with a string of hits like 'The Boys Are Back in Town' and 'Dancing in the Moonlight'.

Alongside the singer and bassist Phil Lynott, Robbo was the star of the show in Lizzy. He was also, as Lynott once put it to me, 'a right fucking pain in the arse, with his fighting and his big fucking mouth'. The former had cost Robbo his job in Lizzy – and nearly his career as a musician – when a brawl involving Frankie Miller at the Speakeasy in 1976 resulted in Robbo blocking a broken glass to Miller's face, severing a tendon in his left hand. But Robbo taught himself to play again and was back in the band six months later. It was the latter that finally got him kicked out for good a year after that.

After he formed a new band, Wild Horses, with Rainbow's former bassist Jimmy Bain on lead vocals, I had come to know Robbo when the PR firm I then worked for was hired to promote them. Robbo was a brilliant player, far smarter than your average bear when it came to performing and recording, but, as Thin Lizzy could attest, he could also be his own worst enemy. He was charismatic, but almost always either drunk or coked out when you saw him. Usually both. He also dabbled in smack. But then he also dabbled in quadruple tequilas, Mandrax, strong black hash and staying up for days at a time. Everybody loved Robbo, until you hated him. Or more likely simply grew bored with his constant growling, his endlessly confrontational conversation. Nobody knew more about music, or indeed anything, than Robbo. In that respect, he reminded me a lot of Lemmy. Except Lemmy was genuinely funnier. When he was in the mood, anyway.

When after two albums that barely scratched the UK charts Wild Horses turned into a power struggle between him and Bain, Robbo walked out. Having sunk all his earnings from Thin Lizzy into the band he was broke and, by his own admission, 'pretty desperate for a gig', when he got the call from Doug inviting him to join up with Motörhead.

Speaking now from the small apartment he lives in alone, above a pub in Essex, Robbo, who still calls Phil Taylor 'one of my best friends ever', says he first met Lemmy when he was in Lizzy. 'We all used to go to the same clubs, drinking together and taking drugs together, whatever. Him and Philthy were close to me way before I joined. They were big fans of Lizzy.'

Yet when he was first approached to join Motörhead, he says, 'I told them to fuck off.' Because, 'I was totally ill. I'd just split up from my wife. I was seven and a half stone. I had double pneumonia and pleurisy. I was a fucking mess. I thought, naw. Physically, I can't do this. I was a skinny little shit. But I was desperate for a gig. I wanted to go back on the road.'

So he flew out to New York. Where Lemmy was shocked to discover that the long brown hair Robbo had worn in Thin Lizzy was now a short, curly orange mop. Says Doug, 'The first day in New York I said, "Look, here's a hundred bucks. Can you please go and buy some like black jeans and black T-shirts, and a black leather jacket." Cos a hundred bucks would do that in those days. "Ah, fuck that!" Robbo says. "I'm not doing what I'm told! I don't wear those clothes." I said, "This is Motörhead, man. You've just got to be part of the image." But he wouldn't do it.'

It was a harbinger of things to come. The first time he got up and played with them though, any doubts Lemmy and Phil had vanished. 'He was fucking great for those first few shows,' recalled Lemmy. 'It was only later, once he got comfortable about his place in the band, the trouble started.'

At their first gig, in Calgary, says Robbo, 'I jumped on that stage. I thought, I've had sixteen hours of rehearsals. I've had speed stuck up my nose. I haven't a fucking clue what the hell's going on. What am I gonna do? Just jump on the stage and play E. They didn't tell me about the fucking lighting rig coming down! And the flash bombs! So I got my bollocks burned off. Then the Bomber came down and I'm going, "Oh shit!" I had to keep moving back until I was at my stacks, and I'm thinking, fuck me!' When someone in the crowd began heckling, shouting for Eddie, Robbo jumped off the stage and went for him. 'I took off my guitar, gave it to the roadie, then jumped over the monitors and just nutted him. Then the roadies grabbed me by the arms and brought me back up. Lemmy was still singing and playing so there was no interruption . . .'

Suddenly there was a whole new dynamic to the band. As a player, technically Robbo was on another level to Eddie. Phil Taylor, in particular, became extremely excited over what he saw as a new, much better phase for the band. For all their success and notoriety over the past few years,

Motörhead had never been taken seriously as musicians. For all their dark, biker glamour, they were still seen as the runt of the litter compared to bands like . . . well, Thin Lizzy. Even Lemmy became sold on the idea. Robbo was a handful all right, but his energy was bringing new life to old material and suddenly things were becoming fun again. Returning to London to start making their first album together, at the start of 1983, hopes were high that something very new and very exciting was about to happen for Motörhead.

Instead, the resulting album, titled *Another Perfect Day*, would become the most divisive of their career. For some, it remains their best, most adventurous work. For others, especially at the time, it betrayed everything they held dear about Motörhead. Forget the immense finesse Robbo's writing and playing brought to the band – most especially on tracks like 'Back at the Funny Farm', their most brilliantly conceived rocker since 'Ace of Spades' (and featuring an almost identical bass riff), the powerful, rangy 'I Got Mine', where Lemmy's lyrics find a whole new previously unguessed at depth, the so catchy it hurts 'Shine' and the shattering, epically scaled title track – it was as if the staunchest fans were at a loss as to how to assimilate a Motörhead record that didn't just repeat slogans of rebellion at them, that didn't just share in the joke and dare you to disagree. It was as if this stuff was simply too good for them. And as soon as that feeling became known to the band – via snippy reviews, odd looks on the faces of fans they met at the stage door, via the way the album simply didn't sell – Lemmy went from loving the new direction to utterly disowning it. Dismissing it in the press as 'Robbo's solo album'. Indeed, it would be years before he had a good word to say for it again. And then always tinged with bitterness and regret.

'Well, it was Robbo's fault and it was our fault,' he would tell me. 'You see, when he was with Thin Lizzy he was great. And I hoped he'd work with us like he worked with them. Really give everything, go for it. And he didn't. He had this thing, he was the guest artiste, you know. It was Motörhead *featuring* Brian Robertson. And that was never my idea at all, I like a band, you know. Otherwise I would have let them keep Lemmy's Motörhead, which was what we started off with, in order just to get some decent gigs. But I fought like fuck for eighteen months to stop that, because the only fame we had was that I used to be in Hawkwind. Ex-Hawkwind, Lemmy's Motörhead, you know? It took me ages to stop them doing that.

'A band stands or falls on its own merits, you can't have ex-so-and-so. Who gives a fuck? You're not playing like that any more anyway!' *Another Perfect Day*, he said, 'was torture to make but it was a great album. Me and Phil had finished all our parts and we left Robbo to do his. We came back three weeks later and he was still doing them. All the same, it *was* a great album. I always thought it was one of our best albums actually, up until then. But what can you do, you know? The kids hated it.'

When I relate Lemmy's words to Robbo now he leans out of his chair and scowls at me. 'It wasn't my solo album . . . I'm used to being in a studio *all* the time. I don't fuck off. The thing is, once Philthy had done his drums he was out of there. Once Lemmy had done his bass and he got to write his lyrics and do his vocals, he was out of there. Down the fucking pub playing the one-arm bandit! For him to hold it against me to stay in there, it's fucking nonsense. I didn't treat it like my solo album. It was *our* album.'

Before, he rightly points out, 'They'd always just gone in and gone dang-dang-dang-dang-dang and then boof! Fucked off and left it to the producer. I'd never done that. I was brought up in the Phil Lynott School. You *learn* the desk. You *learn* everything and you get involved. I put shed loads of guitars on there and I enjoyed every second of it, I have to tell you. I'm *proud* of that album. I really am. I worked so hard on that thing . . . I wanted to make sure it was something special and I think I achieved that. It was something in my heart and I really wanted to do it. My heart was in that band. Why would I spend all that time in the studio and then touring and everything?

'There was a lot of, "This is *my* band. Don't take it away." And I can totally understand that. But at the point I was at in the band, I wanted to get that album done *properly*. That's for me and I don't care about anybody else at that point. Because I'm not gonna have my name on it if it is shit.'

Another Perfect Day was, nonetheless, the worst-selling album since their first, released in June 1983, tiptoeing its way to No. 20 then disappearing from sight. What really put the nail in the coffin of the Lemmy–Philthy–Robbo line-up though was the tour that followed. However conflicted Lemmy may now have felt about the new album, he was more than willing to give it a go onstage. As far as he and everyone else could tell, though, as he put it, 'Robbo would purposely alienate the audience. He would come on stage in shorts and shit, and baggy trousers tied up with bits of towel. It's a very strange thing. But then again, Robbo's always been his worst enemy . . .'

When I put this to Robbo, ask him why he couldn't have tried to fit in better image-wise, I get a flash of what Lemmy was up against back then. 'It was just *me*. And I don't like being told what to do – by anybody. Right? The Animal never told me what to do cos the Animal was hisself as well. I mean that was a great image, the Animal. Fucking brilliant. And Lemmy's image – dead cool. So stop getting on me cos I've got fucking red hair. Bollocks. No . . . Lemmy didn't want it a certain way or whatever and he thought that I was . . . I don't know, sort of disrespectful to his fans or whatever. But I really don't care. Nothing to do with me.'

Things only got worse on tour, not least as Phil was now siding almost exclusively with Robbo. 'Yeah, we had a couple of fallings out,' says the guitarist, pouring himself another large glass of wine. 'I nearly wrapped a chair round Lemmy's head once. He wasn't listening. You'd get off the stage and me and the Animal would go, "That was a great gig." Lemmy would walk in and go, "That was shit." You'd go, "Are you fucking deaf?" Me and Philthy would go against him and he would go off into one and then I just picked up a chair. I said, "I'm gonna fucking wrap this round your head!" So he ran out the dressing room.'

Things finally came to a head when ticket sales for an autumn tour of Europe were so bad Doug decided they would have to pull the tour. 'We couldn't sell tickets anywhere. Couldn't sell merchandising even. So I said to the tour manager maybe we need a doctor to find out if any members of the band are in a state they can't continue touring.'

A doctor was brought in. He made the required diagnosis, wrote the appropriate note for the tour insurers. Robbo was selected as the one to be ill. 'Next thing I knew the tour manager had filled Robbo with lots of booze and took it upon himself to party that night and get everybody really drunk. And in the morning Robbo was in a state. We all thought it was just a scam, though.' But the doctor came out looking serious, telling them Robbo needed to go into hospital and rest. They flew him home separately, at once.

Part of the formalities meant also being checked out by a UK doctor, 'to get the insurance cleared . . . The doctor rang me and said, "He has to go into hospital straight away because he's on the verge of a breakdown."' Doug shakes his head. 'Robbo was a real alcoholic. We didn't realise until he joined the band. He would drink a bottle of Jack Daniel's in one fell swoop. Then sit and suck his thumb. I used to hate that, riding in the van with him when he was sucking his fucking thumb. And he was into downers.'

Robbo was taken to Nightingale Hospital in Lisson Grove, then given heavy meds and allowed to go home on condition he went straight to bed. Meanwhile, back at the real funny farm, Lemmy and Doug and Phil had come to the conclusion that none of them could continue like this. The future of the band was at stake. Robbo would have to go. Lemmy and Phil, to their credit, decided they should be the ones to break the news to Robbo personally.

'They came round to my house in Richmond,' Robbo recalls, looking down. 'I was in such a state, I was in bed. I was really ill. And the two of them came up to my bedroom, sat on the end of the bed and said, "Look, it's gotta go this way, Robbo." And I just lay there and went, "Okay, I'll deal with that . . ." All I wanted to do was get better. Cos I was really ill by that point.'

Looking back now, I ask him, how does he feel? 'Ah, fuck . . . what does it matter? Lemmy, I loved the man to death, and I'm so sad that he's gone. Even though he was a fucking toe rag, I still have so much love for the guy. And Phil was a real friend too, even after that. So . . .' He looks down again.

Like prisoners given a last-minute reprieve from the gallows, Doug and Lemmy set about the rebuilding operation immediately. Ads were placed in the music press, feelers put out among trusted and loyal friends. Literally thousands of tapes flooded in from hopeful guitarists all over Britain, some well known, most completely unknown. Eventually they whittled the candidates down to two strong contenders. Lemmy decreed there should be a play-off between them. A battle to see who was best for the band.

Then on the morning they were due to go to rehearsals to make their final choice between the two, Doug got a phone call from Philthy. Asking him to come and see him immediately, and to bring Lemmy.

He gave them the news as soon as they arrived an hour later. Phil was leaving, he said. To join Robbo.

'Fuck,' said Lemmy, as he and Doug walked back to the car. 'I'm fucked. The band's over . . .'

EIGHT

Killed by Death

Though he would deny it until his dying day, Lemmy was right. The exit of first Eddie Clarke then, barely a year later, Phil Taylor marked the end of Motörhead. The various replacements Lemmy brought in over the next 30 years were all well-meaning, talented players, but the music they helped Lemmy make rarely produced material on the same amphetamine-fuelled level as 'Overkill', 'Bomber', 'Ace of Spades', '(We Are) The Road Crew' or 'Motorhead'. Nor did any of them even come close to exuding the menacing stage presence of the three amigos. How could they? There could only ever be one 'Fast' Eddie, one 'Philthy Animal' Taylor.

The only thing that kept them going was the fact that there could only ever be one Lemmy, too. So that while Lemmy's fame continued to grow, the music he made with Motörhead began to matter less and less. If you were 15 years old and had just discovered Motörhead, the chances were you had done it through listening to one of the three classic albums they made for Bronze in the early Eighties. Lemmy railed against this truth but in his heart he knew. The glory days were never coming back. Instead, he grew comfortable in his newfound aura as rock elder statesman, enjoyed having a band at last that rarely challenged his authority, and carried on with his voluminous daily intake of speed and cigarettes and whiskey and anything else he fancied.

Says Doug, 'Lemmy was a man that really didn't need friends, he needed people. If he had a lot of people around him, in the right situation, he was happy. But even in my days he used to try and get a dressing room on his own. And more often than not if there were two dressing rooms, you would see the other two give it up and let him have the dressing room on his own.'

The new, four-man line-up he initially put together comprised not one but two guitarists – the very two he had first thought to fight it out amongst themselves – Phil Campbell and Michael Burston. Campbell, 22 years old, was the Welsh-born guitarist in heavy metal also-rans Persian Risk, who had supported the Robbo line-up at the last show of their ill-fated UK tour. 'It was terrible,' Campbell recalled. 'I don't think they played any songs I even recognised. I think at that time Robbo was refusing to play "Ace of Spades" and "Overkill", and I think he had pink leg warmers on. Robbo is a great player, but it just didn't work.'

According to Lemmy the decision to hire both guitarists was practically made for him. 'They sounded great together, simple as, and we'd always wanted the band to be a four-piece.' He told how on his way to the rehearsal that Saturday morning, still dazed by the news that Phil was jacking it in to join Robbo, his first thought was to turn around and go home. But what would he have done then? 'I stopped off in the boozer and played the one-arm bandit for ten minutes while I thought about it and when I got there they were already talking about, "Well, I can play this bit and you can play that . . ." So I hired them both.'

As a 12-year-old Phil Campbell had been taken by his dad to see Hawkwind play in Cardiff. Lemmy recalled signing an autograph for him after the show. 'I was the only one who came out afterwards to sign autographs,' Lemmy said, shrugging off the idea that Phil had always looked up to him first and foremost as a fan. 'Talk about come back to haunt you . . .' But as Phil admitted, 'If you'd have told me that I would have been on stage with this guy in the same band one day, I'd have laughed at you.'

Hawkwind fan he may have been, but as Campbell confessed to me years later, when it came to Motörhead, 'I wasn't over-familiar with what they'd done before I joined. I knew the singles and I knew them from what I'd seen on TV but I didn't own any of the albums. When I first joined the band Lemmy said to me, "I trust you musically to play anything you like. Just go for it. There's only one rule: no shorts on stage." I said, no problem, mate. But there were no musical restrictions whatsoever. Lemmy just trusted you to do the right thing.'

But while Phil was a good player, he was largely un-schooled in the art of entertaining a live audience with anything more than his musical competence. No matter that Lemmy nicknamed him 'Wizzo' when he hired him, no one ever actually called Phil that. As Eddie Clarke notes, somewhat unkindly, if summing up the views of many other long-time Motörhead followers, 'That's one thing I've got against Phil Campbell. He never fucking stepped up to the plate. He looked like a man shuffling around in his slippers. You've got Lemmy standing tall, looking like the real deal. Then you've got Phil Campbell waddling around on the other side.'

Campbell's new partner in crime, however, Michael Burston – who arrived with his own nickname, Wurzel, after the TV character Worzel Gummidge, from his days as an army corporal when he was mercilessly ribbed for being so scruffy – was the opposite. From Cheltenham, Wurzel was another decent enough guitar player but his real calling card and key to how quickly the Motörhead fans took to him was his exuberant personality. With his beaming planet-wide smile and his clownish onstage antics, the fans saw him as one of their own. They were right to do so. Before joining the band he'd worked on a building site, playing in pub bands at weekends. Already 30 at the time he read that Motörhead were looking for a new guitarist, he thought his time was almost gone.

'I knew deep down that the only thing I would really be happy doing was playing rock'n'roll,' he recalled, 'but I did think, "I'm thirty years old – am I going to do anything? How am I going to carry on playing these pubs for ever?"' So he wrote Lemmy a letter, enclosed a cassette tape of his playing – and was amazed when a couple of days later Lemmy actually phoned and invited him to audition. 'He also said, "We'll probably end up with an unknown guitarist", and there was no one in the country who was more unknown than I was.'

Lemmy encouraged him to put himself about on stage, suggesting he add an umlaut to his name so that it became Würzel, and generally vibing off his apparently limitless energy. The first gig they did together – with Philthy Phil coming back to help out – was for a now famous appearance playing 'Ace of Spades' on a February 1984 episode of *The Young Ones*, then the most hilariously anarchic and critically acclaimed show on TV. Not that Lemmy thought much of it at the time, he told me. 'I didn't think much of it. People say it was great but I don't know that because I was doing it. I don't know how it was seen. I don't know how anything is *seen*. I'm at ground zero, right? I don't know the effect the explosion has, I really don't.'

Although Doug Smith now says Lemmy secretly always preferred the playing and personality of Phil Campbell, especially as time went by and Würzel began to agitate more for some of the changes that Eddie had first signalled, Lemmy appreciated the value of having another big character in the band. Not least as the last of his new recruits, Pete Gill, didn't seem to know who he was supposed to be in Motörhead. Formerly of Saxon (and before that the Glitter Band), where he liked to rock in a colourful bandana, neckerchief, and tiger-stripe spandex stage costume, now downgraded to a sleeveless Motörhead T-shirt, clean blue jeans and big Boots sunglasses, Pete Gill was a skilled drummer – and completely anonymous. Where Phil Taylor looked like he absolutely lived up to his nickname, Pete Gill looked like someone's dad dressed up for the night. 'I knew he was a great drummer,' said Lemmy. 'I didn't know what a lemon he was but I knew he was a great drummer.'

None of which might have mattered so much if the music they made together with Lemmy had been half as good as what had come before. Instead, the first tracks they recorded with each other – included as four 'bonus' additions to a double-album compilation Bronze released in September 1984 titled *No Remorse* – sounded like what they were: ersatz Motörhead, Lemmy-by-numbers. Plain Janes compared to the siren-like motorcycle sluts of yore.

Lemmy, of course, was having none of it. 'Having two guitars in the line-up totally worked,' he insisted, ignoring the face I was making. He was so determined to get the new line-up off to a winning start he had forced Bronze to include the four new tracks on *No Remorse*, he said. 'I made them put them on there, otherwise it would just have been a greatest hits package. I said, "If you don't put these four [new] tracks on I'm not fucking endorsing it. I'll go in every interview and denounce it."'

In truth, though, there were only two really good tracks. The first, the one they released as their first single, a bit of pantomime villainy called 'Killed by Death', replete with their first ever full-production video – Lemmy on a motorbike bursting through the walls of Mum's and Dad's front room to rescue their underdressed over-made-up daughter from suburban gloom and whisk her away to some biker party where our hero ends up being shot to death. This, plus images of Lemmy's green-lit face doing a horrible fake monster laugh as the band continues to march on with the kind of plodding riff Eddie used to snort for breakfast, leaves the video with a weary, cliché-ridden mid-Eighties metal-mindlessness that makes the band look cartoonish and fake. There was very little that was Fast or Philthy about this Motörhead. This was no longer music for bad guys to stomp their boots to, this was a video-nasty for a generation that was barely old enough to smoke. It was not a hit. Nor would anything else be that the band released over the remainder of Lemmy's career.

The only one of the four new tracks that came close to the original Motörhead ire was 'Snaggletooth', a self-consciously anthemic song apparently about the band's logo, about the only thing left from their original hellfire incarnation that remained intact. But the riff really does hurt this time, not so much an earworm as a drill through the side of the head as Lemmy grits what's left of his teeth and spits out the chorus: *'Speed don't kill and I'm the proof / Just call me Snaggletooth . . .'*

At first, though, it looked like Lemmy may have salvaged the band's career. Magazines like *Kerrang!* that had fallen upon *Another Perfect Day* like a ton of shitbricks came out in favour of the new line-up, treating 'Killed by Death' like the return of the Messiah and running endless pictures of the new Lemmy–Campbell–Würzel–Gill line-up goofing around in sawn-off Motörhead T-shirts and cheap sunglasses. When the new band returned to Britain in May after several warm-up dates in Europe, the flags were out. Lemmy, especially, was flying high again.

'We played six shows in Finland, which was great fun. It was like the old days. Fucking everything that moved and just laughing. All I remember of Finland is laughing. All the way through the fucking six shows.' The first big gig Doug got them was the Poperinge festival. 'Würzel spewed in the lift before the show.' Then, after the show, Doug recalls the band doing 'The dance of the seven tissues, which meant stuffing tissue paper up your arse and lighting it. And they did it on the table in the fucking bar!' 'And then I remember we came and did Hammersmith on the seventh of May,' said Lemmy, 'which was Phil Campbell's twenty-third birthday, and we murdered them. The one before that was with Brian and they weren't crazy about it. But we came back with these two and we fucking creamed them. I remember going back upstairs and going, "Yes!"'

The real test, though, would come with the first album the new line-up recorded. Here they deserved enormous credit, even if the results were sometimes disappointing or even baffling. As Doug says, 'The choice had been whether to try and make another Motörhead album just like all the other Motörhead albums, or go for broke and try something different.'

Change was definitely in the air, though. As well as a brand-new Motörhead line-up, their deal with Bronze had now expired. With the company in dire financial straits suddenly, Doug was able to do a deal that bought back all the Motörhead back catalogue for £25,000 and enabled him to start up his own label, GWR – named after the Great Western Road, where his office was based. New band, new label, new approach to making an album – that's how Lemmy looked at it. When Doug suggested bringing in Bill Laswell as producer Lemmy began to have second thoughts.

Laswell was a 30-year-old Michigan-born musical

innovator who played bass, but whose main interest lay in what he liked to call 'collision music'. That is, making music that lay beyond any one fixed genre, mixing elements of funk and jazz with hardcore punk and heavy metal. He liked manicured noise, out-there rock with a pulsing neon ooze that could be traced back to dance and hip hop. As a producer, most of all, Bill liked fucking with you, undermining preconceptions, offering up the unexpected, the undeserved, the undeniable.

How much of this the rest of the band knew is debatable, but what Lemmy was hoping for, he later told me, was the same sort of transformative effect on the classic Motörhead sound that the introduction of synthesisers and computers had brought to ZZ Top's *Eliminator* album in 1983. That is, a contemporising of the music to the extent that it now appealed to everybody, hardcore fans and chart flies, the same sort of thing that had rewarded ZZ Top with over 20 million sales worldwide. 'Actually, a tenth of that would have done us,' he joked.

Instead what they got was an album, titled *Orgasmatron*, a suitably 'computerish-sounding name', that was neither fish nor fowl. In his memoir, Lemmy blamed Laswell for 'fucking everything up in the mix'. Recorded in London over 11 manic days then taken by the producer to New York to be mixed, Lemmy was apoplectic when he heard what Bill had done. 'I know a lot of fans still like it,' he said, 'but I absolutely hated it.'

A pity as there are some top-drawer tracks on *Orgasmatron*, most especially the opening track and first single, 'Deaf Forever', and the title track, which closes the album.

Both tracks slow Motörhead's usual manic pace to a crawl, yet both are as powerful as anything they had done till then. Like giant attack-robots lumbering towards you over some distant bomb-blasted horizon. Elsewhere, though, it was as you were. Fast, furious, and given such a machine-like sheen by Laswell's taut, button-pushing embrace, it really was as though Lemmy had finally found a tunnel into the future. Maybe he had. He still didn't like it. Which is a shame because *Orgasmatron* was the last Motörhead album that dared wander off on its own into the darkest parts of the woods. Future albums would occasionally fuck with the template, bring in strings or even pianos, slow things down to a slither, or weight things so much it was like dancing with a deep-sea diver. But that was just messing with the kid. *Orgasmatron* was about finding the musical Tardis and closing the door behind you.

Sales of the new album seemed to bear Lemmy's view out though, as the album tottered to No. 21 – one place less than *Another Perfect Day* and far less than *No Remorse*. It didn't help that at the same time they were trying to sell *Orgasmatron*, GWR reissued the entire back catalogue, which now began to sell to a new younger generation of rock fans who simply hadn't been there first time around, or had seen the band live and wanted the records with 'Ace of Spades' and 'Overkill' on them. According to Doug, he had no choice. Money was now so tight the band was starting to run up a sizeable debt.

The excesses of a US tour that autumn also didn't help. Originally scheduled around the hope that the more modern-sounding *Orgasmatron* might open up new pathways for them, an ambitious 32-date schedule was put into place with Motörhead at the top of a three-band bill that included special guests Megadeth, whose second album, *Peace Sells . . . But Who's Buying?*, had also just been released and was already heading for platinum status.

'I flew in for the first show in San Francisco,' says Doug, 'I get to the hotel and I realise they've all been at it for days, rehearsing. Just coked out of their minds.' The band had decided they wanted to take a coke dealer on the road, 'because they had had him on the road already. He did the towels! He brought the towels on stage. So stupid!' And with the cocaine came its usual companions, fear and paranoia. Then, at the show, a fight broke out after Lemmy had ordered the power to be cut halfway through Megadeth's set. A furious and embarrassed Doug recalls storming into the dressing room to find Lemmy smirking. 'This will teach them . . .'

To make matters ten times worse, when Megadeth's booking agent, Andy Summers, complained too loudly, Motörhead's then tour manager, Tommy, hit him with a plank of wood. Summers had to be taken to hospital. Doug was aghast but not in the least surprised when he received a phone call from Summers the following morning informing him that Megadeth would no longer be participating in the tour and that Lemmy could go fuck himself.

'Megadeth cancelled and the tickets immediately stopped selling,' Doug says. 'This is now in LA, Santa Monica Civic. 3500-capacity.' And the place is empty. 'Next day we discover that Megadeth have sent out the message that they won't be appearing on the tour and that was it. Game over.

I had this huge row with Lemmy. His attitude was "They shouldn't have been so cheeky." I said, "Are you stupid or something? We need them for the rest of the tour." I just walked out the dressing room and said, "That's it, fuck you all."' After that they did two more European tours, which they were already committed to. 'But by then we weren't talking.'

Things were falling apart again but Lemmy seemed unwilling or unable to do anything about it. If Phil Campbell and Würzel were overly concerned they kept their mouths shut. But Pete Gill, who'd been around, became the latest to complain of Lemmy's bad habits. In his memoir, Lemmy claims to have sacked Gill when Phil Taylor came back, cap in hand, and begged for his old job back. (The dream of forming a new Thin Lizzy-type band with Robbo had never got off the ground and, despite a high-earning US tour with Frankie Miller, by 1987 the Animal had no place left to go.) Others recall Gill's own frustration boiling over during the filming of a video for the band's next single, 'Eat the Rich' – written as the title song for actor-director Peter Richardson's 1987 *Comic Strip* comedy film, in which Lemmy gives a very stilted cameo playing a two-dimensional version of himself.

When Lemmy wouldn't come down from his hotel room, keeping the rest of the band and driver waiting for hours, Pete finally lost it. When Lemmy eventually emerged Pete went for the jugular and Lemmy responded in kind. After that, Pete quit. And Phil jumped in. Having Phil back was just more fun, says Doug. 'Phil had a fight one night with a roadie called Roach. Phil went for a knife, went to attack him with this knife. And Roach jumped back and Phil's arm went straight the way down into his own foot! He was so drunk we had to laugh.' They were on the tour bus on a boat going across the Channel. When they got to customs the crew threw Phil on the luggage carousel. 'He was so drunk he just sat there going round and round.'

But if the return of the Philthy Animal was meant to signal a return to their roots, the subsequent album, un-imaginatively titled simply *Rock'n'Roll*, with its over-eager attempt to get exactly that message across, was another disappointment sales-wise. Thin production, sketchy songs, Motörhead were becoming obvious and predictable. When the album didn't even make the Top 30, Lemmy knew who was to blame, though. When the promoter Maurice Jones then casually informed Lemmy that he didn't think Motörhead could sell enough tickets any more to make a nationwide tour of Britain worthwhile, urging him to keep Motörhead's live commitments from now on to just a single show a year in London, Lemmy really knew who to blame.

The first indication Doug had that anything was afoot was when Lemmy stopped returning his calls. Next he got a letter. 'I remember driving Lemmy to do a live interview at what was then Greater London Radio – the Krusher show. It was a Sunday and we were chatting away making plans. I can't remember who they were but I remember him telling me there were some other bands also on the show. His last words to me as he got out of the car were, "Right, let's show them who the real fucking boss is." I laughed, and drove off. That was the last time I ever talked to him.'

Lemmy had fired Doug Smith again. But this time there

would be no going back. Lemmy had found a new saviour. His name was Phil Carson and he was about to make at least one of Lemmy's dreams come true by helping him relocate permanently from London to Los Angeles. A former president of Atlantic Records, where he had overseen the careers of such rock giants as Led Zeppelin, Yes and AC/DC, by 1988 Carson was one of the most successful managers in the world, responsible for Foreigner, Bad Company, Robert Plant and Jimmy Page, to name just a few. With offices in London and Los Angeles, and contacts with every heavy hitter in the business, when Lemmy had requested a meeting with him, he didn't even know if Phil would get back to him.

'But I did, because I'd always taken an interest in Lemmy,' he says now, down the line from his home in Los Angeles. 'I knew Motörhead's most successful days were probably behind them in the UK but they'd never really done anything in America, and I was happy to meet them, just to see what they were all about.'

Lemmy took the whole band with him to meet Phil at his London office, where they poured out their woes. Chief of which, says Carson, 'was the fact they were skint and couldn't understand how that could be'. As first Lemmy and then Würzel, who was equally vocal, Carson recalls, laid out their position – that Doug managed them and owned their record company as well as their merchandising company, in essence having complete control over their finances – Carson immediately grasped the problem. 'What we in the business call a conflict of interest,' he explains patiently. 'It wasn't that Doug Smith had done anything wrong, he was perfectly within his rights to conduct his business the way he did.' But with GWR remaining a small independent UK label reliant on licensing its product to other similarly independent labels around the world on a country-by-country basis, it made it harder for the band to collect royalties, not least as their albums were rarely recouping the advances GWR had won for them.

Carson is reluctant to go into any more detail but the main thrust of his point to Lemmy and the band was that were the band managed by someone unconnected to their record company, as was now normal practice among major labels, their outlook would potentially look very different, with that manager in a position to renegotiate more favourable terms with the label. 'It's very hard to do that though when you'd have to renegotiate with yourself,' Carson chuckles. 'I emphasise, Doug wasn't doing anything wrong. But it seemed clear the band had a knot to untangle.'

Carson proposed a simple solution: switch to his company for management. Upon which he would find them a record deal with a major label company, specifically in America, where, as Carson says, 'They hadn't really done much yet, the waters weren't muddied for them there like they were in Britain.' Lemmy didn't have to be asked twice. When Phil told him it would be hugely beneficial for Lemmy also to go and live there he nearly bit his arm off.

When I ask Carson why he was prepared to take such a risk on what for many was now seen to be a broken down band, he is thoughtful. 'I liked Lemmy. I thought he still had a great deal of potential as an artist. And he *looked* like a rock star. There really wasn't anything else he could be.

I thought, all right, let's give him another chance. See what he does with it.'

The fall-out from the break with Doug Smith, though, was such that he and Lemmy would never speak again. Having turned his back on Doug, Lemmy now felt free to blame him for every mistake he and the band had made over the past five years. Doug, for his part, was equally angry, not least because Lemmy kept badmouthing him in the press. 'I kept reading in the press how the band were taking court action against me,' he says. 'There was never any court action! It was all bullshit designed to make me look bad.'

In fact, insists Doug, he was currently overseeing a large overdraft in the band's name, which he and his wife Eve eventually had to sell their house to settle. He admits to a certain amount of bitterness still about the way it all ended with Lemmy. But when I ask why he even put up with him for so long, he smiles indulgently. 'I'm a sucker. I've always had a soft spot for Lemmy. At the end of the day, underneath it all, he was really a lovely man. He had a very gentle side which he rarely allowed anyone to see.'

He tells of one gig at a festival in Poland right before the split where someone from the audience threw a razor blade superglued between two coins at the stage and it sliced right through Lemmy's hand. 'Probably because of the amount of speed and god knows what else in his insides, he hadn't really noticed when it happened. Next thing his hand blew up to twice the size and back in London he had to be admitted to hospital for an operation. As I was leaving he said to me, 'Can you go to my flat and water my plants?' He was

Early promo shot of the short-lived mid-80s line-up. L-R: Würzel, Lemmy, Phil Campbell, Pete Gill. (Getty Images)

The same line-up, recording their only album together, *Orgasmatron*. (Getty Images)

Lemmy spreading good cheer outside his then local the Carlton Bridge Tavern, on the Grand Union Canal, London, 1985, nearby to the houseboat he was living on. (Getty Images)

A shockingly tanned Lemmy just after he'd moved to Los Angeles in 1991. 'I like
Hollywood gals – and they seem to like me.' (Getty Images)

'It's not a costume I change out of when I go home.' Lemmy at his fabled one-bedroom Hollywood apartment, 'just a stagger from the Rainbow.' Note Nazi memorabilia. 'Hitler was the first rock star.' (PA Images)

Lemmy at the five-star Royal
Garden Hotel, in London, June
20th 2006. 'It's not me that's
changed. It's everyone else.'
(Getty Images)

Lemmy and Slash being
inducted into the Rock
Walk at Hollywood's
Whiskey a Go Go in
September 2003.
(Getty Images)

With friends like these... Dave Grohl meets his hero, LA, February 2004.
(Getty Images)

The final Motörhead line-up, pictured in 2010. L-R: Mikkey Dee, Lemmy, Phil Campbell. (Getty Images)

Lemmy in one of his final performances, Helsinki, Finland, December 6th 2015. He died exactly three weeks later. (Jarno Mela/REX/Shutterstock)

A fond farewell at the Rainbow Bar & Grill, Roxy Theatre and Whisky a Go Go, where simultaneous public gatherings for Lemmy were held after his funeral, January 9th 2016. (Getty Images)

into the idea of watching things grow, he loved it, and, yes, he had plants. A long rope with pots of plants in it.'

Within a few months of going with Phil Carson, Motör-head had what was to be their first – and, as it turned out, last – deal with a major record company – Sony Records, no less, one of the biggest in the world. And Lemmy had a new home in Los Angeles.

'He told me he wanted somewhere that he didn't have to drive from to get to the Rainbow,' Carson chuckles. 'And somehow my office in LA managed to find him a place a stone's throw from the Rainbow. This is West Hollywood, mind, not a cheap place to live. But somehow we got Lemmy into his own two-room apartment. Not just any apartment either. A *rent-controlled* apartment! I don't think the rent ever went up the whole time he was there. Or not by very much anyway. Talk about the luck of the devil!'

Suddenly, out of the embers of a thoroughly wasted career, Lemmy was back where he'd always known he belonged. LA, baby! The big kahuna, girls shaking their asses in his face, boys in bands all wanting to hang with him. Dealers lining up to be the first to take care of him. Lemmy, who'd never really cared where he lived, was home.

'I said, "Give me a place close to the Rainbow. Cos I don't drive, right? And LA's like a sprawl. I didn't want to get anywhere where you have to drive five miles to be somewhere. I want to walk there. And luckily I got a place which is relatively cheap. I mean, $700 a month [just over £400], one block from Sunset Boulevard. It compares very favourably with Fulham. One block from Sunset. What is it here for a two-room flat adjacent to Oxford Circus?'

Black Flag's singer, Henry Rollins, who'd just split to go solo and was fast becoming the darling of the US rock press, recalls meeting Lemmy around this time. They were on a panel together at the New Music Seminar in New York. 'I was sitting with Leonard Cohen, Diamanda Galás, Jelly-bean Benitez, Hank Ballard and Lemmy,' he later recalled in an article for *LA Weekly*. 'It was all a little much for me to take in. Lemmy looked at me, then wrote a note on a piece of paper and slid it in front of me. It read, 'What am I doing here?' I admired his overall disgust with the event. Still, Lemmy ended up winning the day by being the only one of us, besides the great Leonard Cohen, to connect with the audience. I was asked a question and, after I answered, Lemmy leaned into his mike and said, "That's a lot of bull." The audience went nuts.'

An acclaimed author, journalist and esteemed figure of the underground counterculture scene in London and New York since the Sixties, Barry Miles also shares a memory of meeting Lemmy at around this time. As he relates, 'The times I remember best are the three Christmas Days spent with him, in the mid-Eighties, in New York City. There was quite a sizeable expat Brit community in Manhattan in those days: we gathered only rarely in that capacity – Guy Fawkes Night being one of them, when someone would bring in fire-works from one of the Southern States where they were legal and we would make a bonfire and set them off, usually on the landfill site where they were building the World Trade Center. The other time was Christmas, when even the most downtown and hip members of the New York arts-drug-music scene went home to see Mom and Pop. Betsy Volk, then married to Mickey Farren, always cooked a Christmas meal. They lived in a late-eighteenth-century Federal building, with its own tiny backyard, just yards from the entrance to the Holland Tunnel, an extraordinary survivor of old New York on a site presumably too small to develop. They had the whole place, which was tiny, and were slowly doing it up. I hope it is still there.

'Betsy would begin the cooking and a dozen or so of us would gather. Sometimes she would need a rest and I would take over, trying to pace myself with the wine. These were not abstemious people. Apart from Lemmy, Mickey and myself, the other Brits were Felix Dennis and usually Victor Bockris. Lemmy was always very relaxed; though he took a lot of speed, he also drank a lot of Jack Daniel's, which tended to smooth it out. He enjoyed talking about the early-Seventies Notting Hill scene that he and Mickey were so much a part of.

'I remember one long conversation about H, one of Jimi Hendrix's roadies, who used to live in a room in the house I rented in Westminster in the late Sixties. Lemmy was fed up with talking about his days as one of Jimi's roadies with journalists, but in fact he had very fond memories of those days and we knew a lot of people in common. He said it was where he learned how to live the life of a rock star . . . I remember him laughing and saying, "They call me the godfather of punk. I don't know why, I've got the long hair and all these hippie connections." It was of course his attitude.'

Another friend Lemmy made during his early years in America was the beautiful and celebrated rock socialite and mother of Liv Tyler, Bebe Buell. She recalls how 'If you were lucky enough to have had a conversation with Lemmy about life, the Beatles or just silly nonsense you found one thing for certain – he was genuine and the real deal. Smart, a gentleman and, yes, a bit of an indestructible warrior.

'I first met him in the late Eighties after being invited by Joey Ramone to perform with my band The Gargoyles at the Ritz for one of his great Circus of the Perverse parties. Joey told me I should cover Janis Joplin's "Piece of My Heart" and after I walked offstage Lemmy came over and told me it was the best version he'd ever heard of such a difficult song to sing. He said I sounded like a "teenage boy".

'Shortly after this meeting Lemmy called me and said he had a song for me. A Motörhead song that he had originally, believe it or not, written for Tina Turner! But she told him it wasn't right for her. He gave a cassette to Joey, who promptly got it to me. I lived about a five-minute walk from Joey's apartment on 9th Street so we would often hang out there and submerge ourselves in music, discussion and Chinese takeout. I went on to record "I'll Be Your Sister", which came out on my 1994 *Retrosexual* album. I sent it to Lemmy and he rang me up immediately to tell me that I sang it exactly as he envisioned I would and how "proud" he was of our version.

'Partying with Lemmy and crew took a lot of stamina, to say the least. I wasn't able to keep up but he never once made me feel bad for it. He might call me a "German Irish lightweight" but never forced his party preferences on others. I always left his presence feeling confident and like I could take on the world with a song. He once even punched a guy square in the nose who was being pushy and gross after one of my shows. He turned to me and said, "There you go, young lady. He won't be bothering you any more tonight. Care for a shot?"

'We then proceeded to throw down a few and talk about the Beatles for hours. That's when I found out about the other side of Lemmy – the musical scholar and true romantic. A couple of my girlfriends had massive crushes on him. Not because he was the prettiest boy in the room but he really did love women and he respected them equally. I hear he was a tender and dear, sweet lover . . . Why do I not find that hard to believe? He was a loyal friend, too. You could call him for advice about everything from boyfriends to song choices. Lem was wise and very funny, one of a kind, that I can confirm.'

The first Motörhead album under the new Phil Carson-brokered deal with Sony was *1916* – taken from the most momentous track on it, about the young First World War soldiers that lost their lives at the Battle of the Somme, one of the bloodiest battles in human history. It was the only sombre moment on an album otherwise bristling with its own bedazzled power, and utterly unlike any Motörhead album before or since. Recorded in LA with the Grammy-nominated producer Pete Solley, *1916* came with all the production bells and whistles one would expect from any major label American album of the time.

'Yeah, it's a beauty that one,' said Phil Campbell. 'Lemmy had relocated over to the US. It was the first time we'd had a major record deal and the first time we had everything we'd ever wanted to do an album – time, a good producer, and the money to make it happen without rushing everything. I remember, I was there in LA for sixteen weeks and it only rained for one hour throughout the whole sixteen weeks! Peter Solley [also] came in for a couple of weeks while we were writing the songs and that helped us develop them, it was great, we'd never had that before in England.'

Indeed, it's by far the most American of any Motörhead album, the band's signature speed metal replaced by cocky, strutting, turbocharged rock – like a cross between Guns N' Roses and Metallica. A calculated move, no doubt, to try and finally capture the American market, the album was not a big seller but was nominated for Best Metal Performance at the 1992 Grammy Awards, only losing out to Metallica, who had just released one of the biggest-selling metal albums of all time with *Metallica*. 'We were all really pleased but I remember we were also really shocked,' remembered Campbell. 'We were having a drink one day, trying to avoid going in and actually rehearsing, and someone came in and said, boys, your album has been nominated for a Grammy – and we thought they were taking the piss!'

They tried to repeat the trick with their next album, *March or Die*, but this time, despite the occasional highlight like the stark and moving 'I Ain't No Nice Guy', it didn't work. 'That was when Philthy was going through a bad time and it affected the album,' recalls Campbell. 'He was overdoing it and had lost control and finally it started to affect his playing. It was so bad by that point that we finally had to let him go. After repeatedly and repeatedly talking to him about it, begging him to get it together again, it got to the point where he simply couldn't drum, so that's when we had to act. Which he didn't take too well, he was so bogged up in his mind he just couldn't see it.'

Lemmy was more to the point. 'Phil came and asked me for his job back and like a cunt I give it to him. And he never forgave me for giving him his job back, because the thing he really believed in [with Robbo] had failed. I think it damaged him. Cos he believed completely that he had gone beyond this Motörhead thing now, and he could do better. And Brian was this incredible musician that was gonna help him. So with me he was just doing it for the wages. We put up with a lot from Phil Taylor. The last two years he didn't even bother keeping a beat properly. He'd start "Killed by Death" like this [hurried motion] and finish it like that [knackered, out of puff] . . .' His legs had gone, said Lemmy. 'In the end we couldn't rely on him to even do "Overkill". I mean, "Overkill". The song he fucking invented practically. But it was beyond him.'

His replacement was Mikkey Dee, a former drummer with Dokken and Helloween. Mikkey was 30, in thrall to all things Motörhead, and could hit the drums harder than anyone Lemmy had ever heard. 'He took a pay cut to be in this band, can you believe that?' Lemmy told me. Mikkey was in and here to stay.

That was it also for the band's deal with Sony. 'They never really believed in us, it was only through Phil Carson that they signed us,' said Lemmy. When Carson was forced to step down as Motörhead's manager though, after accepting an offer to run Victory Records in LA, things changed again for the band. For a while they were managed by Sharon Osbourne. But Sharon soon changed her mind, deciding perhaps that one madman of rock was enough for her to cope with, and Lemmy turned to the man he would entrust his career to for the rest of his life: Todd Singerman. 'Todd just showed up at my house one day,' Lemmy recalled in his memoir. 'He wouldn't leave until I said he could manage us.'

What Singerman lacked in music business experience, he made up for with sheer hard work, passion and, that most important quality of all to Lemmy, loyalty. Todd had previously run campaigns for an American congressman. He *never* took no for an answer. Lemmy told me the story of Todd going to Sony and asking if the then head of promotion could get 'I Ain't No Nice Guy', an acoustic ballad, onto AOR radio, 'and he said "No, we tried it, they wouldn't take it." We said, "You're a fucking liar, you've had no time to try it. It's a three-week campaign. You haven't got time? Fuck you!" We got two guys on two phones and suddenly the song was on eighty-three AOR stations in America, four of them on rotation, New York, LA, Arizona, Chicago, all rotating.' They were now No. 7 in the US radio charts so Todd asked the record company for money for a video and it still said no. 'So we made our own video, it cost eight grand. It wasn't the greatest video but it certainly wasn't the worst. Ozzy and Slash were both in it.' But the record company deliberately held up giving it to MTV until the record was dead on the radio. 'They even called radio guys and told them to stop playing it because it hadn't come from them. This is the band calling up [radio stations] on their own initiative. My god, we can't have that, right?'

Todd called the manager, explained he came from a big family in South Central LA and how 'there will never be a moment again that you are not in danger', if the record wasn't back on the airwaves by 9.30 that night. 'Otherwise, "I'll come over there and cut you a new fucking asshole." It was back on at 8.30. But isn't it awful that we had to resort to that? They signed a contract to promote us to the best of their ability. Then they're ringing DJs saying don't play this band. See what is that? All that is down to is pique. Cos they didn't give it to 'em. As far as whether the record's good enough they've probably never heard it. So that's when I thought, fuck it, we're better on our own.'

It was their last album for Sony. It wasn't long though before Todd had fixed the band with another record deal. It was back to the indies but this one at least paid. 'There were a few interested,' said Lemmy. 'We went with the one that offered the most money. What I call sensible management,' he grinned, showing off his shiny new American teeth.

Lemmy's luck really did change, though, when Sharon Osbourne called him one day and invited him to write some lyrics for the next Ozzy album, *No More Tears*. He came back with half a dozen complete sets which he later reckoned he'd written in one late-night burst of speed. When one of them he wrote the words to, 'Mama, I'm Coming Home', became a big US hit single for Ozzy, said Lemmy, 'I made more from that song than I had from Motörhead at that point!'

There was one more big turn in the road for Lemmy, in the Nineties, when Würzel, who had never really taken to life almost permanently on the American road, as Motörhead now were, decided he'd finally had enough and quit. As Phil Campbell would later tell me, 'Würzel had a lot of personal stuff going on, he was so disillusioned with the business, he was having trouble playing, the poor guy.' One night, while working on 'Out of the Sun', from their 1995 *Sacrifice* album, 'he couldn't get his solo right. He was in there for hours and hours. He came down in the end, he just stopped playing, like that, grabbed his guitar and jumped into his car, and was gone. He was so bitter with himself, I guess, but that's what he was down to in the end. He got so annoyed with himself he couldn't play.'

The next day Würzel sent a fax. 'It was a blow,' admitted Lemmy. 'But when Würzel left, Phil came into his own.' He certainly did. 'I felt sorry for him to go but I knew his heart wasn't in it and, believe me, if your heart's not in it this is the wrong band to be in. So it was kind of a relief when he decided to go off and sort his head out. And I thought, well, here's my chance to really shine, you know? I told the boys, look, I believe I can make it work and that it will be great. But if you let me give it a try, believe me, if it isn't happening, I'll be the first one to say we need somebody else. Then we went to rehearsals and the boys said that after two or three songs they already knew that it was gonna work musically. And then the first gigs we did, I couldn't just stand there any more, and that's when my performing life changed completely. On a good night I cover about ten miles onstage – and I enjoy it! It made me a much better performer being in a three-piece.'

Lemmy: 'The guy who's most out of control in my band is Phil Campbell and he's been with me for years, longer than any of the others, ever. He's the longest-serving member in Motörhead and he's completely out of control. He's unemployable, for a start. If he was actually on the street all the time he'd probably get locked up as a lunatic. But he plays very, very good guitar and he's my brother.'

Off the road, Lemmy had carved a new, more relaxing, if solitary life for himself at his tiny West Hollywood apartment. 'I think that if we hadn't have moved to America we'd have been gone now,' he told me earnestly. 'We couldn't survive here. The last album went in at No. 79 and went out again. We had no base here. Everyone had dumped us. It's only because I went to live in America that when we come back now we're treated like a visiting American band. It's funny. I couldn't have predicted that either. I thought England would just never be interested again.'

I reminded him how he once told me he didn't want to tour America, he joked he just wanted to tour LA. 'That was no joke. Since I've been in America I've found out a lot of stuff about America I didn't know before, and a lot of it is negative. But I still say, America is the promised land, you know? And it is. For every Englishman, to go to America is an adventure because you've watched it all your life on TV. And all them great movies that came out of LA, Hollywood . . . I walk down the sidewalk and it's still a knockout, you know? It's the palm trees that do it though. Flying to LA for the first time you see that every house has a blue swimming pool and the palm trees are yay high. You think, fucking hell, Disneyland!' he laughed.

When he wasn't working Lemmy now spent most of his time at the Rainbow, killing afternoons and evenings draining Jack-and-Cokes and playing the fruit machine at the end of the bar, gamely taking breaks to pose for photos with fans, tourists and the throng of musicians gathered there on the weekends.

Asked why he maintained such modest accommodation rather than something a bit more rock star-ish, Lemmy flatly explained, 'I can't afford it. We didn't sell many albums. I'm not going to die broke, but I'm not rich. I pay taxes here, but I'm not a citizen – they won't give me citizenship. I got busted for two sleeping pills on New Year's Eve in 1971, so obviously I'm a threat to the kids in America, you know.'

He looked at me. 'That's why people get down on you. It's not that you menace them. It's that they don't understand it. And anything they don't understand menaces them. And yet I never had any idea of overthrowing the government. I never had any idea of subverting their children. All I wanted to do was play music that I love and that other people want. And that was it. And that still is it.' It was the same when he flew, he told me. 'Customs all over the world still search me first. I mean, why? Do they think dope smugglers look like me? I don't think so. And how long have they had to absorb this information? The dope smugglers are the [well-dressed] people with briefcases going right behind me. And they still haven't got the brains to figure that out. They say, "Everyone with long hair is a drug smuggler." Well good fucking luck. Apparently we are doomed. If stupidity is the mark of doom then we're fucking doomed. There's no point. We might as well all just fucking cut our own throats.'

He laughed and lit himself yet another cigarette, lighting it with the dying tip of the previous one. Picked up his glass and began to gargle. Enough seriousness, he said, he would tell me a funny story about Phil Campbell.

'Eddie was always leaving the band. He'd use it as a threat. Well, Phil Campbell did it for a long time too. He was always leaving, always packing his bags, you know? I finally said to him, "Listen, you're gonna have to stop leaving the band or I'm gonna let you." He thought about it for a minute and he said okay and he's never said it since. See as much as he's wild, he knows what he's doing. Cos I spoke to him. I just said, enough, you know? Cos he left all the time. Halfway across the mountains of Croatia. That's not a good place to leave. In the middle of the night. "Stop this bus!" Stopped the bus. He's parading up and down the aisle, packing his fucking stuff. "Open these doors!" Opened the doors. Stepped out into three feet of snow. A blizzard horizontally passed him. And all one side of him is white immediately. He looks around. There's one light on, miles away, across the valley. One light on in the whole universe. And as he looks at it, it went out. One of them golden moments. He got back on the bus.'

Another time . . . 'He left the band once on the way into Berlin. We're going down the road. He said, "Take me to the airport!" I said, "Listen, you're a civilian now. You left the band. This is a band bus. We're going to the gig. When we get there you can get a fucking taxi." He said, "I've got no money." I said, "We don't pay civilians either." Grumble, grumble. But I'll give him his due. Since I had that chat with him he's never threatened us with that again. Cos that's a big thing in a band. A lot of band guys do that. "I'm leaving unless you do so-and-so." It works for a while. But then people think, fuck it, you know?'

Mainly, though, he said, life was good. Even if his LA

home was now full to bursting with his Nazi memorabilia collection. 'When I left for America I had one dagger and two Iron Crosses. Now I've got twenty display cases full of medals and badges. About ten flags, over 250 daggers. I've got some real good stuff too. I've got it from all over the world but mostly in America. Some from here. There's a very good store down on Marylebone High Street called Blunderbuss Antiques. They sell everything. They sell Napoleonic stuff too, Indian swords. They sell *incredible* shit there. They've got the British army stuff going all the way back, from the Indian Mutiny, all of that stuff. Some of the swords are incredible. All the helmets, square flat tops, Napoleon ones, and a lot of Second World War stuff. Beautiful, and it's all polished up, you know.

'I was always interested in it. I'm interested in the whole phenomenon. It's the most important thing that happened in the twentieth century. The whole world fought it and it took the whole world to beat it. If you look at Germany on the map and you look at the other powers that were fighting it, we were all smaller. Then look at the size of Russia and America, and it took both of them to beat them. And America had to be bombed into it too.

'I love reminding Americans of this. "You know, you didn't declare war on Hitler. He declared war on you." They go, "No, no . . ." I go, "Oh yeah! He declared war on you eight days after Pearl Harbor. You never declared war on Germany. You never would have either. You had your hands full with the Japanese." They don't tell them at school. They don't tell them, American kids, except the Civil War, gung-ho, fucking pledge allegiance. Criminal state of affairs. Meanwhile kids in America are taking guns to school. Nine-year-old children are walking into school with a .44 automatic. Insane. We have become insane. The world is now run by nutters.

'Anybody that doesn't want to reform the gun programme in the States is insane, because when you put guns in anybody's hands, man . . . when you think of all the friends you've got. How many would you trust with a gun? One per cent, maybe? Anybody with a violent temper, going red and cross-eyed, look out! Instead of arguing, it's just so much simpler. You can't get beaten in an argument if you've got a .44, right? Just blow their fucking head right off! They say it's written into the constitution – the right to arm bears!' He cackled. 'A bear with a Kalashnikov.'

The Nazis had a very powerful and glamorous and exciting image they projected. Did that have something to do with his own fascination for that stuff? 'Yes.' Hitler's rallies were almost like rock concerts, weren't they? 'He was the first rock star. I mean, the one at the Nuremberg Stadium with those two big bronze eagles . . . The Cathedral of Lights they called it. Hundreds of searchlights up into the sky like pillars of white fire. Then as Hitler ascends onto the podium they all met above him and one light hit him in the face. I mean, that's fucking amazing shit! You would go for it. If you were twenty in 1933 you would go for it like a knife! Because of the unemployment and because he always kept all of his promises. He said he'd kill the Jews. He killed the Jews. He said he'd turn around the economy. He turned around the economy. Massive inflation. He got rid of that. Froze all the foreign assets. Just froze it, said you can't have it. And we put up with it because we'd won [the First World War]. We were suffering from victor's ailment. We'd won so we thought that would be it for ever.

'He said he'd unify Germany and give them a new purpose for life. He did that too. Made them proud to be German again. They were the scum of the earth before then. Europe kicked them all over the place. The French occupied the Ruhr. Hitler got them out of there . . . and he ran rings round us in the Thirties. See Neville Chamberlain standing there with that agreement, shaking. He gave that bastard Czechoslovakia. To take his eyes off us. *Appease* him. Why not just lick his rectum?'

He said he'd 'learned a lot of shit' since starting his Nazi collection. 'When you collect something you want something you haven't got. And the way you collect something you have to find out about it otherwise you won't know what it's worth. Although I don't collect it for the money side. I collect it because I like it. I like the way it looks. I like the way it's made. The daggers are fantastic, beautiful, works of art in themselves some of them. Like the German foreign office dagger is a *fantastic* thing to look at. If you put it on a stand in the Tate Gallery and if it wasn't for the connotations of the swastika, you call it a work of art. It ranks alongside a rapier from Toledo in the 1760s. Beautiful workmanship and quality stitching.

'The swastika is the strongest symbol ever invented.' He showed me a swastika from his suitcase. 'This is from present-day India. It's a good luck sign. Before the swastika was a good luck symbol it was a regeneration thing, the four seasons. The cycle. That's what it means. That's what it always meant. It's in every culture, from the Indians, to the Red Indians, to the Chinese, to us. The Druids used it. You see it on the tunics of the Druids.' In India, he said, 'It's a regeneration symbol . . . One culture used it for twelve years. But twelve other cultures used it for 20,000 years.'

He wouldn't go on stage though with a big swastika behind him, would he? 'No. I go on with an Iron Cross around my neck. But it's a First World War Iron Cross. So it's nothing to do with Hitler. In America they point and go, 'Swastika!' *Swastika?* It's a fucking Iron Cross you dolt! From 1813! What's the matter with you people? Don't you know *anything*? And the answer of course is, no they don't.'

As he liked to tell people, 'I've always liked a good uniform, and throughout history it's always been the bad guy who dressed the best. Napoleon, the Confederates, the Nazis. If [England] had a good uniform, I'd collect ours as well, but what does the British Army have? Khaki!'

Once, he told me, apropos of nothing special that I could see but he told me anyway: 'I'd like to say, by the way, that I don't particularly promote drugs as any answer to anything. Because I'm all right but most of my friends died. So I don't promote them. I would say acid is good for you. But you've got to be very lucky for it to be good for you, because I know a lot of people are in the rubber room now. And smoking dope is cool. But I know it does lead people to downers. I know it does because it's the same sort of thing.

'I wouldn't espouse anything to anybody. I'd say have your own experiences and don't come to me with the results, that's all. Don't come crying to me because it's your life and you have to be responsible for it. You can't blame God or the devil or the man who sold you the reefer cigarette. You can't blame anybody for it. It's your fucking life. Be responsible and do it properly. And if you fuck up, put your hand up and take the fucking blame. It's only your fault. Nobody forced you to do anything. It's true.'

A pause, and then: 'Some kid came up to me once and said, "Wow, Lemmy – you're God!" I said, "No, I've seen God, and he's much, much taller." And he is too. And God doesn't play bass. He hates that. God goes to church. You won't see me there . . .'

In 1997 I asked him if he was becoming at all health-conscious as he gets older? Would he ever consider jogging, for example?

'Fuck off! That jogging affects you worse than the fucking disease it's supposed to cure! People dropping like flies all over the fucking place on one-in-seven gradients, like big red faces, dying. It's great, isn't it? Doggedly not smoking, then sitting on the pavement outside the Café Barfly, about two feet from the traffic. How smart is that? It's like lemmings, man. They have no idea why they do it, they just know they have to. It's like England. They're fond of slogans. You know, get a new banner. We don't care what the banner is, just get a new one, we need one. And if anyone says anything against it, it's *heresy!*'

I remarked that looking at pictures of him from, say, ten or even 15 years ago, he hadn't changed much – at least, not from the outside. But what about the inside? Had that changed over the years?

'Not much, man. A few more scars, maybe. You get a bit more impatient a bit quicker as time goes by. I liked my life ten or fifteen years ago, and I don't see why I should change it, if I like it. I just lived my life how I lived it, and people can like it or lump it, you know? It's always that way if you want to be an individual. I was always like that. That's why I kept getting fired out of all the other bands I was in. I had to form me own band to stop getting fired.'

And those white boots – were they the same ones he'd always had? 'Do you know something, I've got about fucking six *left* white boots. Cos I wear the right ones out first, right? And I would only wear one pair at a time, you know? So if you know any fucking one-legged left-footed dancers, ask them to get in touch. Cos they might be really glad of these. Mint condition. Only run away in twice . . .'

NINE

Dead Man's Hand

As the Nineties faded into the black, Planet Earth had entered the throes of its most significant cultural transformation since the Industrial Revolution. The internet – once a brain-freezing futuristic movie plot – was now a real thing, and with it came the dawn of the Information Age. Two parallel technologies – cable modems and file-sharing services – emerged from the neo-primordial ooze, creating a glitzy new platform for twenty-first-century music. Fans exploited the opportunity with greedy, wild-eyed abandon, but the bands and labels who rose up before the late Nineties couldn't help but see this polished new architecture as little more than a gallows for the old guard.

As far as Lemmy was concerned, he told me, 'The internet is the death of civilisation. It will turn people into frightened recluses, as if they aren't bad enough now. What they mean is that we'll all be connected up to the giant industrial brain, and if that fucks up then we're all fucked up. It's like, "Hello, please arrest me, here I am." I just don't like that much information going out to people who don't deserve to have it and are not qualified to understand it. All those people sitting at their computers making contact without being able to see the face. It's incredibly dangerous. And the upshot of it all will be them all sitting like nerds in their little attic rooms with a fucking glowing screen that will be our fond friend.'

Nevertheless, online communities such as AOL and MySpace suddenly empowered ordinary people with broad, sophisticated technologies that allowed a video of a cat playing with its tail to routinely find more viewers in an hour than some bands from the Seventies could have hoped to reach in a lifetime. While many embraced the first day of 2000 as the arrival of a brave new world, for Lemmy it was just another Saturday. 'It isn't going to do much for me,' he snorted derisively. 'They've got the wrong date anyway. This is the last year of the old millennium, not the first year of the next. Do you know how they invented Christmas? Emperor Constantine became a Christian and wanted to give the Jews a holiday. Nice one, centurion!' he added, referencing one of his favourite Monty Python films, *Life of Brian*.

Whether or not Lemmy would adapt to this brave new world of modems, social media and the coming death of the record industry was never a question, not because the answer was rhetorical but because Lemmy had never viewed life as an adapt-or-die proposition. His course had been firmly set the very first time he heard rock'n'roll and the rest of his life arranged itself accordingly, trends be damned.

Like AC/DC, his resistance to change would underpin his legacy, at times calling into question his creative vitality, but ultimately endearing him to fans and artists from across the genre spectrum for holding fast to his utterly unshakeable sense of self. It's not that Lemmy was impervious to change, he simply wasn't interested in it. With regard to Motörhead's sound, he would tell *Rolling Stone*, 'I don't see why one would change it for the sake of fashion . . . fuck that.'

Released in May 2000, *We Are Motörhead* righted the ship after the lacklustre *Snake Bite Love* and reaffirmed the band's commitment to eardrum-punishing, four-on-the-floor rock music, as heard in the gasoline-soaked roar of 'See Me Burning' and a reverentially sleazy cover of the Sex Pistols' 'God Save the Queen'. As with previous albums, Motörhead balanced the speed-driven punch-ups with down-tempo numbers like 'One More Fucking Time' and sprawling, tempo-shifting belters like 'Wake the Dead'. Produced by Bob Kulick and the band, their fifteenth album galvanised the fan-base, but, as was now the norm, the mainstream would remain blissfully unaware of its illicit charms.

By summer's end, *We Are Motörhead* faced familiar competition in the record stores. Adding to the catalogue-exsanguinating list of Motörhead compilations clamouring for shelf space, Import Records released *Deaf Forever: The Best of Motörhead* (produced by the Midas-fingered Ken Caillat, who had produced Fleetwood Mac's *Rumours*) and *The Best of* . . . released in September. Such wanton oversaturation was down to the sale of their classic three-amigos Bronze Records catalogue, which would nonetheless continue to earn royalties for the band, albeit without any controlling interests over the distribution.

On 21 October, Lemmy temporarily reunited with Hawkwind for 'Hawkestra' – an ambitious celebration that convened past and present members of the band running through years of old set lists. Musicians rotated on- and offstage like a benefit gig, with Lemmy coming out for the second set (nearly two and a half hours into the show), for sloppily aggressive numbers like 'You Shouldn't Do That', 'Psychic Warlords' and 'Space is Deep', sharing a stage with Dave Brock for the first time since the old 'irksome days' of his sacking. Lemmy would later insist that the night had been an unmitigated disaster behind the scenes, telling the journalist Scott Heller it was 'The worst thing I've ever been involved in. I don't know how Brock could have let it slide so bad. He didn't seem to know what he's doing any more. I don't know what's up. I know the songs, it's him that has forgotten them.' As for arranging to have the topless model Sam Fox come on and sing 'Master of the Universe', Lemmy was almost speechless. 'This is such an unbelievable idea, I can't even grasp it. I just don't understand that at all. I don't know what he was thinking, do you?' For Doug Smith, the whole proposition of Brock and Lemmy getting together again was a bad joke. 'For [Brock] and Lemmy to become friends after *years* of anger and nastiness . . .' He shook his head.

When I spoke to Lemmy ahead of the show, he seemed far more relaxed about the prospect of getting back together with Dave Brock. 'There were always long periods when we didn't stay in touch. But, like, I've always known where Dave is kind of thing. Yeah, we stayed in touch. He's even older than me, you know? Fucking crusty old cunt. Last time I saw him he was on his way to Hawaii. Had a grass skirt on and everything. Fucking flowers round his neck . . .'

And how were the two of them together after all this time? Were they very polite, were they able just to slip back into the groove? 'Oh, we'll always be Dave and Lemmy, you know? It's not like that. You spend five years in a band together, you don't get like that. That's like lovers get, we're not lovers. "Oh, I feel like a schoolboy again when he's around!" It's not like that. More like, "I feel like a Teddy Boy again."'

The following night at the Brixton Academy it was different though, with Lemmy and Motörhead celebrating their twenty-fifth anniversary by filming their fourth live album and first live DVD, a double-sided, star-loaded blowout that unfurled an eccentric parade of special guests, including Brian May, Doro Pesch, Ugly Kid Joe's frontman, Whitfield Crane, and Skunk Anansie's guitarist, Ace. One of Lemmy's favourite guests though was Captain Sensible of The Damned. 'He turned up wearing some sort of cow outfit. He came in singing that fucking song, "Happy, happy, happy . . ." Fucking great, Captain! Irrepressible. Can't be killed. Can't be kept down. He *will* be the Captain! He *will* fuck you!'

The most anointed guest though, onstage at least, was Eddie Clarke. Though pleased, and somewhat relieved, to be included, Eddie now reveals there was, in fact, another idea afloat in the months leading up to the Brixton show that he feels might have offered a more spectacular way of marking Motörhead's quarter-century.

'There was talk of us – the original band with Phil – doing an Unplugged reunion.' According to Eddie, his then manager had gone to talk to Lemmy about it when he was in London at the tail end of 1999. 'This was before the 2000 Brixton thing,' Eddie recalls. 'We were gonna have chicks on the cellos with the fucking stockings and suspenders. It was gonna be fantastic!'

Eddie also tells how, alone backstage with Lemmy at the Brixton show, they shared a moment of painful reflection. 'I said to him, "Lem, I never got over fucking leaving this band, you know?" He said, "No, neither did I." But then he might have just been paying lip service, I don't know. But I never got over it and there was no way I was ever gonna get over it.'

But Lemmy wasn't having any of it. He'd just spent the past 15 years trying to get people to focus on the fact that he'd moved on with a new and, he always insisted, better Motörhead line-up. The thought of reactivating the original, most successful band was simply anathema to him. As he told me at the time, he found the growing trend for classic line-ups of rock bands to get back together 'a bit sickening, really. People jumping on the bandwagon the whole time. On the other hand, a lot of them need the bread, you know, so what are you gonna do? It's difficult. I don't know if I'd ever do it. We never stopped, you see, so why should we break up and restart now? Both of the members in my band now have been with me for longer than the original members, so why should I put them on hold? And we're not the people we were then, the three of us, the original three, right? It's not gonna be the same.'

In the event, the 23-song set list at the Academy covered all the bases, pairing new material ('We Are Motörhead', 'God Save the Queen') with classics like 'Overkill', 'Ace of Spades' and 'Bomber'. Sonically, the audio album, *Live at Brixton Academy*, offered a more muscular and contemporary production than *No Sleep 'til Hammersmith*, and the subsequent DVD, *25 & Alive: Boneshaker*, yielded a trove of extra goodies, including music videos of 'God Save the Queen' and 'Sacrifice', and a bluesy, stripped-down acoustic version of 'I Ain't No Nice Guy', filmed with Phil in July 2001.

Lemmy later admitted that while he didn't even own a DVD player at the time, he was quite proud of the whole affair, saying, 'We wanted to record it for the posterity or whatever it is. I nodded off through the tenth anniversary, we never did anything on the twentieth, so the twenty-fifth made sense.' Adding, 'When you form a band, you think, [you'll last] maybe five years if you're lucky. And it sort of stretched a bit. Whether people like it or not is not important. I think we're necessary. I think you deserve us!'

The supporting tour crossed east through Europe for the final three months of the year – a hard campaign marked by long drives and late stage times. A rapacious strain of the flu waylaid all three musicians, eventually forcing the cancellation of ten shows (which they made up later in the year). Of his relentless pace, both on- and offstage, the grizzled frontman admitted, 'You can't keep up the same enthusiasm for twenty-five years, but it's good enough. I still get a charge out of going out there. The one thing is the same, on a good night when you can hear everything perfect and everybody's playing well and the crowd is going nuts, it's still better than sex, you know. And I like sex.'

While such backbreaking touring would send most of today's bands off on a three-month holiday, Lemmy had just a month off before descending on the producer Chuck Reid's Hollywood home to begin work on what would be their sixteenth album, *Hammered*. At the same time, ever game for further diversions, Motörhead would forge a not-entirely-unlikely partnership with America's World Wrestling Entertainment – that bonzo group of oiled-up, muscle-bound actors in spandex, cartoonishly hurling themselves about a wrestling ring and bashing the living daylights out of each other in the service of a preordained result. One wrestler, Paul Levesque, known to his adoring fans as Triple H, adopted one of the new Motörhead songs, 'The Game', as his theme song, and the band returned the favour on April Fool's Day, 2001, by playing it live at *WrestleMania X-Seven* in Houston in front of 68,000 maniacal grapple-fans – a sublime intersection of British headbanging and trailer park Americana deep in the heart of Texas.

'The thing is the fuck you-ness,' Lemmy said. 'It's always a minority at the time. Cos skateboards were a minority music at the time, and wrestling, well, it wasn't in a minority, but it was looked down upon by real sportsmen. I don't particularly like wrestling, it's a bit obvious for me, but at the same time there's some great characters in it. It's not actually a sport any more, it's a show, it's a circus. It's so awful, some of them shouldn't be acting, they should go back to wrestling. But some of that soap opera bullshit is really quite funny. But the guys we met connected to it are total gentlemen.'

Released later that year, *Hammered* was a dramatically darker affair than its predecessor. Written in the wake of the 9/11 terrorist attacks in the US (Phil and Mikkey actually flew to California on the day before the attacks), *Hammered* seemed to mirror America's spiralling disillusionment and gloom, playing out in bluesier tempos, soulful melodies and lyrics like these, from 'Walk a Crooked Mile': *'If you were Armageddon / Who would you spare? / If you were judge and jury / Why would you care?'*

November 2002 saw the release of Lemmy's autobiography, *White Line Fever*, ghosted by the estimable American music journalist Janiss Garza – a nimbly paced, life-in-a-day memoir that Lemmy was more than happy to admit was little more than a pure cash grab that had been laid at his feet. Predictably light on emotional depth and long on delightfully outré Lemmy anecdotes, its charm was in the way Garza had successfully captured Lemmy's voice, part Les Dawson, part defiantly ageless rock rebel. It's pity was that Lemmy didn't allow himself to revisit people and events in his life that had been significant but were no longer considered important by him, either through spite or through plain thoughtlessness, the most glaring example being his arbitrary downscaling of his near 20-year relationship with his former manager, Doug Smith, who is mentioned in passing only a handful of times.

Through constant touring and a steady stream of new

releases every two years, Motörhead eventually infiltrated the American mainstream to a measurable extent, now regularly appearing on talk shows with Conan O'Brian, Jimmy Kimmel, Letterman and Leno, doing the late-night rounds. Lemmy seemingly reconciled, at least somewhat, to the fact that Motörhead's days of having hit records were long over. As long as they still held a reserved table for him at the Rainbow and the ever-younger generations of bands and fans still held him in the same dizzyingly high regard. Now virtually bulletproof from critics, the old stager was fully aware that it was less and less Motörhead the cutting-edge rockers people were paying homage to and more and more the living legend that was Lemmy.

Back in the real world, however, Lemmy's health was becoming worrisome. In 2003, he sought medical treatment for what official sources described as a heart murmur. Meds were prescribed, as was a complete overhaul of his nasty habits. Unlike the so-called Harley Street doctor who he still claimed had once warned him not to stop taking drugs, he was now told in no uncertain terms by his physicians in Los Angeles that the time had come to at least partially start mending his ways. Lemmy listened, patiently, agreed to act. Then left the hospital and lit a cigarette, glanced at his watch and thought about a drink. And some speed. His friend, Mörat, recalls Lemmy telling him around this time: 'Why live to be 120 years if you're bored? Why not do what you want and have however long you get?'

Privately, however, when he thought no one was looking, Lemmy, now approaching his fifty-ninth birthday, was becoming more circumspect. He had even lately begun going to bed early. 'It's not that I had to,' he insisted, 'more that you don't get as much pleasure out of being the last one awake any more.' Pause for wry smile. Then: 'I attempt to get more sleep than I used to, basically because there aren't enough people staying up any more to hang around with.'

In 2004, the band released *Inferno*, spicing the mix with the virtuosic Steve Vai playing guitar on two tracks, including the singularly brutal opener, 'Terminal Show'. Dramatically more influential, however, was the engagement of Cameron Webb, former producer of Monster Magnet and Limp Bizkit, to produce the affair – a relationship that would endure for the remainder of Motörhead's career. Todd Singerman facilitated the introduction over steaks and drinks by the pool of the Sunset Marquis. Speaking in 2010, Webb explained, 'I talked about how I wanted to make a really heavy record for them. That was a mistake, because Lemmy likes to play rock'n'roll, he doesn't like to play heavy music, and he called me on it. He said, "I wanna make a rock'n'roll record", and right then I thought I wasn't gonna get hired. But we kept talking and I said, "I like to give people freedom in the studio, but I'm still gonna bust your balls", and he said, "Okay, see you tomorrow for pre-pro-duction in the rehearsal studio." And that was it. It worked out really well.'

It might have worked 'well', but, as Webb recalled, it was far from easy. 'They're one of the most fun bands to work with, but also one of the most difficult . . . Imagine people having a party, 24/7, every single day. That's their life. Now look at me: I'm the one who has to say, "Hey, can we stop the party for a minute and get some work done?"' As he said,

'Lemmy came out of the Sixties and Seventies when things were a little more free, and bands did what they wanted, but times aren't like that any more. He knows that and that's one thing he hates about now, that it's not as free as it used to be. Sometimes he looks at me as if I'm this mean person who's saying, "Let's do that again", and he says, "I don't wanna fuckin' do it again!" That's the hardest thing for me. It's also really enjoyable, though. They tell great stories and they're fun to be around.'

Critically the album was received as predictably as prior efforts – the metal press and fans once again praised the band's intransigent commitment to the inveterate Motör-head sound. Anybody expecting Motörhead to go off on a psych rock voyage or to slow down and pile into west Texas blues hadn't been following the plot. *Inferno* was not without variety, however. The blues-drenched acoustic blowout 'Whorehouse Blues' delivered an exhilarating stylistic diversion, while tracks like 'Life's a Bitch' and 'Smiling Like a Killer' offered gear-grinding reminders that beyond the paint-stripping rock monster bludgeoning, a steady level of playfulness pervaded the music, a wink and a nudge to the fans.

In January 2005, after 30 years of slogging it out in the trenches, the National Academy of Recording Arts and Sciences of the United States recognised Motörhead with their first Grammy award – though not for *Inferno*, nor for any of their own material. Ironically, the band earned the award for their cover of Metallica's 1983 song 'Whiplash', on the Metallica tribute album, *Metallic Attack* – that very same quartet of Bay Area fan-boys who arguably based their whole sound on wanting to out-Motörhead Motörhead. Unsurprisingly, Lemmy considered the honour dubious, grumbling, 'Of course, they poisoned it for us by giving us one for somebody else's song. We didn't get to go to the real Grammys cos we're distasteful. Us and the Mexican jazz bands all had to line up and get our stuff the previous afternoon.'

Lemmy could still shock his interlocutors from the media, it seemed. Though he didn't do himself any favours when Reuters UK quoted him as saying that Hermann Goering was 'the only one I admire at all', from the Third Reich, for establishing the Gestapo, accepting blame in the Nuremberg trials and committing suicide prior to the execution of his death sentence, which Lemmy was quoted as describing as 'fantastic'. Likewise, drawing parallels between 9/11 and the Second World War was not always received in the US with the intellectual detachment Lemmy felt it should.

'I think it's historically important that you remember that shit, because otherwise it'll get done to you again,' he told *Spin* magazine. 'I don't get any thanks when I tell Americans to put 9/11 into perspective. We did that to Berlin every night for three years during World War II, and 19,000 British were killed before lunchtime on the first day of the Battle of the Somme. Napoleon, the Confederates, Hitler – it's always the bad guys who have the best uniforms. The black hat beats the shit out of the white hat anytime. The Lone Ranger looked like a twat to me, with his little mask. I also collect Kinder Egg toys and skulls. I've got a dog and a pig skull and a couple of human ones. I've seen museums with less shit in them than I've got in my home.'

In his autobiography, *The Lost Gospels According to Al Jourgensen*, the Ministry frontman shared a story which revealed that Lemmy's Nazi fascinations occasionally went beyond strictly artefacts. Meeting up with Motörhead at a show in Austin, Texas, in 1995, Al recalled, 'I knocked [on Motörhead's] bus. No answer. So I open the fuckin' door and there's Lemmy in a complete full-on Gestapo uniform spanking a naked chick with a riding crop. She was loving it. So was he. I apologised and closed the door.'

Years later, another bit of play acting would land Lemmy in hot water when, in Germany, he posed for a photo shoot wearing a Nazi hat to promote Motörhead's performance at the upcoming Wacken Rocks Seaside Concert in Schleswig-Holstein, Germany, that July. As Mörat says in his friend's defence, 'One thing I'm not sure everyone got was his sense of humour. He had a wicked sense of humour. He had a very surreal and English sense of humour. Even though he moved to LA, he retained that Monty Python sense of humour.' Under German law, however, it is illegal to openly wear Nazi symbols, display Nazi banners or to even make Nazi gestures, as such conduct could be viewed as 'anti-constitutional propaganda' pursuant to articles 86 and 86a of the German penal code. Needless to say, no one saw the funny side of Lemmy's gesture and an investigation was launched but no action was taken, although the conflict thrust Lemmy into a broader global spotlight and, once again, he was asked to discuss his fascination with the Nazis.

'I don't only collect Nazi stuff,' he explained to *New York Waste*, 'I collect objects from all the Axis countries.

Also from countries who aren't even mentioned any more as former parts of the Axis, like Latvia, Lithuania, Estonia, Finland, Hungary.' It was a subject he would still find himself explaining over and over until his dying day. 'World War II was only just over my shoulder,' he told *Spin*, years later. 'Somebody gave me a flag and then a dagger. I don't know why they gave them to me, but that started me off with collecting. I learned that if I had known how much of this Nazi memorabilia there was to collect, I never would have started in the first place. It's crowding me out of my house. But it's a good hobby, because it's so recent, that period, that there's still plenty to collect. This was in the twentieth century so there's still all the good stuff. It's only a collection, it's not because I believe [in Nazism]. You do realise that, right?'

The year ended with one of Lemmy's most surreal episodes, when, at the invitation of a Conservative AM, William Graham, Lemmy addressed the Welsh Assembly regarding the dangers of heroin. In true rock'n'roll form, Lemmy promptly lit a cigarette inside the National Assembly, under AM Graham's assurance that it was permissible. Moments later, after a brusque reminder from security of the building's exception-free no-smoking policy, he stabbed out his smoke and made his way into the hall. Graham, in a spirited bid to unite with the country's disaffected youth, had quite obviously failed to vet Lemmy's remarks prior to delivery – a costly blunder that played out in spectacularly embarrassing fashion when Lemmy, wearing a black shirt buttoned mid-chest with a pack of Marlboro Reds poking out of the pocket, rattled off the dangers of heroin abuse, ultimately concluding that the only solution to the country's heroin epidemic was decriminalisation. Graham's face froze in icy chagrin, clearly as surprised as the room full of ministers and journalists in attendance, though not nearly as amused. Graham's mortification was rendered complete when, during a Q&A after the address, Lemmy was asked about politics, prompting the following response: 'I don't believe in any politics. If anything, I'm an anarchist.'

Some months later, Lemmy recounted the incident for *Decibel* magazine, stating, 'Some dummy Conservative trying to get the youth on his side, you know? Like he gives a fuck. I just spoke about what I thought they should know about the heroin problem. I figure they've been throwing police at it, right, for the last thirty years, and it's worse than ever. So that hasn't worked, has it? The only thing they haven't tried is legalising it and controlling it. Which, I mean, I hate the idea, but it's the only one I can think of. I've never done anything like that before, but it's just like any other audience, I suppose. And quite a few of the English papers reported it very favourably.'

Motörhead released *Kiss of Death* in 2006, reuniting with Cameron Webb and inviting glam metal refugee C. C. DeVille of Poison and Mike Inez of Alice in Chains as guests. Although the album rehashed the old playbook to the letter, fans and the metal press accepted it with swivel-eyed fervour. Discussing the songwriting approach for *Kiss of Death* and Motörhead's approach to confining innovation within the context of the band's ironclad sound, Lemmy explained, 'We're one of the few bands that never let you down. We've been true right through. We've never had a plan of any kind, we just played the music we like. We don't like people telling us what to do: "Get your hair cut, it's out of fashion." Fuck off! How does that sound? There's that much of the Northerner in me still. I don't like being told what to do by grotty Southerners: "What the fuck do you know about it? You sit on your arse all day listening to opinion polls." I just wanted to be the MC5 basically. But two of them bailed and we became the MC3. Us against the world, mate.'

Lemmy's heroic mythology would expand in the spring of 2010 with the premiere of his own documentary, affectionately referred to as 'The Lemmy Movie'. Released in March 2010 and directed by Greg Olliver and Wes Orshoski, *Lemmy: 49% Motherf**ker, 51% Son of a Bitch* followed the archetypal rockumentary format of stitching together years of live and archival footage with contemporary interviews with recognisable talking heads such as Ozzy Osbourne, members of Metallica and Slash, as well as Peter Hook (Joy Division, New Order), Marky Ramone (the Ramones) and former Hawkwind band-mates Nik Turner, Dave Brock and, rather sweetly, Stacia. 'I kept saying no to the director,' she tells me. 'But Lemmy kept giving me full glasses of vodka so in the end I just talked.'

Lemmy seemed to view the finished film from his usual stoic perspective. 'I think he enjoyed it,' says Mörat. 'He always told me he had no complaints about it, really. Other than the state of his apartment.'

Commentary from actor Billy Bob Thornton and rapper/ actor Ice-T underscored Lemmy's genre-crossing appeal. That and the cinéma vérité scenes of Lemmy playing Xbox or making French fries at his small, cramped abode, investing his mythology with an almost elegiac sense of ordinariness that cast the film as an affectionate portrait of one of music's last living lions in the autumn of his life. Notably, no one voiced any disappointment at the utterly mundane and, in some places, lonely aspects of Lemmy's off-tour life; quite the opposite, such footage only bolstered his legend, reinforcing that, for the denim-and-leather masses, Lemmy was always 'one of us', while radiating an ineffable charisma that captivated attentions far beyond the sweaty circle pits of the concert halls.

Whether on the road or at home in Hollywood, Lemmy may have been getting older but he still liked to hint at a sex life that harkened back to those halcyon days of the early Seventies, when wild backstage trysts with anonymous, doe-eyed groupies were not simply the spoils of war, but widely considered as inextricably part of a music career as singing or playing an instrument. And while Lemmy would never be confused with a Calvin Klein model, he offered unassailable proof that sex appeal was simply a state of mind. When one journalist asked why he never underwent plastic surgery to remove his moles, Lemmy replied, 'Cos I don't give a fuck. After all, you're lookin' at 'em and I'm not short of birds!'

His own admitted estimates were jaw-dropping; he once stated, 'There was a magazine in England who said I screwed 2000 women and I didn't, I said 1000. When you think about it, it isn't that unreasonable. I'm not even married, and I've been doing this since I was sixteen. And I'm now sixty-six, so that's like fifty years. I could've done more if I'd tried, I guess. I didn't even fool myself with that. My father was a stranger to me, and I learned that my stepfather was fighting a losing battle with my mother. Almost everyone is unhappy with themselves when they realise what they've done. And the lot of them get married because of the kids and that's a really bad idea. People just rip each other to shreds over the years. Nothing kills a relationship like commitment.'

Lemmy then added, 'It might be up to 2000 by now. Between sex and drugs and rock'n'roll, I might put rock'n'roll first, but sex would be a very close second. Rock'n'roll is only a means to get more sex. But I don't chase as much these days. When you're younger, you'll sell your soul to the devil for some pussy, but you get over that. You don't have to be special to get my interest now.'

Asked if he ever hoped to find a real, lasting love, Lemmy replied, 'Doesn't everybody? But falling in love is terrible. It makes you act foolish, like an idiot. You sign your life over when you fall in love, and it's awful, it's torture. You end up walking past their house at night and looking up longingly at their window . . . Who wants to live like that?' Such jadedness was, of course, rooted in more than a few heartbreaks along the way, fuelling a voracious fear of abandonment. 'Women always left me because I wouldn't commit,' he said, 'but then nothing changes a relationship like commitment. If you move in with someone, you lose all respect for them. All them dirty knickers on the towel rail, all that snorting and farting. Does that appeal to you? Because it doesn't to me. When you first start dating someone, it's all about being on your best behaviour, and that initial magic. I never wanted the magic to stop.'

When one reporter committed the unpardonable error of suggesting that Lemmy's heroic libidinous excesses might include bisexual escapades, Lemmy's response was swift and merciless. 'I didn't threaten him. I just said it would be difficult for him to kneel down and get his floppy disk with a screwdriver through both knees. He said, yeah, he could really see that problem, and he hoped it wouldn't arise.' He laughed. Hack, hack, hack. 'The next day there was an apology on the internet. I'll tell you what, though, man, if it was somebody who couldn't have fought back, that bastard could've ruined somebody's life for ever. They could've lost their job, their wife, the whole fuckin' movie, you know? Seeing as how I've got no family axe to grind, it didn't hurt me, but he could've fucked somebody's life completely just for being a smart cunt on the internet. I should've done his knees anyway, even after the apology.'

Behind the biker bravado, in reality Lemmy managed to keep a fairly steady American girlfriend – Cheryl Keuleman – mostly hidden from public view for over the last two decades of his life. As Mörat observes, 'They had, I wouldn't say a troubled relationship, but she had quite a lot to put up with in some ways. But they were together for twenty years, on and off. He'd write songs for her, every now and again. "In the Black" [from *Inferno*] is about his girlfriend. I didn't know that until years later. It was kind of funny because his girlfriend was black. Cheryl deserves a lot more credit than she gets. She was seen as the girlfriend but she was with him for twenty years and at the end she looked after him a lot. He was seriously fucking ill.'

Mörat first met Lemmy in 1981 as a snotty 20-something punk rocker, following Motörhead around England on his motorbike. Once Lemmy heard that Mörat was following the band across the English countryside in the dead of winter, he put him on the band's permanent guest list, ensuring that food and drink awaited Mörat at every stop. These days a successful writer and photographer living in Los Angeles, he would forge a powerful and enduring friendship with Lemmy over the next three decades that would see the two of them living half a block away from each other in LA, killing many an afternoon in Lemmy's apartment listening to music over drinks and watching the History Channel. Despite their friendship, there was one thing Lemmy refused to do for his good friend. 'He refused to marry me,' Mörat laughs. 'Not in that way – he was an ordained minister but he wouldn't do marriages. He said he'd do deaths, but he wasn't going to do marriages.'

Strange but true, Lemmy, the man who right up to the end professed to 'dislike religion quite intensely', claiming that if there was a god he must be 'senile like George III', had been ordained as a minister – online.

As he laughingly recalled, 'Yeah, it's funny, isn't it? This guy wanted me to marry him and his girlfriend at the Rainbow. He's ex-Special Forces, so that might be something to do with it. He got me ordained on the internet into this Church of Universal Peace or something so I'm the Reverend Lemmy Kilmister.'

Motörhead's next notable album, *The Wörld Is Yours*, was initially included as a bonus with issues of *Classic Rock* magazine before the album's formal worldwide release, in

January 2011, via their own label, Motörhead Music. Funnelling the trademark Motörhead sound into pummelling condemnations of global greed ('Brotherhood of Man'), death ('I Know How to Die') and, of course, bad, bad women ('Bye Bye Bitch Bye Bye'), this was Motörhead as any self-respecting 15-year-old rebel might wish them to be. Reflecting on the theme of death in 'I Know How to Die', though, Lemmy was in more sombre mood. 'In your twenties, you think you are immortal. In your thirties, you hope you are immortal. In your forties, you just pray it doesn't hurt too much, and by the time you reach my age, you become convinced that, well, it could be just around the corner. Do I think about death a lot? It's difficult not to when you're sixty-five, son.'

Commercially the album reached a wider, and possibly younger, audience, claiming the No. 1 spot on the UK's Official Rock & Metal Albums chart, edging out new material from contemporary heavy-hitters such as Pearl Jam and Muse, as well as collections from Led Zeppelin and the Foo Fighters. The album also reached No. 4 on Billboard's Top Hard Rock Albums chart. No longer seen as brutish reprobates, Motörhead had now evolved into standard-bearers of the heavy metal culture – regardless of Lemmy's insistence that they were never heavy metal, just 'a fucking good rock'n'roll band'. From the thoroughly over-the-top War Pig logo to the steroidal gusts of speed freak rock that dominated their every release, Motörhead now stood shoulder-to-shoulder with Metallica, Slayer and the newer members of heavy metal's pantheon of golden gods, if not in sales, then surely in stature.

The Noughties would also see Lemmy's stature solidify as a kindly, if curmudgeonly grandfather figure in rock'n'roll. Terms like 'gentleman' were now woven into seemingly every interview, due largely to Lemmy's ineffable candour and good manners. The days of the chest-beating hellion, menacing the British countryside with bikers, speed freaks and other triptonauts were now dwindling in the rear-view mirror. Chatting amiably about history, music or mortality, it became harder and harder to see the wild-eyed thug who was deported from Finland and scolded by an airline pilot as a disgrace to England. For the first time in six decades, your daughters were safe around Lemmy. Instead, you'd regularly find him playing his fruit machine at the back bar of the Rainbow, gamely posing for social media photos with 20-something girls, starry-eyed metal-heads and passing tourists looking for a brush with fame.

A goodly bit of this was due to mounting health problems that had as much to do with age as with a lifetime of 60 cigarettes a day, a bottle of Jack Daniel's to go with them and three grams of speed. Though he was diagnosed with Type 2 diabetes in 2000, his unwavering dedication to his beloved vices charged on. Even in 2006, Lemmy boasted that his steady diet of booze and drugs left him remarkably unscathed, insisting, 'I got checked over in Berlin two weeks ago and my doctor said I have the liver of a newborn baby. That's some justice, isn't it, eh? I'm sure everybody who's switched to fucking nut cutlets is really pissed off by that. I don't do anything to keep in shape. I eat junk food, I drink all day, I still take speed. What the fuck. I think the secret is you find out which bits work for you, and then do only them. Don't fuck with the programme. Everybody I ever knew who went on heroin or downers then fucked up. They were asleep when the phone call came. I much prefer to see my enemies coming, even if they are imaginary.'

This, though, was a Lemmy full of defensive bravado – the young man whistling as he walks through the cemetery. Unfortunately, Lemmy the older man's problems were now to begin in earnest.

One bright spot was the blossoming relationship that Lemmy enjoyed with his son, Paul Inder, a musician and producer based in Los Angeles. 'Great guitarist and piano player, too,' Lemmy would boast. He had missed the first six years of Paul's life ('Have you ever changed a diaper?' Lemmy would remonstrate with anyone foolish enough to try and pull him up on this. 'It's rotten. As a lifestyle, it sucks. I could never imagine looking at the same face over the cornflakes for the rest of my life. I don't know how people do it'), but Lemmy and Paul forged a profoundly close bond, spending time at Lemmy's flat, at gigs and of course, at the Rainbow, where the two began and recovered from many a joyfully noisy father–son bender.

In his latter years, in fact, Lemmy sometimes spoke of having 'half a kid' in France, explaining, 'Me and my roadie went with this girl one night and the next night . . . I was young. I was a fool. Anyway she's called it Lemmy, but it has glasses like, so I'm not sure. And it speaks only French. I met him when he was about eight. He didn't look like me. But then he didn't look like Graham either. Maybe it was a third party. Under cover of darkness.'

There was also Lemmy's rockabilly side project, The Head Cat, a three-piece featuring Lemmy on acoustic guitar and harmonica alongside The Stray Cats' drummer, Slim Jim Phantom, and multi-instrumentalist Danny B. Harvey, of The Rockats (mashing the three feeder bands together to derive their name). Lemmy had first met Slim Jim in 1980, when The Stray Cats had moved to London, joining them onstage a couple of times during that period. The Head Cat was fun on those nights on the town in LA, but their 2006 album *Fool's Paradise* was actually something of an embarrassment. Presented as a hip-shaking backyard blowout of barrelhouse jams and rockabilly classics like Carl Perkins's 'Matchbox', Johnny Cash's 'Big River' and Buddy Holly tracks like 'Not Fade Away' and 'Well . . . All Right', all it really did was highlight Lemmy's now wincingly shaky voice and the lowering of whatever quality control he'd once possessed in the heyday of both Hawkwind and Motörhead, ultimately pleasing neither hardcore Motörhead fans nor genuine lovers of rockabilly.

A 2011 follow-up called *Walk the Walk . . . Talk the Talk* was much better, broadening the scope to include two Lemmy/Phantom originals in 'American Beat' and 'The Eagles Flies on Friday', both of which were good enough to have been used on any Motörhead album from the same period – and concentrating covers less on rockabilly classics and more on the kind of stone cold rock'n'roll floor-fillers Lemmy could sing in his sleep, like Chuck Berry's 'Let It Rock', Eddie Cochran's 'Something Else' and, most affectingly, Robert Johnson's 'Crossroads'. More fun than any Motörhead album in recent memory, the end result was still the same: puzzlement from metal fans, indifference from the mainstream.

Lemmy was happy, though, taking the trio out on the American road – a welcome respite from the strictures of tour life with Motörhead, where the set had now evolved into a tightly orchestrated production of Motör-highlights. Lemmy still insisted on including material from whatever the band's latest album was, but it was now generally accepted that what most people in his audience – mainly metal kids young enough to be his grandchildren – were coming to see was the legend playing his greatest hits.

In 2011, doctors diagnosed Lemmy with a dangerous arrhythmia, requiring the implantation of a cardioverter-defibrillator into his chest. Lemmy's PR team did a good job of managing the news by making it sound like Lemmy was having a fairly standard procedure, like fixing a broken bone. In fact, ICDs are only fitted in people with dangerously abnormal heart rhythms. That is, those with significant risk of dying from heart failure or stroke. Lemmy made a joke of it, telling *Rolling Stone* that after the surgery he had cut back to one alcoholic drink a day, eventually switching from Jack-and-Cokes to vodka and orange juice. That, though, had been in response to his diabetic condition, and would have had little or no impact on his blood-sugar levels. The heart surgery was something else. His doctors warned him that if he did not quit smoking, he would die. His response: a promise to try and cut down to one pack of cigarettes a week. Something he hardly, if ever, kept to, no more than he did his promise of just one alcoholic drink a day. The drinking and smoking and drugging had been such an enormous part of his identity, professionally and personally, that he simply couldn't separate them in his mind from the day-to-day normalities of life. He told one journalist, 'I've been smoking since I was eleven, so I wasn't really looking forward to putting out my final cigarette. [But] I faced it like a real man – no plasters or pills, just cold turkey. I feared I'd have all kinds of side effects, but I didn't notice anything.' In reality, the old stager was struggling.

When Eddie Clarke, whose own health had also taken a pummelling due to his years in Motörhead ('I've had some trouble with my heart, some stents were put in. I'm on blood pressure pills and I've got emphysema through smoking. They've discovered that I've got prostate problems as well, so I'm also on pills for that. I quit the cigs in 2008, though I still have the odd reefer. The drinking stopped in 1989 because I didn't feel the need to go back to it . . .'), got word of the seriousness of Lemmy's condition he began phoning him. 'I called Lemmy every couple of weeks to see how he was doing. He'd been in hospital and he'd knocked it all on the head. I remember one conversation, he said, "Fucking hell, man! I'm fucking drinking water!" When I asked why he replied, "My kidneys have gone." He's on heart pills and he's got diabetes, when you get older these things creep up on you. He was moaning on but I thought to myself, well, he's obviously having a stab at it. If I'm honest, though, I didn't ever see Lemmy quitting the things that he loved so much, the things that were killing him. But he did [albeit temporarily] and it surprised me. He even gave up smoking for a while. He was back on the cigarettes in the end, though.'

LEMMY

A few months later he suffered a hematoma. His veins and arteries were now splitting open, sending clotted blood leaking into tissues where it does not belong. A tiny drop can cause pain and swelling. A more significant leakage can cause serious clot formations in the body, inviting stroke or even death.

Lemmy's bravado could no longer shield him from the brutal truth. As he told a Dutch journalist, 'During my last surgery I was close to death. It was the only moment I was stalked by the devil called doubt. I wondered if I'd make it. I'm not afraid of death – I often sing about it. So I wasn't shaking in my bed, but I did have the feeling I wasn't done yet. I still wanted to do shows and make records. That feeling pulled me through all this.'

On daily medication now for the rest of his life, Lemmy was finding it increasingly difficult to walk or even stand for prolonged periods, and Motörhead's next serious tour, a run of American arenas on the 2012 *Gigantour*, with Megadeth, Volbeat and Lacuna Coil, was cut short by four dates when a viral upper-respiratory infection and voice strain conspired to put him off his feet again. Official cause: severe laryngitis. The band announced the cancellation on Facebook, stating, 'We want to sincerely apologise . . . We would never miss a chance to play for our fans unless it was impossible. And in this case, it was.' Lemmy was quoted as saying, 'I'm giving my voice a good rest, and will be better than ever for our shows on the Mayhem tour this summer. Hope to see you all there!' Nice, hopeful words written for him by his ever faithful PR, Ute Kromrey.

If Lemmy was growing tired of questions about his

health, the death of Würzel in July 2011 would only inspire more speculation surrounding his own encroaching mortality. Würzel's death from heart disease at the age of 61 would affect Lemmy on a deep and profound level. Lemmy released another press statement saying, this time in his own words, 'Wurzel was my friend and my brother and he's never going to laugh with me again or bitch me out or do . . . anything. And that truly and cosmically SUCKS. RIP Wurz. Godspeed. Good man.'

Motörhead began recording their next studio album in February 2013, originally scheduled for a mid-year release, though it wouldn't be until October that *Aftershock* would finally see the light of day. Once again, while the sonic elements remained predictable, the delivery of the 14 bone-shaking tracks sounded familiar and yet somehow just out of reach. With so many killer Motörhead classics now available at the tap of an iPhone, on YouTube, on Spotify, on iTunes, *Aftershock* would become just another tour souvenir. As was the case now with all the bands from the classic rock era. It sold more than 11,000 copies in its first week of release in America, and practically nothing after that, and the year would end with more show cancellations, Lemmy's on-going ill-health forcing the postponement of a series of dates with Saxon. Another press statement was issued in Lemmy's name: 'I have to sadly let you know that Motörhead has had to postpone the forthcoming European tour until early next year, 2014. We have made the decision because I am not quite ready to hit the road yet, and am working my way back to full fitness and rude health.'

Lemmy now needed a walking stick to get about. 'As long

as I can walk the few yards from the back to the front of the stage without a stick,' he told the *Guardian*, he would continue to perform. 'Or even if I do have to use a stick.' Others reported seeing him ambling about backstage at festivals on a mobility scooter, a sad comedown from the iron horses he had once ridden so proudly. The wonder was that he allowed the Motörhead machine to keep on going. As Doug Smith observes, 'It's not like he needed the money any more. The others probably did though.'

Mörat describes the toll on his old friend as 'massive', explaining, 'He'd try and hide it a lot, or at least he'd try to be stronger than he was but you could tell. His hands had started to shake. One time I came in and he said, "I'm sorry you have to see me like this", and I was like, "Mate, we're fucking friends. It doesn't matter to me. I mean, it does, but not in *that* way." But it definitely affected him. He felt like he was letting people down if he cancelled a gig. He had fucking two weeks off after his heart operation and went straight back out on tour. I wasn't alone in telling him he should cancel it, but he was very aware that people had planned for the shows. Some bands will cancel a show if one of the guys breaks a fucking fingernail but Lemmy was always very aware that people had saved up for his shows and that they had planned travel and such.'

As cancellations and doctor visits increased in tandem, more and more interviewers raised the imminence of death, which Lemmy fielded with typical matter-of-factness, though it was sometimes hard to tell if that was the Lemmy persona speaking or if he authentically embraced both the past and his uncertain future with equal acceptance. Asked by *Classic Rock* if he harboured any regrets over his hard living, in view of the physical damage it seemed to have caused, Lemmy demurred, stating, 'I don't do regrets. Regrets are pointless. It's too late for regrets. You've already done it, haven't you? You've lived your life. No point wishing you could change it. There are a couple of things I might have done differently, but nothing major; nothing that would have made that much of a difference. I'm pretty happy with the way things have turned out. I like to think I've brought a lot of joy to a lot of people all over the world. I'm true to myself and I'm straight with people.'

Of his looming mortality, Lemmy simply said, 'Death is an inevitability, isn't it? You become more aware of that when you get to my age. I don't worry about it. I'm ready for it. When I go, I want to go doing what I do best. If I died tomorrow, I couldn't complain. It's been good.'

More cancellations followed. In February 2014, the band scratched a European tour due they said to severe complications with Lemmy's diabetes. The band's statement read, 'Many concerted, diligent and focused efforts were made by founding member, and international icon Lemmy Kilmister to deal with a range of health issues relating to diabetes. While there has been undoubted progress, Lemmy and the band were advised by doctors that it was still too soon to resume full touring activities, and so for the good of the future, the band and Lemmy reluctantly agreed to cancel.'

It went on: 'No one is hurting more over this than Lemmy, and he feels the aggravation and inconvenience of every ticket, and every method of transportation, already paid for by loyal fans in anticipation of the tour. Being a road warrior of over 50 dedicated, non-stop years, it is equally distressing for him to be unable to occupy the top lounge of the trusty tour bus (his spiritual home) but Lemmy recognises that his long-term health must win. It goes without saying that Lemmy profusely apologises for inconveniences caused, but he does want everyone to know that he is continuing on the road to a full recovery, and that the prognosis long term is very good.'

Discussing the increasingly grave developments with Lemmy's health, Motörhead's long-time manager, Todd Singerman, told *Decibel* magazine, '[Lemmy's] been up and down. He's got a really bad diabetic problem, and it changes on a daily basis. A lot of it is just fighting the bad habits, the things that he's not supposed to do any more. He's stopped smoking, but he probably sneaks Jack and Coke here and there. He'd be lying to you if he said he stopped. He's been trying to substitute it with wine, and I'm sure he's slowed down on the speed. He thinks wine's better than Jack, but it's still got tons of sugar, you know? He doesn't grasp that he's just trading one demon for the other. That was the compromise with the doctors, by the way – trade the Jack for the wine. But he doesn't tell them he's drinking two fucking bottles, either. These are the battles we're up against. Keep in mind he's been doing all this stuff on a daily basis since Hendrix. And it's coming to roost. It's sad for him, because he's gotten away with this stuff for all this time.

'I made them cancel [last fall's European tour], because Lemmy's not ready,' Singerman continued. 'He didn't wanna cancel. But what was gonna go down is what happened in Europe over the summer. See, he fucked up in Europe. He was supposed to rest for three months, and he refused. He ended up doing that show [Wacken Open Air in August 2013], which he wasn't supposed to do, and it ended up being 105 degrees out there. He's playing direct in the fucking sun. The only thing I'm proud of him for is stopping when it didn't feel good. That was smart of him. The bottom line is that he needs to find a balance and then live that balance for a few months. But we can't find the balance yet. He has great days and then he fucks it up. And when you fuck up, you go backwards.'

While Lemmy now generally refused to discuss his own prodigious drug habits in interviews, he continued using speed through all his worst days. Mörat recalls, 'He was still taking speed at the end as well. He cut down on it a lot, obviously, because we used to do massive amounts . . . well, *he* used to do massive amounts and I used to do small amounts and get the same effect. It was like rocket fuel that stuff. Like proper stuff, you'd be up for three days. I asked him about it towards the end. I said, "I'm glad you stopped doing that", and he said, "No, no! I haven't stopped doing that. I just do less of it." I said, "Why are you still doing it?" and he said, "Because it makes me happy."'

Though the early-2014 dates were set aside, Motörhead confirmed slots in the two weekends of the Coachella Valley Music and Arts Festival, held every April in the arid California desert, three hours southeast of Los Angeles. Traditionally a hipster-infested, cross-genre celebration of alt-rock, pop and hip hop, the festival rarely ceded more than a handful of slots to heavy music, though past years had featured the likes of Tool, Queens of the Stone Age, the Mars Volta, Rage Against the Machine and Nine Inch Nails – stadium-friendly super-rock acts who had managed the feat of achieving mainstream success while concurrently finding acceptance in the underground rock community. To accommodate fans, the festival occurs over two consecutive weekends, which invariably sees the local clubs ablaze with 'secret shows' in the four days between.

But if the teen-bangers and art-stoners in the desert found themselves agape at the three ageing figures who took the stage in the Mojave tent, they caught on quickly, as mosh pits opened up and the energy reached feverish heights while the band ran through their arsenal of classics. Lemmy's son Paul joined the band for a number, and on both weekends Slash joined the band for 'Ace of Spades', to the noisy approval of the sweaty desert legion. 'Don't forget us now,' Lemmy called out towards the end of the set. 'We are fucking Motörhead and we play rock'n'roll.'

Though hardly approaching the backbreaking pace of previous years, the band then played a run of dates through Europe and a handful of dates in the US that summer. In September, they also held the first annual Motörhead's Motörboat cruise, in the tradition of similar heavy metal-themed cruises such as Shiprocked and 70,000 Tons of Metal. The promoter Alan Koenig, whose company, Ask4 Entertainment, produces such cruises and who organised the first Motörboat, recalls, 'Motörhead had expressed interest to their booking agent, TKO, about doing a cruise, so [they] reached out to me and I said, "I'm in!" They came up with the name "Motörhead's Motörboat". How could you call it anything else, really?'

Joined by Anthrax and Megadeth, the cruise set sail from Miami, making stops in Key West and Mexico, while at night the bands would play loose, free-flowing sets in the most chilled-out of environments. Ever a creature of habit, Lemmy spent much of his days in the ship's casino, pumping cash into the fruit machine. 'The first Motörboat in 2014,' Alan recalled, 'Lemmy won quite a bit of money! I don't remember the total, but I remember that he did very well at the slot machine.'

Elsewhere, however, the odds were now heavily stacked against him.

TEN

I Have Never Drunk Milk

On Christmas Eve, 2014, the old, now-ailing warrior turned 69. His plans were the same as they had been for the last few years: to head off to Las Vegas for a few days, play the slot machines and check out the chicks. Some things, though, were now different. Having swapped Jack Daniel's and Coke for vodka and orange, he was now dutifully doing his best to stick to wine. Of course, it would have been much better for Lemmy to drink nothing at all, but as he'd joked in the past with me, 'I don't mind living longer. I just don't want it to *seem* longer.' The thought of going through a day and night without at least something to help him on his way he considered intolerable and, moreover, grossly unfair. Nevertheless, he'd been spending less and less time in the Rainbow recently, sometimes going only twice a week.

The rest of the world might still have preferred to think of Lemmy as somehow immortal, but the man himself knew he wasn't. Fast approaching his eighth decade, and beset by aches, pains and more serious ailments, he knew he had to make some serious lifestyle changes, however grudgingly. 'Getting old is the worst thing that can happen to anybody,' he told *Metal Hammer*. 'I don't recommend it. It's no fun waking up in hospital.'

The very last time I spoke to Lemmy, during a fleeting promotional visit to London, the mood was reflective, sombre. He was flying back to LA the next morning. 'I've got to water my plants, man. Cos they never get watered enough. I might have a dead vine, who knows?' I asked if, as he got older, his relationship to God had changed at all. He looked at me, was I taking the piss? No. I meant in a spiritual sense, not a religious one. He puffed out his cheeks. 'They say God moves in mysterious ways. Well, it's too fucking mysterious for me, buddy. How about solving a few of them fucking mysteries for once. Oh, we have to take what God says . . . WHY?' he shouted. 'I don't like him! I think he's a sadistic fucking maniac! How's that? Or he's out of the office whenever we call, you know? God, you know, big deal. Spelled backwards is dog.'

He had always been a loner. At this time of his life though, did he ever think he might prefer to have someone share his bed on a more permanent basis? I expected another look. But this time he was more thoughtful.

'Well, it didn't work out that way for me, you know. Cos I always felt . . .' Pause. 'A set, a concert, lasts for an hour and a half. Sex is what, half an hour at most. The concert won. And also, I've never been able to find a girl that would stop me chasing all the others. If I do, I would be only too happy to stop chasing girls. But I never found it, yeah? And I'm not gonna get married and *lie*. And then run around. Cos I'm an honest man. If I get married to somebody I will never chase another woman. But I haven't found it yet.

'These guys get married then run around on the day of their wedding, for Christ's sake, don't they, some of them. Fuck that, what's that? It's just poor. To be politically correct and have a wife of a certain age so she can stand next to you and welcome the fucking guests. Balls, I'd rather hire a hooker. "Hello, baby, dress up good and come on over. We gotta welcome some guests!"'

I asked him which of the many Motörhead albums he would play to anyone who had never heard his music and being Lemmy he immediately named his newest few. No mention of *Overkill* or *Bomber*. He was still professing the superiority of the final Campbell–Dee line-up over the classic Clarke–Taylor one, even though Motörhead still ended their shows with 'Ace of Spades' each night. Still elicited the greatest reaction from their faithful audiences with all the 'classics'.

At the end of the day, he said, he liked 'brutal' music. And the current band was simply faster, more full-on – he said.

'I'm not a brutal man but I like brutal music. It's good for you, it helps to take you out of that safe cocoon you've got for yourself, you know. What do you want *safe* rock'n'roll for, man? What the fuck is it for? Rock'n'roll was supposed to be rebellion with no apparent goal. It's just rebellion for the sake of it, because it pisses your parents off. If your mother says she likes it there's something wrong with it, it's not rock'n'roll. It's true, though, isn't it? Who the fuck wants your mother to come and listen to it with you? "Oh, I like them harmonies!" Let me play you this one, Mum. "Oh, that's a terrible noise!" You know?

'The trouble with now is everybody's hip. Everybody's hip. The delivery boy, the fucking greengrocer, everybody's hip now. Cos they've all been through some sort of rock'n'roll lifestyle. But it's easily penetrable, isn't it? Say, "How about *this*?" They go, "Oh! It's too loud!" Traitor! Counter-revolutionary! String him up! The guillotine! The Inquisition, the Voice of Christ. We'll kill your immortal soul. Why? In order to make you live in heaven we've got to burn you at the stake now. "Oh, that sounds good, yeah. It's a fair cop . . ."'

Lemmy may have eased back on the hard living, but his dedication to his greatest love and most steadfast addiction – Motörhead – was as intense as ever. In February, the band entered Grandmaster Recorders studio on North Cahuenga Boulevard in Hollywood to start work on their twenty-second album, to be titled *Bad Magic*, and once again with Cameron Webb as producer. According to Mikkey Dee, the trio approached it with deliberate spontaneity. Rather than writing the songs before they entered the studio, this time they plugged in and simply played spontaneously in the room. 'We kind of recorded it live, right away, as we had the song,' said the drummer.

Musically, the album crackled with energy. The volatile opener 'Victory or Die', the high-voltage biker blast 'Electricity', the thunderously grooving 'The Devil' (featuring a guest appearance from Queen's Brian May) and their respectful, if unremarkable, cover of the Stones' 'Sympathy for the Devil' were built-by-numbers Motörhead, the sort of thing they had been blasting out for the previous 40 years, in the best possible way.

But Lemmy's voice was another matter. Webb's on-the-nose production couldn't quite paper over his vocal frailties. While it was still recognisably, undeniably Lemmy, the singer's firepower was no longer the unholy force of nature it was even two years before on *Aftershock*. Most startling of all was 'Till the End', a subdued but striking semi-ballad that found Lemmy laying his cards on the table. *In my years my life has changed*, he intoned hoarsely but defiantly, *I can't turn back the time, I can tell just what made me change*. It sounded for all the world like a lament by a man who knew his time was running out. But then Lemmy always was a realist. 'You wanna live for ever?' he taunted. 'I don't, not with my health. I mean, I wrote 'I Know How to Die' [from *The Wörld is Yours*], but I wrote that before I got bad.' Still, it wasn't all doom and gloom – at least not how Lemmy told it. 'I don't think it's affected me much, because I was always pretty doomy anyway – war and death, the usual subjects. Somehow on this one I've written a lot about being locked up, so I don't know if that's a portent of anything.'

He began to speculate openly about how his health issues now affected his playing. 'They have a little bit,' he admitted, 'but I can play fast. The fast ones are the easy ones – there's only a couple of notes! I can still play all right, touch wood.' Then he admitted with a shrug, 'No, I can't play for much longer.'

'When I was working on [a] feature about their new album, I went to the studio one day and he was fine,' says Mörat, 'just knocking out tunes and stuff. We didn't finish the interview so I went round to his house the next day and he was just really ill. He looked like he'd aged thirty years overnight. Then he'd bounce back again. That was why they had trouble booking tours, because one day he was great, strutting around with that Lemmy strut and the next day he was basically an old man.'

It was hard to escape the air of finality that surrounded *Bad Magic* – something that wasn't helped in April, when the band cancelled an appearance at the Monsters of Rock festival in São Paulo, Brazil, alongside old mates Ozzy Osbourne and Judas Priest, just a few hours before they were due to take the stage. It was reported that Lemmy was suffering from gastric distress and dehydration, and had been hospitalised once more.

As in the previous two years, the 2015 cancellations sparked more worries about the state of his health and questions in the media about whether he should be out on the road. He was discharged from hospital a few days later, but sadly it wouldn't be the last time Motörhead had to pull shows. Despite their frontman's travails, the Motör-machine rolled on regardless. In early June, the imminent release of the new album, *Bad Magic*, was announced, together with what was being billed as their fortieth-anniversary tour. Inevitable speculation suggested that this would be their swansong, though Lemmy emphatically denied it.

The tour would kick off in August, though not before another strength-sapping sweep through the European festival circuit, including an unlikely appearance on the main Pyramid Stage at the Glastonbury Festival in Somerset, the big daddy of the British festival scene, where Motörhead were an unlikely addition to the bill. That year's festival featured everyone from Kanye West to Lionel Ritchie, via The Who, Paul Weller and rodent-masked rave upstart deadmau5. But with a 200,000-strong crowd and a TV audience in the millions, it was a chance for Lemmy to remind the world that Motörhead were still alive and kicking in 2015, and he was damned if he wasn't going to take it. Along with the hefty fee that went with it.

Their early-evening set on Friday, 26 June, was an object lesson in ear-splitting rock'n'roll to a crowd more used to the baroque dramatics of that evening's headliners, Florence and the Machine (who had themselves stepped in for original bill-toppers the Foo Fighters after Dave Grohl broke his leg falling from a stage in Sweden). Lemmy looked small and frail on the vast Pyramid Stage, but 'Ace of Spades' again came to his rescue, the sort of timeless anthem that everyone from 16 to 60 now knew and whose chorus they could sing along to.

The only really shaky moment came when the band launched into 'Overkill' immediately after 'Ace of Spades', only for Lemmy to repeat the lyrics to the latter. 'It was a mental block,' he said afterwards. 'I've sung those songs so many times. First time I've ever sung "Ace of Spades" to it, though. We did it the night before and it was fucking terrible, and I swore I'd never do it again. But we did. Obviously.' An embarrassing YouTube video of the event eventually had its audio track removed for 'copyright' reasons. Though you can still find hundreds of clips of them doing 'Ace of Spades' and 'Overkill' elsewhere on YouTube, including one from the Resurrection Festival in Spain just three weeks after Glastonbury. Lemmy's blushes, it seems, were to be spared. Though not enough, apparently, for anyone to persuade him to call off the tour. To go home perhaps and enjoy what time he had left.

Two months after Glastonbury, on 28 August, *Bad Magic* was released. Critically, it received glowing reviews from sources as disparate as the long-running rock magazine *Kerrang!*, the *Boston Globe* and British broadsheet the *Guardian*. Commercially, it was their biggest hit in years, giving them their first Top 10 hit in Britain since *Iron Fist* more than 30 years before. It also hit No. 1 in France and Germany. From the outside looking in, Motörhead's career was in robust health again.

Sadly, the same thing couldn't be said for their leader. The US leg of Motörhead's fortieth-anniversary tour started in Riverside, California, on 19 August and was set to run through to 25 September. On the road with them were their friends Saxon and upcoming US rockers Crobot. Things started to go wrong almost immediately. A week into the tour, performing at The Complex in Salt Lake City, Lemmy suddenly left the stage after just three songs. According to onlookers, both Mikkey Dee and a crew member rushed to check on him, while Phil Campbell asked the audience to 'give us a minute, all right?'

Ten minutes later, Lemmy was back on stage. 'Sorry about that, I'm old,' he joked, then added ominously: 'I don't know how long I can do this. Sorry, guys.' They managed just one more song before he left the stage again, complaining he had problems breathing. This time he didn't come back.

Motörhead's team quickly sprang into action. In a Facebook post, they explained that Salt Lake City's high altitude was the cause of the problems. 'He feels very bad to have cut the show short, but being that high up, he had some trouble breathing well,' said the post. 'Lemmy appreciates everyone's concern. The fans always rally round!'

The following night's appearance in Denver was cancelled, prompting a conciliatory quip from management: 'The Rocky Mountain High has affected Lemmy ... It's been quite a while since [he] was this "high" in the US.' Ha, yeah.

The tour was scheduled to restart in Austin, Texas, two days later. But their problems were far from over. Once again, Lemmy was forced to cut the show short just a minute into the third song, 'Metropolis'. He returned to the microphone, using a cane for support, and apologised for not being able to continue. If anyone wasn't concerned for his well-being before, they were now.

Motörhead's camp released yet another statement, announcing the cancellation of further shows: 'This is a direct follow-on from the altitude issues in Colorado, and clearly, Lemmy tried to get back at it too quickly. Lemmy will resume duties the moment he is properly rested and firing on all cylinders again.' What they didn't tell people was that Lemmy wasn't even sound-checking or doing interviews. 'He couldn't do anything,' his manager, Todd Singerman, later told *Rolling Stone*.

It would be a full week before they returned to the stage, this time in St Louis on 8 September. Management claimed that Lemmy had been diagnosed with 'a lung infection (exacerbated by that Denver altitude) which has now been taken care of'. Something certainly seemed to have been fixed. Motörhead – and Lemmy – made it to the end of their 13-song set. When they finished, Phil Campbell raised Lemmy's hand in the air in triumph. As a video of the gig posted on YouTube shows, it was a genuinely moving moment.

By the time the tour finished with the Motörboat Cruise on 28 September in Florida, the official message now was that the worst was over. Plans were announced to extend the Motörhead brand with a new Motörhead whiskey and, even more unlikely, a range of vibrators bearing their logo and the Snaggletooth image made in conjunction with the sex toy company Lovehoney. There were four vibrators in the range, from the Ace of Spades to the Born to Lose. There was also the Overkill, or you could simply go for the Motörhead.

The tagline for the vibrators was suitably 'head-esque: 'Do it hard, do it fast, do it loud.' Amusingly, Lemmy claimed to know nothing about them until the last minute. 'They do a deal with our manager, then he tells us and it's too late to change it,' he said. 'The sex toy thing was a surprise, but it seems to be working out.'

Behind the scenes, though, things were becoming grim. In October a cartoon began to circulate privately among many of Lemmy's oldest friends, in which he is being wheeled out onstage, ordering his bandmates not to announce he's died until the end of the tour. It was cruel but wincingly accurate. 'I laughed when I saw it,' says Doug Smith. 'But only because there was a horrible truth to it.' His wife, Eve, shuddered. 'They shouldn't have let him be seen like that.'

The renowned rock photographer P. G. Brunelli, who took hundreds of shots of Lemmy and Motörhead over the years, told friends of his shock at bumping into Lemmy on the Motörboat cruise. Passing him in the corridor, PG smiled and said 'Hello, Lemmy.' Lemmy stared at him blankly and replied, 'Who are you?'

Dave Ling, one of the founding fathers of *Classic Rock* magazine and someone who also knew Lemmy for more than 30 years and who even named one of his sons Lemmy, told me that PG was still in shock when he related the story to him. 'PG said Lemmy was dead behind the eyes. He shook his hand and said, "Thank you for the music." Then went outside and stood at the balustrade and just cried.'

Outward appearances were still being ferociously maintained when, despite the cancelled shows, the next leg of the anniversary tour had found America rediscovering the band. 'I know he was very proud that Motörhead's final tour of America broke them in that country,' said Saxon's singer, Biff Byford, who had watched the drama unfold at first-hand. 'That's something he had been trying to do for years.'

Lemmy had a few weeks off to recuperate before Motörhead were due to pick up the tour in Europe, although the break didn't do him much good. In early November, he flew to London to attend the annual awards ceremony held by

Classic Rock, where he was due to present an award to Janie Hendrix, on behalf of her late brother Jimi, whom Lemmy had once known and worked for, of course, back when the world was still new.

Walking unsteadily up and down the carpet with the aid of a cane, he looked gaunt and ill. He received a steady stream of well-wishers at his table in front of the stage, like an emperor reaching the sunset of his days. More than one person wondered aloud if they'd see him again. When he did make it onto the stage to present the award, he received a standing ovation, led by Queen's Brian May.

Eddie Clarke, who had paid a visit to catch the band in Birmingham on their previous British tour, says he was deeply shocked by the man he saw at the *Classic Rock* awards show. 'When I saw him in Birmingham he was looking good. He was in good shape. He'd put on a bit of weight. And he was talking fine. Everything was looking the right way. But at the awards, he was gone. I knew then, inside, that he wasn't going to make January,' he adds referring to the fact that Lemmy had invited him up to guest onstage at the Hammersmith show scheduled for January. 'Cos I had my heart set on doing January. Cos Hammersmith Odeon was our home, you know? For us it was the home of Motör-head. No sleep till Hammersmith, you know?'

The same day as the *Classic Rock* ceremony, Lemmy received some bad news. Phil 'Philthy Animal' Taylor had died of liver failure at the age of 61. The pair may have had a fractious relationship over the years but they were still close. At least, as far as Lemmy was concerned. 'One of my best friends died yesterday,' he said. 'I miss him already. His name was Phil Taylor, or Philthy Animal, and he was our drummer twice in our career. Now he's died and it really pisses me off that they take somebody like him and leave George Bush alive. So muse on that. We're still going, we're still going strong, it's just first Würzel and now Philthy, it's a shame, man. I think this rock'n'roll business might be bad for the human life.'

According to Eddie Clarke, though, who had stayed in close contact with Phil over the years, Taylor had spent most of his time grieving over not being in Motörhead any more. 'When he got the sack from the band, he never got over it,' says Eddie now. 'Did you ever see him after that? Bitter and fucking twisted. He never got over it, man. He *never* got over it. There's a man that didn't *ever* get used to it.' Then again, as Eddie says, 'He was prone to doing the wrong drugs. That was his problem. Whereas I picked myself up and got through, even though carrying the fucking bag of sorrow with me, Phil just took drugs. He got into crack and crystal meth. That's why he was in LA, really.

'I tried so hard to get Phil out of America but he wouldn't leave. I always felt I'd get the call that he was dead, you know? Next thing I got a call from Phil, saying, "I'm in England, I've had a fucking aneurysm" and whatever. They saved his life but he [wasn't] the same. He still remembered stuff but he was just a little bit slower than he was. He came and stayed with me for a while after he got back then I took him up to his flat in Chelsea.' Eventually, Eddie had helped move Phil up to Derbyshire where he could be looked after by his sisters. 'It was difficult. His sisters didn't really fully understand him. They did a wonderful job with Phil, but you can't expect them to know. It's its own thing, this rock'n'roll business. For all of our differences I still loved Phil to bits. The three of us . . . what we did together [in Motörhead] was so incredible.' He paused, looking for the right words. 'The way things are turning out, dying at thirty-five of a drug overdose might not have been so bad.'

Was it true then, the rumours that had sprung up over the last few years, that Phil had turned to dealing drugs to make money? 'He didn't need to. He had plenty of money. Loads of it. He was the richest of the three of us, I should think. Though Lemmy might be now.' He gave a morbid chuckle. Taylor, he insists, 'never paid any taxes and he had all the royalties we had. He had his flat in Chelsea. Trust me, Phil was wealthy.'

Asked for his own views on Taylor, Lemmy remained typically bullish. 'Phil was a nutcase – and I do admire that in a person,' he said. 'I think he lost his will to live. He was doing a lot of the wrong drugs and living with the wrong people. It was too much for his constitution. So far I've survived it, because I invented it, more or less.' Privately, he couldn't help but be reminded of his own mortality. 'I don't recommend the lifestyle, because most people die of it. A lot of my friends are dead who shouldn't be. They had a lot more music in them. But that's the way life is – it's all down to luck.'

Motörhead's own luck was also now running out. Lemmy was still reeling from the news of Taylor's death when the tour began four days later. It couldn't have got off to a more inauspicious start. The first date, in Paris on 15 November, was cancelled in the aftermath of the terrorist attacks on the Bataclan theatre and elsewhere two days earlier. 'Our hearts go out to all who have suffered in Paris tonight,' the band said in a statement. 'We are so sorry; it is so utterly horrific.'

It wasn't the only difficulty they faced. The band were forced to cancel two shows in Germany and one in Denmark at the end of November, though this time it wasn't down to Lemmy. Instead, it was Phil Campbell who required urgent hospitalisation for an unspecified ailment. Rumours began to circulate that the guitarist was fine, and the story was just a cover for the ailing frontman – something the band's management quickly stepped in to quash. 'For all members of the media who engage in the modern-age bloodsport of celebrity-death-watch-by-internet-rumour-spreading, we hope you feel the shame and shoddiness of your "work".' Campbell was back on his feet and onstage within a few days.

In early December, in a revealing interview with Dave Ling, Lemmy spoke about his own health issues. He was characteristically truculent when it came to speculation about his health. 'I'm sick of the fucking "Are you going to die?" line of questioning,' he said. 'It's getting really old, that question. I'm all right. I'm going out there and doing my best. I have good days and bad days but mostly I've been doing all right.' When asked whether he thought of death in the wake of his recent problems, his reply was blunt and revealing. 'Death is an inevitability, isn't it? You become more aware of that when you get to my age. I don't worry about it. I'm ready for it. When I go, I want to go doing what

I do best. If I died tomorrow, I couldn't complain. It's been good.'

'It was a horrible experience,' Ling told me afterwards. 'The man you and I knew is no longer there any more, I'm afraid. I knew instantly that this page and a half of questions I'd prepared I was going to get almost nothing out of. It was awful.'

Clearly, Motörhead still meant everything to him though, and he told Dave he saw no reason to slow things down. 'We've just put out two of the best albums we've ever done, you know? To me it's quite obvious that we're not done yet.' He even predicted that there would be another album within the next two years. 'In fact it might be a bit sooner than that.' Sadly, he would be proved wrong.

The final date on the European leg of Motörhead's fortieth-anniversary tour took place in Berlin on 11 December, with a set of follow-up shows in Britain lined up for January 2016. In Berlin, Lemmy looked almost skeletal, but still he soldiered on, bringing the show to its climax with a thunderous 'Overkill'. He hardly moved at all onstage now, standing there like a waxwork dummy, holding fast to his bass, almost leaning on the mic for support, just trying to stay on his feet, his deadened eyes hidden behind mirrored sunglasses, his voice old and trembling, his spirit still stuck somewhere back in 1969. Those of us who had known him since the days when he would boss the stage with his presence, throwing his head back and snarling, jumping around in his white boots like he was dancing on coals, or simply throwing out that gunfight stance, eyes into the sun, those of us who had known him since the days when you could feel the crackle in the room every time he walked in we were horrified and saddened. What none of us knew yet was that it would be the last song he ever played onstage.

When, later on, I emailed Ute Kromrey asking why Lemmy had been allowed to continue touring and making public appearances when it was clear he was desperately ill, the reply was polite but wearily on-message. 'As you know as well as everyone else, playing live for his fans and touring was his life and always came first for Lemmy,' wrote Ute. 'Consideration for health and other issues only came second. And furthermore he did not know (and no one knew) how sick he was, he just felt tired once in a while but didn't feel that bad in his overall disposition that he felt he should cancel.'

The man could not walk unaided, could barely speak any more. To be told he 'didn't feel that bad in his overall disposition' felt faintly ridiculous. On the other hand, as every manager Lemmy ever had soon found out – and now every doctor – trying to get Lemmy to do anything he didn't want to was a frustratingly fruitless endeavour. Invulnerable rock god Lemmy had ceased being plain old Ian Kilmister so long ago, he simply had no way of returning to other people's ideas of 'normal'. The only way to face death was to stare it down and growl, to refuse to be cowed. Even when it hurt just to stand.

Two days later, he was back in Los Angeles. His seventieth birthday wasn't until Christmas Eve, but his friends and fellow musicians had organised an early party at the Whisky a Go Go. And so on the night of 13 December 2015 the great and good of rock'n'roll assembled to pay tribute to the man who had helped write the rulebook. The bash was organised by the former Guns N' Roses drummer Matt Sorum, a long-time friend of the birthday boy, who sent out an invite promising 'chit-chat and general all-round merriment'. The crowd were a Who's Who of Rock. Sorum's old band-mates Slash and Duff McKagan were there, as were Metallica's Lars Ulrich and Robert Trujillo, Scott Ian and Charlie Benante of Anthrax, and Ozzy's guitarist Zakk Wylde. Billy Idol rubbed shoulders with Steve Vai and ex-Skid Row singer Sebastian Bach. Kiss's Gene Simmons and ZZ Top's Billy Gibbons paid tribute via video messages. An all-star jam featured Slash and Anthrax playing '(We Are) The Road Crew', Steve Vai and Lemmy's son, Paul, trading licks, and a climactic set of punk classics featuring Sorum, McKagan, Billy Idol, the Sex Pistols' guitarist Steve Jones and Billy Duffy.

Lemmy himself remained on the balcony all night, though he wasn't short of visitors hoping to catch up. Lars Ulrich went to see his friend and knelt beside him while they talked. 'I got a chance to sit with him for about ten minutes, just him and me,' the Metallica drummer wrote in *Rolling Stone*. 'I told him it was his obligation to live for ever, because he was the reason we could all get together and celebrate hard rock and celebrate Motörhead and see familiar faces because we're all so scattered now. Obviously I could tell that he was in deteriorating health but we had a close bond, one that didn't necessarily need to be reaffirmed or articulated. The less we said the more we knew the connection was there.'

Steve Vai was another one who went over to personally wish him happy birthday. 'He was shockingly thin and frail, but still had that steady awareness of all that was going on in the world around him. I held his shaking hand, told him how nice it was to jam with his son, and then I kissed his hand and said 'God bless you, my brother, and thank you.' There are times when you know you will be saying goodbye to someone for the last time in this life, and though there was a sadness, with Lemmy it was a heartfelt salute and a momentary exchange of deep respect and joy in the knowing of each other.'

Lemmy's other band, rockabilly revivalists The Head Cat, were due to play a short set that night too, and his bass rig was set up just in case. But he never made it down from his seat in the balcony. No one can say if Lemmy knew the end was approaching, but he was no fool. He knew what this so-called birthday party was really about – saying goodbye.

Two days later, he was admitted to hospital after suffering chest pains. He was released the next day, but Todd Singerman was concerned enough to take him for a brain scan. Lemmy was uncharacteristically quiet, and when he did speak, his speech was slurred. Singerman was concerned that he'd had a stroke. 'We took him for the X-rays, and they said, "Oh my God, there's stuff all over his brain and his neck",' Singerman told *Rolling Stone*.

It was cancer. On 26 December, two days after Lemmy's seventieth birthday, his doctor visited his apartment. He had some terrible news: Lemmy's cancer was inoperable, it had spread too far. He informed him he had maybe two months to live, maybe six, if he was lucky. But Lemmy wasn't feeling lucky any more.

'He took it better than all of us,' said Singerman. 'His

only comment was, "Oh, only two months, huh?" The doctor goes, "Yeah, Lem, I don't want to bullshit you. It's bad, and there's nothing anyone can do. I would be lying to you if I told you there was a chance."'

Preparations were made. Lemmy's favourite video console from the Rainbow was brought to his apartment. Close friends were informed. But no one guessed quite how quickly the end would come. Lemmy spent a few hours on Monday, 28 December, playing the video game before the Rainbow's owner, Mikael Maglieri, dropped by for a visit. They talked, then Maglieri watched Lemmy drift off to sleep. He didn't wake up again.

'Mikael called to say, "My God, he just died right in front of me",' Todd Singerman told *Rolling Stone*.

People were understandably shocked. 'I was speaking to a friend of mine who knows Motörhead's manager very well and he told me that things were not well and maybe I should consider going down to LA to see him and pay my respects,' said Lars Ulrich. 'The cancer was very aggressive, and it was end stage and there probably wasn't a lot of time left. That was at one p.m. and then I guess I heard the news around six p.m. That was crazy.'

Ozzy Osbourne, Lemmy's old partner in crime, was just about to leave the house when he heard the news. 'I phoned him up two days ago, and I couldn't make out one word he was saying,' he said the next day. 'Yesterday, I got a text from his manager saying, "Lemmy's on the way [out], and he wants to see some of his friends." So my wife and I were just about leaving the door and the text came saying he'd gone. It shook me up bad.'

The news appeared on the band's Facebook page via a carefully worded statement: 'There is no easy way to say this . . . our mighty, noble friend Lemmy passed away today after a short battle with an extremely aggressive cancer . . . We will say more in the coming days, but for now, please . . . play Motörhead loud, play Hawkwind loud, play Lemmy's music LOUD. Have a drink or few. Share stories. Celebrate the LIFE this lovely, wonderful man celebrated so vibrantly himself. HE WOULD WANT EXACTLY THAT.'

Over the next few hours and days, tributes began to flood in from friends and fans. 'Lost one of my best friends today,' tweeted Ozzy. 'He was a warrior and a legend.' 'I'm going to miss this guy more than words can express,' Slash wrote on Instagram. 'Rock'n'roll personified and the embodiment of everything it stands for and a truly good friend. RIP Lemmy.' Speaking to the *Blackpool Gazette*, Harry Feeney recalled how he and Lemmy had 'kept in touch and whenever he was in the north of England we would meet up. The last time was 2012 at the Apollo in Manchester . . . We all thought we were going to get together in November but he couldn't do it because he wasn't well. So we exchanged greetings through Facebook etc. His death is so sad, but he led the type of life that meant he shouldn't really have been here ten years ago.'

'I couldn't believe it when I heard,' Stacia told me just a few weeks later. 'When you love somebody so much, you can't imagine your life without them.' She and Lemmy hadn't seen each other in some years, she said. 'But you don't have to when you love someone. Then I heard he was ill and I was so sad for him. I never knew he was going to leave us so soon, though.' She began to cry again.

'Words don't come easy, especially when you know Lemmy would have laughed at us all trying to say dignified things about him being a hero,' wrote Queen's Brian May on his website. 'Any time I attempted to say anything complimentary to Lemmy to his face, he would fix me with a kind of amused, contemptuous stare. But a kind of hero he certainly was.'

'Behind the Man and the Legend was a kind man who went out of his way to make you feel special,' wrote Kiss's bassist, Gene Simmons. 'The Lemmy I knew and loved always held out his hand to help new bands. I will miss him.'

There was grief, of course. Eddie Clarke, who had been a member of the classic Motörhead line-up of the late Seventies and early Eighties, referenced both Lemmy and Philthy Animal Taylor. 'As the last man standing, the world seems a really empty place right now,' he said on his own Facebook page. He also rather touchingly shared an extract from a letter Lemmy had written to him, which ended: 'Thanks for the best and the worst and the deeply shared, Eddie. I know you think I treat everything as a joke, and I take the piss, but everyone survives the way they can. I love you. You're my family. God help us both! Cheers, Lemmy xxx.'

'All this outpouring, it's genuine stuff,' says Eddie now. 'He never changed. There was something between us the whole time. I swear to god. And he knew it was there. We had the utmost respect for each other. When Lemmy and I were together, we didn't have to speak a lot. It was just there.' In recent years, 'I was kind of surprised he didn't reach out to me a bit more.' Even with Lemmy gone, he says, it still hurts after all these years how it all ended. 'You think you've got your life back on track but actually you never really have. In the real scheme of things, you never recover from things like that. There are things you've done and you're proud of them when you look back. But the damage is in there.'

In keeping with his wishes, others who knew Lemmy far less well queued up to share their stories of him with the public. Like Black Sabbath's guitarist, Tony Iommi. His old Hawkwind bandmate Dave Brock recalled sharing a room with Lemmy on tour, watching the singer fall asleep with his eyes open while reading a book on account of 'being up for days'. Duff McKagan remembers meeting Lemmy the first time he arrived in London with his band: 'He passed me a beer and asked me how I like the girls in England.' The former Eighties glamour model Samantha Fox revealed that the pair talked about recording a single together, 'Beauty and the Beast', the video for which would feature them dressed as each other. There were many more. A great many more.

A picture of the man emerged that went well beyond the rock'n'roll image: his love of horses, his fondness for astrology, the fact that he once lived two doors down from the actress who played Grandma Walton in the Seventies TV show *The Waltons*, his kindness. Perhaps most surprising of all to the people who had frequented his small, rent-controlled West Hollywood apartment, the fact that he died a millionaire. According to some sources Lemmy had a net worth of £6.75 million ($10 million), and his estate will continue to earn royalties from his recordings worldwide for decades to come. As Doug Smith says, 'Lemmy's success, financially, made him a lot of money. But it hasn't been through Motörhead. It's been through Lemmy. Motörhead has been the vehicle but because of his personality, his verbal and all the rest of it, Lemmy has gained a massive amount of credibility with all his contemporaries.'

A memorial service took place on 9 January at the Forest Lawn Memorial Park in Hollywood. It was an understandably emotional affair. Mikkey Dee, Slash, Dave Grohl, Lars Ulrich, Anthrax's Scott Ian and Lemmy's son, Paul Inder, paid tribute to their old friend, while a quarter of a million people watched the live stream on YouTube, many of them raising Jack Daniel's and Cokes in pubs and bars from London to LA.

Grohl talked about how the first time he met Lemmy, the Motörhead man had commiserated him on 'the death of your friend', Kurt Cobain. Scott Ian compared Lemmy to Elvis, Little Richard, Carl Perkins and the Beatles: 'Lemmy taught us that we could be real.' His son, Paul, said, 'He was one hundred per cent real. I won the lottery when I got Lemmy. You were perfect. Travel well, my dear father. You are back out on the road for a longest tour to the great gig in the sky, we will never, never forget you. I love you.'

At the end of the service, Lemmy's bass was placed against a Marshall stack next to the cowboy hat-shaped urn that contained his ashes, deliberately filling the room with feedback. 'Lemmy has left the building,' said his manager, Todd

Singerman, before mourners convened at the Rainbow for a public memorial. He might have been physically gone but his presence remained, like the afterimage from a camera flash.

In the weeks that followed, an online campaign was mounted to rechristen Jack Daniel's and Coke after him; shortly afterwards, the makers of Jack Daniel's announced they were releasing a limited-edition bourbon in his honour. Another petition campaigned to make 'Lemmium' the chemical name for Heavy Metal 115 on the periodic table. Most touching of all was a Finnish advert for milk filmed less than a month before Lemmy's death that featured the great man standing outside a gas station. Waving his cane at the camera, he scornfully intoned: 'I have never drunk milk and I never will. You asshole', before turning away and breaking into a grin that stripped away his frailties and rolled back the years. It ended with the lines: Ian 'Lemmy' Kilmister 1945–2015 – We raise our glasses to you.' It was as good a memorial to the man as anything.

There was still the question of Motörhead's future. Unthinkable as it was, there was always the chance the band could continue without him – other outfits had done the same. But Mikkey Dee, a man who cared about his band almost as much as Lemmy, quickly shot down such outlandish suggestions. 'Motörhead is over, of course,' he told Swedish TV. 'Lemmy was Motörhead. We won't be doing any more tours or anything. And there won't be any more records. But the brand survives, and Lemmy lives on in the hearts of everyone.'

Sales of the Motörhead back catalogue soared in the

weeks that followed Lemmy's death. The single of 'Ace of Spades' re-entered the British charts at No. 13 – two places higher than it achieved on its original release nearly 26 years before. In America, it accrued 1.8 million streams in the week ending 31 December, up 1096 per cent from 149,000, the week before, according to Nielsen Music. Obituaries were run in such august journals as the *Wall Street Journal*, who described him as 'the Keith Richards of the bass', going on to note how 'Lemmy seemed to care not a whit about what anyone thought of him and yet was beloved by his peers.' Or as *Rolling Stone* commented in its obit, 'Kilmister's unique personality and appearance – the muttonchops, the facial moles, the obsession with slot machines, his collection of Nazi memorabilia – endeared him to diehards and casual music fans alike.'

In darker corners of the internet speculation grew that Lemmy had taken his own life. But nobody who knew Lemmy took this seriously. The problem was he had died so quickly after his diagnosis that no one could quite believe it. Perhaps Mikkey Dee came closest to the truth when he speculated that Lemmy had, in some way, willed himself to die. 'When he went home he said, "I've had a good run, fuck it", and then more or less laid down and died,' he was quoted as saying.

Back in that hotel room in London, on that dark rainy day in 1997, the first time around, when I thought he was about to die, I asked towards the end of the evening, 'Do you ever think about death?'

'No,' he lied. 'But as far as I know I don't know what it is. I don't know what happens. I don't know about the tunnel with the lights at the end and the nice music. I think that's probably wishful thinking. Cos all those motherfuckers came back, right? That might just be the bit to get you in there. Bend the knives eye, you bastard.'

More drinks, more cigarettes, everything more than everything else. What about the afterlife, did he ever think about that?

'Who knows what the afterlife is?' he mused. 'Who knows whether there is one, there isn't one. You don't know what form it takes. You don't know what you have to do to achieve it. The devil could walk in and say, "Yes, I'm afraid the Jews were right. Off you go!" It just doesn't compute. So instead of planning for an uncertain afterlife, which is what all these wankers go to church for every week and show off their new hat, I'd rather just . . . I'll find out when I die. And I'm willing to *wait* for this. I don't have to know now. I don't have to know like an evangelist about what's really gonna happen because he doesn't know either.

'You should live your life as if you *do* believe in it and it *should* come true if you're good. And I live my life like that. Decent behaviour is easy. It doesn't cost anything. Same as good manners or a good outlook. It doesn't cost anything to be honourable. All it does is it gets you dirty looks from the people who aren't honourable, and my god I can handle that. You know, so fuck 'em.

'And if we ever come to stand before the Great Desk I'm sure there'll be some bastard behind there with a clipboard. "Ah, yes do you admit that you . . .?" The Inquisition! The Voice of Christ! Will kill your immortal soul! Eaten alive by worms, scorpions, snakes and ants while your old lady does it with a million black men! That's the Catholic Church for you.

'I live my life as decent as I can, you know, and I'm an honourable man. I never made . . . I hardly ever made a promise I didn't keep. I'm not talking about social. I'm talking about shit that matters, you know? And I don't like people who are dishonourable. And I especially hate people who are proud of being dishonourable. Of which there are more and more as time goes on.

'But I beat them. I'm still here. You come and see Motörhead you have seen one of the best rock'n'roll bands in the fucking world! I don't care. I got that. And that's good enough. That's what I set out to do. That's what I've done.'

And all the hard living, the drinking, the drugging, any regrets at all?

'It wasn't hard,' he cackled. 'This is easy. The hard part was not dying.'

Anyway, he said, death was not about how you lived your life.

'It's not related to your fucking lifestyle. It's being in the wrong place at the wrong time . . . Death doesn't care. Death doesn't mind where you are. Death gets you anyplace . . . There are no rules. It doesn't matter how careful you are. That fucking girder on that truck can still come through your windshield and cut you off at the fucking neck. You can't be careful of life. Life fucks you anyway. When it gets ready, you're gone. There isn't no appeal. You can't go, I want a second opinion . . .'

So no thoughts about slowing down or cutting down . . .?

'If it starts to hurt me that I can feel then I'll cut down.

Till then – why? It's so much fun. People having a good time only cut down because they think they should, cos of their age, that worries me.'

We're bombarded by these messages all the time, aren't we?

'Well, you don't have to listen to them. You're bombarded all the time by gamma rays, you don't know. The ozone layer's melting, I mean, people say save the planet, fucking arrogance. The planet is made of volcanoes, yeah? You don't give a fuck you're gonna hurt the planet. You're gonna dissipate the air *we* breathe, that's all. The planet isn't going anywhere – we are! People talk about save the environment, they mean what it takes to keep us alive. The planet will invent something else when we go. The planet don't give a shit. We've only been around for five minutes anyway, compared to the dinosaurs. They were around 150 million *years*. We've been around for one million. Do you think the planet's even noticed us yet? It's probably still looking back to its golden days with the dinosaurs, right? What's this? Ants? Oh no, humans. Okay?

'We don't mean shit. The human race is a blight upon the face of the earth, if you ask me. We're a disease. We deserve to die.'

And now Lemmy is dead, but he's not gone. He never will be. The music he made with Hawkwind and especially with Motörhead is for ever out there for everyone to hear, changing the course of rock'n'roll as much today as it did 40 – or 30, or even 20 – years ago. And anyone who professes to be 'rock'n'roll' – whatever that means in the twenty-first century – is now standing on the shoulders of a real giant.

In 2010, when he was a mere stripling of 65 and long before his health began to decline, Lemmy was asked what he thought his legacy would be.

'When Motörhead leaves,' he predicted, 'there will be a hole that just can't be filled. That's fine with me. It means I've achieved what I set out to do – which was to make an unforgettable rock'n'roll band.'

A man of his word, that's exactly what Lemmy did. Born to lose. Lived to win.

NOTES AND SOURCES

The bulk of the quotes in this book are taken from my own extensive interviews over many years with Lemmy, as well as the great many conversations we had together over the course of the more than 35 years we knew each other. Lemmy was always a remarkable raconteur, mythmaker, bullshit-detector and disciple of the truth – his truth, anyway. He was also a brilliant joker and master of the straight face. One thing he never was: boring.

Others interviewed for the book include: 'Fast' Eddie Clarke, Doug and Eve Smith, Brian 'Robbo' Robertson, Phil Carson, Ted Carroll, Stacia Blake, Tony Platt, Chris Greenaway of Blunderbuss Antiques, Dave Ling, Mörat, Bebe Buell, Joel McIver, and some who would prefer to remain anonymous. Others who I have interviewed in the past include: Phil 'Philthy Animal' Taylor, Phil Campbell, Mikkey Dee, Dave Brock and Nik Turner. There are also a great many people who spoke to me about their experiences with Lemmy that also informed the writing of this book, including: Ozzy Osbourne, Phil Lynott, Lars Ulrich, Slash, Duff McKagan, Ute Kromrey, Motorcycle Irene, and many others.

In terms of research, special mention must also be made of Lemmy's own highly entertaining autobiography, *White Line Fever*, co-written with the brilliant Janiss Garza, and Joel McIver's Motorhead biography, *Overkill*.

There are also a handful of beautiful magazine articles published over the years that brought both a tear to my eye and a roar of laughter in rereading them again, and that also inform parts of this book. They are: Chris Salewicz's brilliant 1979 *NME* feature, Dave Ling's wincingly acute *Classic Rock* article from 2000, and Mick Farren's 1970s-vintage *NME* pieces on both Hawkwind and Mötorhead. Plus some truly lovely pieces across the years from proper 'Head stalwarts like Pete Makowski in *Sounds* and Kris Needs in *ZigZag*.

Other notable background sources quoted come from *The Times*, *The Guardian*, *Q*, *Rolling Stone*, *The Independent*, *The Telegraph*, *Sunday Times*, *Classic Rock*, *Metal Hammer*, *Kerrang!*, *Melody Maker*, *Uncut*, *Record Collector*, *Bass Guitar Magazine*, *Spin*, *The Quietus*, and *Billboard*. Along with the various websites attached to these estimable publications. Some excellent websites also provided useful insights, including www.aural-innovations.com, www.bravewords. com, www.blabbermouth.net, www.loudwire.com, www. ultimateclassicrock.com, and others, not least the superb Eddie Clarke official site, www.fasteddieclarke.com.

INDEX

9/11 attacks 242, 246
25 & Alive: Boneshaker
    (Motörhead DVD) 240
1916 (Motörhead) 219–20

Ace of Spades (album)
    (Motörhead) 161–2, 163
'Ace of Spades' (single)
    (Motörhead) 143, 144,
    160–1, 267, 275, 276, 294
Action, The 53–4
Adverts, The 147
Aftershock (Motörhead) 262
Anderson, Dave 83
Another Perfect Day
    (Motörhead) 193–5
Anthrax 268
Armstrong, Roger 128, 129, 130
Artwoods, The 57

Bach, Sebastian 286
Bad Magic (Motörhead) 272–3,
    274, 276
Bain, Jimmy 190, 191
Barnes, Peter 154
Beatles, the 27, 31, 33–5, 47, 54
Beer Drinkers and Hell Raisers
    (Motörhead) 156
Benante, Charlie 286
Bennett, Brian 23
Bennett, Susan 47, 98–9, 103
Berry, Chuck 31
Betteridge, Dave 137, 138,
    139–40
Beyond the Threshold of Pain
    tour 134
Birds, The 52–4
Blue Cheer 115
Blue Öyster Cult 117
Bomber (Motörhead) 153–5

'Brainstorm' (Hawkwind) 86–7, 94
Brixton Academy 238–9, 240
Brock, Dave 72, 73–6, 78, 84, 92, 108–9
and Lemmy 104–5, 111, 237–8, 291
Bron, Gerry 138, 139–40, 156
Bronze Records 137–8, 139–40, 144, 159, 206
Brunelli, P. G. 279
Bubbles, Barney 77, 83, 84–5
Buell, Bebe 217–19
Burston, Michael 'Würzel' 200, 202–3, 223–4, 262

Calvert, Robert 77, 79, 84, 85, 102
and rock theatre 96
and 'Silver Machine' 91–3
Campbell, Phil 200, 201–2, 203, 219–20, 224–5, 227, 283
Captain Sensible 147, 238
Carr, Roy 131
Carroll, Ted 128–9, 130, 156
Carson, Phil 212–14, 215, 221
Chas McDevitt Skiffle Group 21
'Chase is Better Than the Catch, The' (Motörhead) 160, 161, 188
Chesters, Neville 58–9, 60–1
Chiswick Records 128, 130, 137, 156
Clapton, Eric 170
Clarke, 'Fast' Eddie 115, 121–4, 127, 183–9, 238–9
and Lemmy 135–6, 280, 290–1
and money 172, 173–4

and production 179–80
and singing 153–4
and Taylor 163–4, 281–2
Classic Rock (magazine) 254, 264, 279–80
Coachella Valley Music and Arts Festival 266–7
Comic Strip (film) 210
Cooper, Alice 100
Crabtree, Shirley 37–8
Crobot 276

Damned, The 8, 139, 147–8
'Dandy' (Rockin' Vicars) 48–9
'Dead Men Tell No Tales' (Motörhead) 153, 159
Dee, Mikkey 221, 272, 293
Dettmar, Del 89, 92, 94, 102
DeVille, C. C. 249
Dikmik (Michael Davis) 69–70, 72, 77, 90, 102
Donegan, Lonnie 19, 21
Doremi Fasol Latido (Hawkwind) 94–5
Douglas, Shirley 21
Dr Feelgood 120
drugs 31–2, 62–3, 171–2
acid 54, 60–2, 87–8
heroin 98–9, 180, 248–9
speed 4–5, 8, 32, 125, 149, 158–9
Duffy, Billy 286

'Eat the Rich' (Motörhead) 210
Edmunds, Dave 117, 120
Edwards, Jimmy 95
Edwards, Malcolm 175, 176, 177
Eliminator (ZZ Top) 207

Ellsmore, Andrew 175–7
Epstein, Brian 34
Escalator (Sam Gopal) 64–5
Escape Studios 129, 156

Faithfull, Marianne 135
Farren, Mick 81, 112, 170
Feeney, Harry 'Reverend Black'
 42, 49, 55–6, 289
Finland 43–4, 151–2, 205–6
Fool's Paradise (Head Cat) 258
Ford, Clinton 49
Four Plus One 52
Fox, Lucas 115, 116, 117–18,
 119
Fox, Samantha 237, 291
Frank, 'English' 126
Frendz (magazine) 81, 83, 84, 94
Friends of the Earth 87
Fury, Billy 33

Gardner, Kim 52–3
Garza, Janiss 242
Genesis 108
Gibbons, Billy 286
Gigantour 261
Gill, Pete 203–4, 210
Girl Can't Help It, The (film) 29
Girlschool 164, 174
Glastonbury Festival 275–6
Goering, Hermann 246
Golden Years, The (Motörhead)
 159
Graham, William 248, 249
Grammy Awards 220, 245–6
Grateful Dead 101
Greasy Truckers Party
 (Hawkwind) 91
Greenslade 116, 117

Grohl, Dave 292
Grosvenor, Luther 116
Guns N' Roses 11, 220
GWR Records 206–7, 208, 213

Hammered (Motörhead) 241,
 242
Hammersmith Odeon 139–40,
 171, 280
Harris, Jet 23, 24
Harrison, John 76, 83
Harvey, Danny B. 258
Hawkwind 5, 6, 8, 69, 70, 71–4
 and albums 83, 88–9
 and beginnings 76–7, 78–82
 and drugs 90–1
 and 'Hawkestra' 237–8
 and Lemmy 85–8, 89–90,
  106–13
 and line-up 83–4, 102–4
 and Motörhead 131
 and recordings 82–3
 and success 94–7
 and USA 100–2
Hawkwind (album) 83
Head Cat, The 258–9, 287
Heavy Metal Barndance 169–70
Heavy Metal Holocaust 170
Heavy Publicity 8
Hells Angels 5, 81, 107, 118,
 130, 149–50
Hendrix, Jimi 35, 54–5, 59–60,
 62, 159
Hitler, Adolf 9, 229–30
Holly, Buddy 21
House, Simon 102
'Hurry on Sundown'
 (Hawkwind) 82
Hynde, Chrissie 135

'I Ain't No Nice Guy'
(Motörhead) 222–3
Ian, Scott 286, 292
Ice-T 250
Idol, Billy 286
'I'll be Your Sister' (Motörhead)
139
In Search of Space (Hawkwind)
84–5, 88–9
In the Hall of the Mountain Grill
(Hawkwind) 86, 103
Inder, Paul (son) 46, 146, 257,
267, 286, 292
Inez, Mike 249
Inferno (Motörhead) 244–5
internet 234–5
Iommi, Tony 291
IRA 97–8
Iron Fist (Motörhead) 168–9,
179–81
'It's All Right' (Rockin' Vicars)
48

Jagger, Mick 47
Jam, The 147
Jarry, Alfred 92, 93
Johnny Kidd & The Pirates 40
Jones, Allan 125
Jones, Steve 286
Jourgensen, Al 247
Judas Priest 147, 274

Keen, Speedy 129–30, 131, 135
'Keep Us on the Road'
(Motörhead) 129, 139
Kerrang! (magazine) 205
Keuleman, Cheryl 253
'Killed by Death' (Motörhead)
204–5

Kilmister, Ian Fraser *see* Lemmy
King, Simon 68, 89, 92, 111, 112
King Crimson 79
Kinks, The 48
Kiss of Death (Motörhead)
249–50
Koenig, Alan 267, 268

Lacuna Coil 261
Ladbroke Grove 80–1, 86
Lang, Don 21
Langton, Huw Lloyd 83
Laswell, Bill 206–7, 208
Lauder, Andrew 82, 117, 120
Leary, Joanna 100–1
Leary, Timothy 100, 101
'Leaving Here' (Motörhead) 159
Led Zeppelin 120, 159
Lemmy 1, 14–18, 234–6, 285–7
and appearance 3–4, 27–8
and the Beatles 33–5
and Bennett 98–9
and Brock 74, 237–8
and Clarke 122–3, 124,
187–9
and death 288–96
and drugs 4–5, 31–2, 60–3,
87–8, 125, 149, 158–9,
231–2, 248–9
and early career 22–3, 26–8,
29–31, 35–8
and guitar 20–2, 143–4
and Hawkwind 71–3, 79,
85–7, 89–90, 93–4, 96–7,
103–4, 106–13
and health 8–10, 243–4,
256–7, 259–66, 269–70,
273–4
and Hells Angels 149–50

and Hendrix 54–5, 59–60
and LA 10–11, 225–6
and line-up 200–4
and logo 133
and London 57–9, 67–9, 127–9
and Motörhead 113–15, 116–18
and musical influence 18–19, 23–4, 28–9, 50–4, 146–7, 271–2
and Nazi memorabilia 228, 229–31, 246–8
and performance 181–2
and Robertson 193–4
and Rockin' Vicars 39–41, 42–5, 47–50, 55–6
and Sam Gopal 63–6
and Smith 211–12, 214
and songwriting 141, 142, 154, 223, 249–50
and Taylor 118–19
and USA 215–18
and women 19–20, 32–3, 45–7, 66–7, 145–6, 251–3, 270–1
Lemmy: 49% Motherf**ker, 51% Son of a Bitch (documentary) 250–1
Lennon, John 34, 35, 50
Levesque, Paul 241
Lewis, Jerry Lee 31
Ling, Dave 123, 140, 164, 181, 279, 283–4
Little Richard 28–9, 31
Live at Brixton Academy (Motörhead) 240
London 47–8, 57–9, 67–9; *see also* Ladbroke Grove

Lord, Jon 57
Los Angeles (LA) 10–11, 215–16, 285–6
'Lost Johnny' (Hawkwind) 63
'Lost Johnny' (Motörhead) 119
'Louie Louie' (Motörhead) 6, 136, 137, 138–9
Lynott, Phil 190, 195

McIver, Joel 142, 143, 144, 152
McKagan, Duff 286, 291
McVicar, John 176
Maglieri, Mikael 288
Maile, Vic 159, 179
Makowski, Pete 131
'Mama, I'm Coming Home' (Osbourne) 223
Manfred Mann 138
Mankowitz, Gered 48
March or Die (Motörhead) 220–1
Marquee, the 127–9
Marvin, Hank 21, 23
May, Brian 272, 280, 290
MC5 115
Megadeath 209–10, 261, 268
Melody Maker (newspaper) 125, 161
merchandising 172, 173
Metallica 11, 142–3, 220, 245–6
Miles, Barry 216–17
Miller, Frankie 190, 210
Miller, Jimmy 145, 153
'Mirror of Illusion' (Hawkwind) 82
Monsters of Rock festival 274
Moorcock, Michael 77, 79, 83–4, 85, 102

Mörat 243, 247, 250, 253–4, 263, 266
Morely, Paul 165
Morris, Stephen 'Moggsy' 40, 44, 49
Motörboat cruise 267–8, 278
Motorcycle Irene 130, 134
Motörhead 6, 8–9, 113–20, 122–4, 141–2, 255
   and 25th anniversary 238–41
   and final concerts 266–8, 274–5, 276–9, 282–3, 284–5
   and line-up 199, 200–4
   and logo 132–3
   and 'Louie Louie' 137–9
   and the Marquee 127–9
   and money 172–4
   and post-Lemmy 293–4
   and problems 162–4, 174–5, 177–9, 185–9
   and Robertson 191–8
   and stage shows 154–5, 156–7, 169–70
   and USA 11
Motörhead (album) 129–32
'Motorhead' (Hawkwind) 104–5
'Motorhead' (Motörhead) 130, 131–2
Motown Sect 36–8
Mott the Hoople 116
MTV 222

Nash, Graham 59–60
Nazi memorabilia 9, 150, 228, 229, 231, 246–8
New York City 216–17
Nirvana 52

NME (magazine) 5, 94, 131, 148–9
'No Class' (Motörhead) 145
No More Tears (Osbourne) 223
No Remorse (Motörhead) 204–5
No Sleep 'til Hammersmith (Motörhead) 165–6
Nolan Sisters 182–3

Ogden, Richard 113
Oh Boy! (TV show) 19
Ollis, Terry 76–7, 81, 89
On Parole (Motörhead) 120–1, 124, 155–6
Opal Butterfly 68
Orgasmatron (Motörhead) 207–8
Osbourne, Ozzy 12, 163, 165, 223, 274
   and Lemmy death 288, 289
Osbourne, Sharon 221–2, 223
Overkill (album) (Motörhead) 145, 152
'Overkill' (single) (Motörhead) 142–3, 144, 275, 276

Peel, John 80, 139
Petagno, Joe 132–3
Peterson, Dickie 115
Pink Fairies 81
Pink Floyd 54, 73, 79, 108, 120
Plasmatics, The 183–4
Portobello Road 5, 6, 81
Powell, Alan 94, 102, 111, 112
Presley, Elvis 24, 31
Proby, PJ 50–1
psychedelia 95–7
punk music 6–7, 120, 139, 146–7

INDEX

Queen 120

Radio 1 145, 159
Rainbow Bar and Grill 11, 215, 225–6
Rainbow Theatre 97
Rainmakers, the 35–6
Ramone, Joey 218
Rath, Billy 135–6
Reading Festival 148
Red Army Orchestra 44
Reid, Chuck 241
Reid-Dick, Will 180
Richard, Cliff 24
Richards, Keith 9, 47
Richmond, Neil 137
Riviera, Jake 127
Robertson, Brian 'Robbo' 189–98
Robinson, Dave 91
Rockin' Vicars 39–41, 42–6, 47–50, 55–6, 85–6
Rock'n'Roll (Motörhead) 211
rock'n'roll music 29, 31, 271–2
Rolling Stones, the 54
Rollins, Henry 216
Roundhouse, the 89–91, 116, 147
Rudolph, Paul 110, 111, 112
Rydell, Bobby 31

Sacrifice (Motörhead) 224
St Valentine's Day Massacre (Motörhead/Girlschool) 164
Salewicz, Chris 88, 148–52
Sam Gopal 63–6
Sassoon, Vidal 48
Saxon 167, 180, 203, 262, 276

Secunda, Tony 134–5
Sex Pistols 91
Shadows, The 21, 23–4
Shaw, Cyril 'Ciggy' 42, 45, 51, 56
'Silver Machine' (Hawkwind) 5, 89–94
Simmons, Gene 286, 290
Singerman, Todd 222–3, 244, 265–6, 287–8
Six-Five Special (TV show) 19
skiffle music 21
Slash 12, 267, 286, 289
Slattery, Mick 76, 83
Slim Jim Phantom 258
Smeaton, Jonathan (Liquid Len) 83
Smith, Doug 3–4, 8, 172–4, 206–7
  and drugs 9, 10, 171–2
  and Hawkwind 72, 74, 80–1, 82, 90–2, 93–4
  and Lemmy 108, 109–10, 112–14, 157–8, 211–13, 214–15
  and Motörhead 117, 120, 121, 126–7, 128, 134, 136–8
  and Petagno 132
  and USA 101–2, 209–10
'Snaggletooth' (Motörhead) 205
Solley, Peter 219, 220
Sony Records 215, 221, 222, 223
Sorum, Matt 286
Sounds (magazine) 7–8, 145, 161
Sounds Incorporated 51–2
'Space is Deep' (Hawkwind) 95
Space Ritual Alive (Hawkwind) 94, 95–6

INDEX

Speakeasy 47, 65
Springsteen, Bruce 120
Stacia 6, 11, 72, 85, 100, 108,
    289–90
Staff, Ray 130–1
Stanley III, Owsley 60
Steele, Stewart 36
Steele, Tommy 19
'Step Down' (Motörhead) 153–4
Step Forward Records 6, 7
Stiff Records 127
'Stone Dead Forever'
    (Motörhead) 153, 154, 159
Stray Cats, The 258
Stringfellow, Peter 37

Talmy, Shel 48
Tank 179
Taylor, Dick 82
Taylor, Phil 'Philthy Animal'
    118–20, 121–2, 127, 134,
    135, 136
    and Clarke 163–4, 174
    and death 280–2
    and departure 198, 199,
    220–1
    and drumming 142–3
    and heroin 180
    and return 210–11
    and songwriting 141–2
'Tear Ya Down' (Motörhead)
    137, 139
Thin Lizzy 128, 189–90
Thornton, Billy Bob 250
'Time We Left This World
    Today' (Hawkwind) 95
Tiswas (TV show) 165
Tito, General Josip 44
Tomorrow 52

'Too Late, Too Late' (Motörhead)
    159
Top of the Pops (TV show) 9, 49,
    138–9, 145, 154, 161, 164
    and Nolan Sisters 182, 183
Townshend, Pete 170
'Train Kept a Rollin''
    (Motörhead) 129
Trujillo, Robert 286
Tsangarides, Chris 179
Turner, David 'Nodder' 45, 49
Turner, Nik 69, 72, 77–9, 81–2,
    83–4, 111
Tyler, Tony 120

Ulrich, Lars 143, 286, 288
United Artists 82, 117, 120,
    155–6
United States of America 100–2,
    151, 163–4, 208–10,
    225–6, 228–9; see also Los
    Angeles
'Urban Guerrilla' (Hawkwind)
    97–8
Uriah Heep 138

Vai, Steve 286–7
Vicious, Sid 139
Vincent, Gene 50
Volbeat 261

Walk the Walk . . . Talk the Talk
    (Head Cat) 258–9
Walker Brothers, The 54
Wallis, Larry 115, 119, 122
Warnock, Neil 138, 139–40
Warrior on the Edge of Time
    (Hawkwind) 103–5
'Watcher, The' (Hawkwind) 95

INDEX

Watson, Robbie 32
We are Motörhead (Motörhead)
    236
'(We are) The Road Crew'
    (Motörhead) 160, 161
Webb, Cameron 244–5, 249,
    272, 273
Weller, Paul 147
Weston, Gil 178
Whaley, Paul 115
'Whiplash' (Metallica) 245–6
White Line Fever (autobiography)
    242
'White Line Fever' (Motörhead)
    8, 123, 129
Who, The 48, 159
Wild Horses 189, 190, 191
Williams, Wendy O. 183–6, 188

Willis, George (stepfather) 17,
    27, 28
Wonder, Stevie 100
Wood, Ronnie 52, 53, 57–8
World is Yours, The (Motörhead)
    254–5
World Wrestling Entertainment
    241–2
Wylde, Zakk 286

Yes 79, 108
Young & Moody 182
Young Ones, The (TV show)
    203
YouTube 66, 262, 275, 276, 278
Yugoslavia 44

ZZ Top 207